BREAKING FREE *from*
SPIRITUAL STRONGHOLDS

PRAYING
GOD'S
WORD

BETH MOORE

BREAKING FREE *from*
SPIRITUAL STRONGHOLDS

PRAYING GOD'S WORD

NASHVILLE, TENNESSEE

0-8054-2351-6

Published by Broadman & Holman Publishers,
Nashville, Tennessee

Unless otherwise stated all Scripture citation is from the NIV, the Holy
Bible, New International Version, copyright © 1973, 1978, 1984 by
International Bible Society. Other versions used are KJV, the King James
Version, and NASB, the New American Standard Bible, © the Lockman
Foundation, 1960, 1962, 1963, 1968, 1971, 1972, 1973, 1975, 1977;
used by permission.

DEDICATION

To Dale and Cheryl McCleskey,
Comrades in the freedom fight for all prisoners of war:
Thank you for enduring the heat so close to the front
lines of this generation's battle.
May the blaze of enemy fire only cast a clearer light
upon the glorious face of Jesus Christ.
One day in His courts is worth a thousand in battle.
With love and deep appreciation,
Beth and Keith

ACKNOWLEDGMENTS

I owe a debt of love to those who allowed me to share
their insights and testimonies of the grace and power of
God in this book. Joy Conaway, Alison Shanklin,
Jeanine Dooley, Danice Berger, Kim Bankard,
Dale McCleskey, Vickie Arruda, Susan Kirby,
Carole Lewis, and my friends at "First Place."
You are heroes to me.

CONTENTS

B R E A K I N G   F R E E   *from*
S P I R I T U A L   **S** T R O N G H O L D S

P R A Y I N G
G O D ' S
W O R D

INTRODUCTION

As long as I live, I don't think I'll ever comprehend why God has allowed me the unspeakable joy of serving Him through full-time ministry. Goodness knows I didn't deserve it. My entire life has been a mission of God's mercy. I am increasingly awed over my salvation and find the privilege of knowing and loving God to be unfathomable. A long time ago I had to accept the fact that I could do nothing to repay God for His bountiful grace to me, for if I could, grace would be nullified. What I could do instead was pour my life on His altar and make every effort to "press on to take hold of that for which Christ Jesus took hold of me" (Phil. 3:12). Translation? Fulfill my calling. Not anyone else's—just mine. To know Him. To love Him. To serve Him. I believe that is what He's called you to do too.

For reasons equally mind-boggling to me and known only to Him, God has called me to *teach*. I think perhaps because I had so much to *learn*. Still do. In fact, the more I learn, the more I realize I don't know . . . but I hunger to know. I have often been asked how a believer might identify whether God had given her or him the gift of teaching. I believe I have stumbled on at least one possibility: if you are compelled to tell others virtually everything you learn from God, you might be a teacher! My friends who have other spiritual gifts can learn something from God without feeling the overwhelming need to share it with everyone they know. Not me! The second I receive the least spiritual insight or learn anything at all about the practicality of Scripture slapped on the hot pavement of real life, I want to make the world's biggest conference call. Perhaps I should mention that not everyone I tell wants to know. The beauty of a sanguine personality is that I'm too blinded by passion to notice rejection! I am not content to keep to myself any hidden treasure I've discovered. What little I know, I want others to know. Before God tells me a secret, He knows up front I'm going to tell it! By and large, that's our "deal."

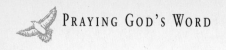

OVERCOMING STRONGHOLDS

Often times, the precepts I feel the most urgency to teach are those lessons I learned the hard way. Somehow I keep hoping that someone else might learn through my mistakes and not their own. Oh, my friend, have I ever learned things the hard way! I've been educated in the power of God and His Word through the field trips of my own failure, weakness, and past bondage. This book is a result of my unquenchable desire to share one of the most effective approaches to the liberated life in Christ that God has ever taught me: *praying Scripture to overcome strongholds.* Actually, I didn't discover what a vital part of my liberation this approach has been until long after I had begun practicing it. I suddenly realized it was no accident that I was finally set free from some areas of bondage that had long hindered the abundant, effective, Spirit-filled life in me. After the failure of all my formulas, in my desperate search for freedom I cast myself entirely upon God. He faithfully led me to several deliberate practices that He knew would work. Stunningly, in fact. He also knew that He had given me a mouth to tell!

The key to freedom from strongholds is found, not surprisingly, in 2 Corinthians 10:3–5. Read the words carefully:

For though we live in the world, we do not wage war as the world does. The weapons we fight with are not the weapons of the world. On the contrary, they have divine power to demolish strongholds. We demolish arguments and every pretension that sets itself up against the knowledge of God, and we take captive every thought to make it obedient to Christ.

Let's lay down a few basic principles so the purpose of this book will become clearer.

WHAT IS A STRONGHOLD?

The apostle Paul, under the inspiration of the Holy Spirit, did a masterful job of explaining it in 2 Corinthians 10:5. Basically, a stronghold is any argument or pretension that "sets itself up against the knowledge of God." The wording in the King James Version draws a clearer image of a stronghold: "every high thing that exalteth itself against the knowledge of God." A stronghold is anything that exalts itself in our minds, "pretending" to be bigger or more powerful than our God. It steals much of our focus and causes us to feel overpowered. Controlled. Mastered. Whether the stronghold is an addiction, unforgiveness toward a person who has hurt us, or despair over a loss, it is something that consumes so much of our emotional and mental energy that abundant life is strangled—our callings remain largely unfulfilled and our believing lives are virtually ineffective. Needless to say, these are the enemy's precise goals.

WHERE IS THE BATTLEFIELD?

In any warfare waged by the enemy against the individual believer, the primary battlefield is the *mind*. The goal of our warfare as stated in 2 Corinthians 10:5 is to steal back our thought life and take it captive to Christ instead. The enemy's chief target is the mind because the most effective way to influence behavior is to influence thinking. Our minds are the control centers of our entire beings. The enemy knows far better than we do that nothing is bigger or more powerful than God. That's why everything that "exalts itself" in our thought life is called a "pretension." Satan plays make-believe. He can only pretend because he lost all rights to presume authority over the believer's life when Christ, "having disarmed the powers and authorities, . . . made a public spectacle of them, triumphing over them by the cross" (Col. 2:15). Unfortunately, Satan is very good at his job because he's had so much experience. He plays make-believe and does a remarkable job of trying to make us believe it. Repeat after me: *nothing is bigger or more powerful than God!* Absolutely nothing! Not even the strongest addiction or over-whelming feeling of rage. One of the purposes of this book is to help you downsize anything that has a hold on you until you have, in effect, commanded it to bend the knee to the authority of Christ. Is this really possible? You bet it is!

WHAT ARE OUR WEAPONS?

According to the 2 Corinthians 10:3–5 passage, we have four vital pieces of information identifying the weapons of our warfare:

1. They are not the weapons of the world.
2. They have divine power.
3. They are associated with the "knowledge of God."
4. Their purpose in warfare is to take our thoughts captive.

In Ephesians 6:10–18, Paul listed the whole armor of God. Only one piece of the armor is actually a weapon. The figurative belt, shield, breastplate, shoes, and helmet are all defensive pieces of armor intended to keep us from being injured by the weapons of the evil one. The sword of the Spirit, clearly identified as the Word of God, is the only offensive weapon listed in the whole armor of God. Second Corinthians 10:3 uses the plural, assuring us we have *weapons* for warfare. What would the other primary weapon be? Perhaps additional weapons might be identified elsewhere, but I believe the other *primary* weapon of our warfare is stated right after the words identifying the sword of the Spirit as the Word of God in Ephesians 6:17. The next verse says, "And pray in the Spirit on all occasions." I am utterly convinced that the two major weapons with divine power in our warfare are the Word of God and Spirit-empowered prayer.

These two weapons have *divine power.* The original Greek word for *power* is the adjective form of the term *dunamai* meaning "to be able." It is the *achieving* power of God applied.[1] Perhaps this Greek term might pack a little more punch if we meditated on the fact that our English word *dynamite* is derived from the same root word. Stick with me here, because this is important: Virtually nothing we come up against in our individual Christian lives is more formidable than a stronghold. The very nature of the term tells us that whatever it is, it has a "strong hold" on us. Strongholds can't be swept away with a spiritual broom. We can't fuss at them and make them flee. We can't ignore them until they disappear. Strongholds are broken one way only: *they have to be demolished.* Have you ever seen a building demolished? In the Word of God, the term *fortress* is the closest equivalent to a literal, ancient stronghold. Both were fortified buildings. The most common way a modern "fortress" is demolished today is by deliberately and strategically placing dynamite in the building and then detonating it. Imagine the demolition crew showing up at the building with sticks and stones. They could holler at that building with all their might and throw sticks and stones until they fainted from exhaustion and it would still be standing. No one would doubt they had tried. They simply had the wrong tools. What they needed was dynamite.

You and I are just about as effective as the crew with loud mouths, sticks, and stones when we try to break down our strongholds with carnal weapons like pure determination, secular psychology, and denial. Many of us have expended unknown energy trying *hard* to topple these strongholds on our own, but they won't fall, will they? That's because they must be demolished. God has handed us two sticks of dynamite with which to demolish our strongholds: His Word and prayer. What is more powerful than two sticks of dynamite placed in separate locations? Two strapped together. Now, *that's what this book is all about:* taking our two primary sticks of dynamite—prayer and the Word—strapping them together, and igniting them with faith in what God says He can do. Hallelujah! I'm getting excited just thinking about it!

What makes these two sticks of dynamite so powerfully effective when strapped together? Let's consider the stick of prayer first. Prayer keeps us in constant communion with God, which is the goal of our entire believing lives. Without a doubt, prayerless lives are powerless lives, and prayerful lives are powerful lives; but, believe it or not, the ultimate goal God has for us is not power but personal intimacy with Him. Yes, God wants to bring us healing, but more than anything, He wants us to know our Healer. Yes, He wants to give us resurrection life, but more than that, He wants us to know the Resurrection and the Life. Please let this truth sink in deeply: It is never the will of God for warfare to become our focus. The fastest way to lose our balance in warfare is to rebuke the devil more than we relate to God. The primary strength we have in warfare is godliness, which is achieved only through intimacy with God; therefore, God will undoubtedly enforce prayer as one of the weapons of our warfare because His chief objective is to keep us connected entirely to Him. We will never win any spiritual battle without prayer, but when the heat of battle has momentarily cooled, the plunder from the battle is a far greater intimacy with God. Prayer is not the means to an end. In so many ways, it is the end itself.

Then what makes the Word such a powerful stick of dynamite to demolish strongholds? Take a look once again at 2 Corinthians 10:3–5. In the process of demolishing strongholds, our objectives are to cast down anything that exalts itself in our thought life and to take our thoughts captive to Christ. What does Scripture mean by "taking captive every thought to make it obedient to Christ"? This is the key that I finally recognized after many months of studying these verses: We take our thoughts captive, making them obedient to Christ, *every time we choose to think Christ's thoughts about any situation or stronghold instead of Satan's or our own.* What are Christ's thoughts? The Word of God revealed to us. I finally learned that the way to make our exalted, overpowering thoughts bow down in obedience to Jesus Christ is to choose to think His thoughts about the matter rather than my own or those influenced by the enemy. In this book, I am sharing with you exactly how I began to think God's thoughts over controlling strongholds in my life. I've also applied the same approach to several other strongholds that I have not personally experienced. For fourteen different strongholds, I have identified numerous Scriptures suggesting God's thoughts on the matter and reworded them into prayer. In praying Scripture, I not only find myself in intimate communication with God, but my mind is being retrained, or renewed (Rom. 12:2), to think *His* thoughts about my situation rather than mine. Ultimately, He resumes His proper place in my thought life as huge and indomitable, and my obstacle shrinks. This approach has worked powerfully every time I've applied it. It takes belief, diligence, and *time,* but the effects are dramatically liberating and eternal.

I am anticipating the following question: Beth, do you use Scripture every time you pray? The answer is no. We have such a tendency toward extremes. We find security in "always" and "nevers." I don't *always* pray *any* certain way, but I can confidently tell you this: I have never discovered a more powerful way to demolish strongholds in my life than praying Scripture. When it comes to warfare, this approach is without question the one I most often apply. Take note of a rule of thumb I've tried to apply in each Scripture-prayer. The words preceding the Scripture reference appearing in parentheses are a paraphrase of that reference. Any words following the parentheses are my own additional prayer suggestions. The following is a Scripture-prayer excerpt out of the chapter on overcoming the stronghold of unbelief:

Lord, Your Spirit clearly says that in the later times some will abandon the faith and follow deceiving spirits and things taught by demons. (1 Tim. 4:1) Please help me to be very discerning of deceptive teaching. Help me never to abandon the faith to follow after a lie.

In addition to the Scripture-prayers, I have included other encouraging quotes relating to each chapter's topic. If the quote is mine, it is unidentified. Otherwise, the author of the quote is referenced.

Please hear my heart as we conclude this portion of the book. The last thing I want to do is set myself up as any kind of proper example. Remember, our objective here is to learn not to allow anything or anyone to be exalted in our minds but Christ! I am a fellow sojourner with you. I have made so many mistakes and learned so many hard lessons. Please don't misunderstand my intention and think I'm suggesting my own formula here. This is not my formula. With all my heart, I believe it is one of God's. This book is about Him and the divine weapons He's given us to demolish strongholds. If I am an example of anything at all, I am an example of life after failure. *Abundant life.* And I am living proof that God can liberate *anyone.*

TO GET THE MOST OUT OF YOUR BOOK . . .

1. *Consider praying a few Scriptures out of chapters 1 and 2, "Overcoming Idolatry" and "Overcoming Unbelief," every single day,* no matter which other stronghold you're specifically seeking to

demolish. These Scriptures will remind you how powerful God is and will work to increase your faith in His Word. Please do not confuse this book with a name-it-and-claim-it philosophy. Our chief purpose here is to develop the mind of Christ in areas that seek to hold us captive. With every Scripture-prayer, we are asking God to fill our minds with His thoughts instead of ours. One thing of which you can be absolutely certain is this: It is most definitely God's will for you to be free from all areas of bondage. Galatians 5:1 says, "It is for freedom that Christ has set us free. Stand firm, then, and do not let yourselves be burdened again by a yoke of slavery." God may not always will for us to be physically healed in these earthly bodies or tangibly prosperous, but He always wills for us to be free from strongholds. You'll never fail to have His cooperation as long as He has yours.

2. *When seeking to demolish a specific stronghold, don't just pray through the list of Scriptures once,* unless you experience the rarity of immediate release without sensing any threat of relapse. Pray the Scriptures over and over until you experience lasting freedom. Even after freedom comes, you are wise to pray occasionally the Scriptures that God seemed to use most powerfully. I can think of a particular stronghold that hasn't had power over me in years, but I pray certain truths on a fairly regular basis for maintenance purposes. That stronghold was costly! I never want to go back to it as long as I live! Be wise. Some strongholds are simply more threatening than others. Never take for granted that you are beyond a return to captivity, but also do not live in inappropriate fear. I often think of the apostle Paul's words in 2 Corinthians 1:9–11 when I think about my former captivity and the freedom God has given me. "But this happened that we might not rely on ourselves but on God, who raises the dead. He *has* delivered us from such a deadly peril, and He *will* deliver us. On Him we have set our hope that he *will continue* to deliver us, as you help us by your prayers" (emphasis mine). God has all the power we need to free us and keep us free, but in the matter of demolishing strongholds, He also demands our prayerful cooperation.

3. *If you like the approach of strapping two sticks of dynamite together, prayer and the Word, to demolish strongholds, let this practice spur you on to write your own Scripture-prayers.* You will

find lined pages at the end of each chapter so that you can continue on by searching the Scriptures and compiling your own. Look for any Scripture that you believe reflects the mind of Christ toward your stronghold, reword it into a prayer, write it at the end of the chapter, and pray it! My hope is that you will learn a practice that will be beneficial for the rest of your life.

4. *Allow this approach to be a complement to any other means by which God may be teaching you and leading you to freedom.* For instance, if your obstacle has been overwhelming and God has led you to sound, godly counseling, don't stop the counseling as long as it's beneficial. Simply add this practice to it. Praying Scripture is not the only means of demolishing strongholds; I've just found it to be among the most effective. God may use many different elements to usher you to freedom, but one thing I believe with all my heart: The Word of God will be the absolute common denominator in all genuine deliverance from captivity. "Then you will know the truth, and the truth will set you free" (John 8:32). "He sent forth his word and healed them" (Ps. 107:20). "I will walk about in freedom, for I have sought out your precepts" (Ps. 119:45).

5. *As you single out one obstacle you desire to overcome, don't forget that other issues may be involved too.* In other words, if you are praying to overcome the stronghold of unforgiveness or the stronghold of anger, pride is virtually always involved. Ask God to give you discernment about coinciding areas that may be hindering your freedom and abundant life in Christ. Pray the mind of Christ in those areas as well.

6. *Consider using this prayer guide as a preventive measure as well as a prescriptive measure.* For example, if a situation arises that suddenly fuels fear in your heart, don't wait for Satan to bind it into a stronghold. Pray about it long before it becomes a serious, abundant-life-strangling problem. If you happen to feel a little depressed one particular day, pray a few of the pertaining Scripture-prayers in this book, and I think you'll sense the Spirit of Truth ministering to you. You don't have to have a stronghold to pray these Scriptures! On the contrary, perhaps they'll help us avoid a few. Whether you're

facing a stronghold or a momentary struggle, I believe you'll find grace and mercy in your time of need.

7. *Use the book any way and at any time you wish!* Consider keeping it with your daily prayer time materials and pick it up any time you desire a little extra guidance in prayer. Turn to several chapters and pray a number of Scriptures . . . out loud if possible. The Scriptures will help you develop the mind of Christ in all sorts of areas, whether or not you presently battle a stronghold. As I prepared the book, I was delightfully surprised to be immeasurably blessed by chapters addressing strongholds that really had never been my personal struggle. One of my coworkers who helped with some of the data processing remarked, "I've found that you don't have to have a problem in an area to be blessed by praying Scripture over it!" I shared several of the chapters with my Sunday school class along the way in my preparation. We all laughed as we remarked that some of us had been set free from strongholds we never even had! Praise God!

8. *Pray pertinent Scriptures as intercession for someone else whom you know is struggling to be free.* Be careful, however! The enemy is very shrewd. Sometimes he successfully schemes to keep us in bondage by fueling our focus on others' strongholds rather than our own. We have such a tendency to see the speck in the other person's eye when a log is lodged deeply in our own. I am convinced that as a general rule, strongholds are almost always broken between God and the individual captive. As 2 Corinthians 1:10–11 tells us, we can *help* others with our prayers, but we cannot do it for them. We can and should pray for an individual's willingness to let God set him or her free. We can and should pray for the enemy to be withheld and for the individual's eyes to be opened to truth, but freedom rarely comes to a person who does not get intimately involved with God for himself/herself. You see, God is far more interested in our getting to know the Deliverer than our being delivered. Remember, freedom comes through taking thoughts captive to Christ. We cannot take another person's thoughts captive. The thought life is the most intensely personal part of each individual. We may have *influence* upon another person's thought life, but God is the only one who has *direct access.* As Psalm 139:2 says, God perceives each of our thoughts from afar.

In concluding this section, please allow me to say that I would be thrilled for God to use these pages in *any* possible way to enhance your walk with Him. I hope you'll feel like it's *your* book. Let Him completely personalize it to you just as He has to me. The truths of each book God has given me have been deeply engraved upon my heart. I have a feeling, however, that this will be the first book He's allowed me to compile that I will actually keep with me and use over and over. Why? Because it's far more of His Word than mine . . . and we've got a written guarantee on His.

> *So is my word that goes out from my mouth:*
> *It will not return to me empty,*
> *but will accomplish what I desire*
> *and achieve the purpose for which I sent it.*
> *You will go out in joy*
> *and be led forth in peace;*
> *the mountains and hills*
> *will burst into song before you,*
> *and all the trees of the field*
> *will clap their hands. Isaiah 55:11–12*

FOUR COMMON QUESTIONS
ABOUT STRONGHOLDS

1. Do only unbelievers have strongholds?

Absolutely not! The Book of Galatians, the New Testament's primary treatise for freedom, was addressed to *believers* in Galatia. Galatians 5:1 says, "It is for freedom that Christ has set us free. Stand firm, then, and do not let yourselves be burdened again by a yoke of slavery." Likewise, 2 Corinthians 10:3–5, which addresses the demolition of strongholds, was written to believers. The Word is very practical. God never addresses "nonissues." If a believer could not return to a yoke of slavery, He would never have warned us of the potentiality of it. If we would never have to deal with a stronghold, God would never have told us how. It is interesting that the great majority of Scripture addressing captivity and liberty concerns God's own people. Without a doubt, all people who have never accepted Christ as Savior are held captive by the enemy, their primary stronghold being unbelief. This book, however, is primarily for the believer. Based on my understanding of Scripture, anything that steals, kills, or destroys the abundant, fruitful life of a believer can be considered a stronghold of the enemy. God used my own battle with strongholds coupled with years of traveling and speaking to open my eyes to the disturbing numbers of believers who live in daily defeat. Yes, believers can have strongholds!

2. Why has the subject of strongholds suddenly swelled in "popularity"?

I believe that the primary answer is the timing of our generation on God's kingdom calendar. The Word of God clearly teaches us that satanic activity and influence will increase dramatically as the day of Christ's return draws nearer. Revelation 12:12 says of Satan, "He is filled with fury, because he knows his time is short." This Scripture appears in context concerning believers and their war with the enemy who is called "the accuser of our brothers." In other words, Scripture intimates that much of Satan's fury will be directed specifically toward Christians as the clock ticks closer toward Christ's return. Please understand that Satan knows the Word better than we do. He knows the signs of Christ's coming. He knows every detail characterizing the last generations. He sees the present evidence of 2 Timothy 3:1–5 in our generation with clearer vision than we do. Satan is in a time bind; therefore, like the heat of Nebuchadnezzar's blazing furnace, he's turning up the fire on every modern-day Shadrach, Meshach, and Abednego. As Louie Giglio, a fellow bondslave to Christ, says, "We're dead center in the crosshairs of Satan's weapons."[2] So, do we run scared? God forbid! We put on the full armor of God, take our stand, and fight the good fight. Satan's already been defeated. Most of the power he wields is from pure deception and bluffing. Greater is He who is in us! (1 John 4:4). But we've got to learn how to live like the overcomers we are.

3. Is it possible to become unbalanced in our approach to warfare and strongholds?

No doubt about it! Please understand that Satan's utmost goal is to be worshiped (Isa. 14:12–17). Much of worship is focus.

Satan wins a tremendous victory and derives much satisfaction when he can get us to focus more upon him than upon God. That's why this book centers on our communication with God through prayer and His Word far more than directives on what to say to the devil. Christ set a perfect example for us in Matthew 4:1–11. Satan is most effectively rebuked by the believer taking his or her stand in the Word of God. If we know God's Word and how to pray the mind of Christ in a matter, we will be equipped with specific Scriptures when the need arises to face our foe and rebuke him verbally. Throughout this book, I will echo my absolute conviction that the most effective way to live in victory over the devil is to walk in righteousness with God. Strongholds are thoughts taken captive to anything but Christ. If Satan can take our thoughts captive simply to warfare, all he's done is successfully mounted another stronghold. I often ask God to keep me balanced in the whole counsel of His Word and to help me discern when I'm getting off track. Let's all stay balanced in God's Word. We may be at war with a powerful, unseen enemy, but we are at peace with the Lord God omnipotent, and He still reigns!

4. *Can we be set free from strongholds instantly?*

It's possible, but we must remember that God is far more interested in our relationship with the Deliverer than our being delivered. Sometimes the overwhelming power of a stronghold may be instantly broken, but the renewing of our minds can take a little longer. Remember, strongholds are demolished when we are able to take our minds captive to Christ. Let's face it, some "holds" in our lives are simply "stronger" than others. If God is getting our full cooperation, the length of the process or the intensity of the struggle is really up to Him. You see, it all depends on His objective. I am certainly no expert, but after about eighteen months of researching the biblical topic of strongholds and the Christian, I've come to believe that God generally prioritizes one of two objectives: showing us His *supremacy* or teaching us His *sufficiency.*

For example, I have a sister in Christ whom God set free from an addiction to both alcohol and tobacco years ago. Instantaneously, God broke the stronghold of addiction to tobacco and renewed her mind so that she had no desire whatsoever to smoke. In contrast, she makes the choice to walk in freedom over alcohol addiction almost every day of her life. She still has the desire to drink although she has lived in victory many years. From which stronghold did God set her free? Both! Neither area is controlling her. The instantaneous release from tobacco addiction taught her that God's dominion is over all things. She saw that nothing is impossible for God. She beheld His absolute *supremacy*. However, if God had broken her free of every stronghold that easily and rapidly, she would never have learned to depend on Him. The lingering desire to drink coupled with an exceeding desire to overcome has challenged her to choose the authority and power of Christ every single day. In His sovereign wisdom, God chose to leave her a thorn in the flesh so that she could be taught His strength in her weakness. She has learned God's *sufficiency*.

The same will probably be true for you and me. Some strongholds will never threaten to take our minds captive again. Others may contest their defeat and demand a rematch every single day. Either way, God has equipped us to overcome. We are wise not to judge others when they struggle to be free and seem to relapse over and over for a while. None of us is beyond facing the same challenge. Matthew 7:1–2 offers wise counsel when we are tempted to judge a person for his or her inability to attain immediate and lasting victory over a stronghold. "Do not judge, or you too will be judged. For in the same way you judge others, you will be judged, and with the measure you use, it will be measured to you." Renewing the mind means learning to think new thoughts. That can take some time . . . but let's not waste another minute of it, OK? It's time to start igniting some dynamite!

Chapter 1
OVERCOMING IDOLATRY

W hen I first began to research the biblical history of captivity among God's people, I kept running into a conspicuous common denominator: *idolatry*. I don't know why it was such a news flash. God warned His people over and over that if they did not resist the false gods of the nations surrounding them they would be snared, and He would ultimately allow them to be taken captive. They didn't and He did. One sobering thing about the faithfulness of God is that He keeps His promises, even when they are promises of judgment or discipline. Over and over the Book of Isaiah seems to plead the question, "Why in the world would you worship idols when you have been chosen by the sovereign God of the universe to be His own?" Isaiah 43:10–12 packs a powerful punch:

"You are my witnesses," declares the LORD,
    "and my servant whom I have chosen,
so that you may know and believe me
    and understand that I am he.
Before me no god was formed,
    nor will there be one after me.
I, even I, am the LORD,
    and apart from me there is no savior.
I have revealed and saved and proclaimed—
    I, and not some foreign god among you.
You are my witnesses," declares the LORD, "that I am
    God."

You and I as believers in Christ have also been chosen to know and believe and understand that He is God. Our lives have been sanctified by the one true God. Heaven is His throne. Earth is His footstool. Awesome creatures never cease day or night singing,

"Holy, Holy, Holy, Lord God Almighty!" Lightning flashes from His throne. The winds do His bidding. The clouds are His chariot. The earth trembles at the sound of His voice. When He stands to His feet, His enemies are scattered. He is transcendent over all things. Absolute. Uncontested. Omniscient. Omnipresent. The Lord God omnipotent reigneth. He is God and there is no other.

And, yet, this very One is our Father. Our Abba. He demands, deserves, our respect. Without it, for all practical purposes, we are powerless. Consider three reasons why praying Scripture regarding the "Godness" of God is so critical in the process of breaking free from strongholds:

1. *Virtually every stronghold involves the worship of some kind of idol.* For instance, the stronghold of pride is associated with the worship of self. The stronghold of addiction is often associated with the worship of some kind of substance or habit. In one way or another, something else has become "god" in our lives: the object of our chief focus. Filling our minds with Scripture acknowledging the "Godship" of God is a crucial part of renewing our minds. Until we turn from our idols to the one true God, we will never find liberty, for "where the Spirit of the Lord is, there is freedom" (2 Cor. 3:17). One missing link in almost every captive life is the spirit of God's *lordship.*

2. *As long as our minds rehearse the strength of our stronghold more than the strength of our God, we will be impotent.* As we pray the Word of God acknowledging His limitless strength and transcendent dominion, Truth will begin to eclipse the lies. We will realize that in our weakness He is strong and that as we bend the knee to His lordship God is more than able to deliver us.

3. *We may be forced to realize that our perception of God is something that we, ourselves, have conjured up and not the one true God at all.* This point may be a little hard to swallow. We may see ourselves as conventional Christians, but if we believe our God is small, that's not God at all. Truth sets us free. The truth may be that we've carved a "God" out of our own image, assigned Him the utmost and noblest of human characteristics, unintentionally envi-

sioning Him to be more of a "superhuman" than the sovereign *El Elyon*—The Most High God. I am praying that this chapter will aid the development of a more accurate perception of God. I think sometimes that God must listen to our pitifully small acclamations, expectations, and petitions in prayer, and want to say, "Are you talking to *Me?* I'm not recognizing Myself in this conversation. Are you sure you have the right God?"

I will never forget the story I once heard about a Sunday school teacher giving his elementary school class an assignment on Easter Sunday. He asked them to make an acrostic of the word "Easter." He was stunned by one student's perception. The child had written: Every Alternative Savior Takes Early Retirement. What a thought-provoking statement! Hear this from a former captive: every alternative savior *must* take early retirement if we are ever to be free. Only one God can deliver us. The most monumental leap we take toward freedom is the leap to our knees—the lordship of Jesus Christ.

I suggest using several of these Scripture-prayers or others like them every single day. May God remind us daily—no matter what kind of obstacles we face—that we are loved and empowered by the One who brought the universe into existence with the mere sound of His voice. Nothing is impossible for Him.

<hr/>

My Father, I acknowledge that You are the Lord Almighty. You are the first and You are the last, and apart from You there is no other God. Make me witness to the fact that there is no other Rock but You. Enable me to say with full assurance, "I know not one." (Isa. 44:6, 8)

My Father, You are my Lord, my Holy One, my Creator, my King. You are the One who made a way through the sea, a path through mighty waters. (Isa. 43:15–16)

My Father, You are the Lord my God. I desire to love You, listen to Your voice, and hold fast to You, for You, Lord, are my life. (Deut. 30:20)

> *The giant step in the walk of faith is the one we take when we decide God no longer is a part of our lives. He is our life.*

You alone are the Lord. You made the heavens, even the highest heavens, and all their starry host, the earth and all that is on it, the seas and all that is in them. You give life to everything, and the multitudes of heaven worship You. (Neh. 9:6)

My Father, how I thank You that it is unthinkable that You would do wrong, that the Almighty would pervert justice. Who appointed You over the earth? Who put You in charge of the whole world? If it were Your intention and You withdrew Your Spirit and breath, all mankind would perish together and man would return to the dust. (Job 34:12–15) Instead, my Lord, You have promised that Your plans for Your people are plans to prosper and not to harm, plans to give us hope and a future. (Jer. 29:11)

Yours, my Lord, is the greatness and the power and the glory and the majesty and the splendor, for everything in heaven and earth is Yours. Yours, my own heavenly Father, is the kingdom and You are exalted as head above all. (1 Chron. 29:11)

My mighty God, in Your hand is the life of every creature and the breath of all mankind. (Job 12:10) You, my God, open Your hand and satisfy the desires of every living thing. (Ps. 145:16)

The earth is Yours, O Lord, and everything in it, the world and all who live in it. (Ps. 24:1) For You, my Lord, are a great God, the great King above all gods. In Your hand are the depths of the earth, and the mountain peaks belong to You. The sea is Yours, for You made it, and Your hands formed the dry land. (Ps. 95:3–5)

Lord, I know that You are great—greater than all gods. You do whatever pleases You, in the heavens and on the earth, in the seas and all their depths. (Ps. 135:5) Although You are sovereign and You do what You please, You are righteous in all Your ways and loving toward all You have made. (Ps. 145:17)

My Father, Your kingdom is an everlasting kingdom, and Your dominion endures throughout all generations. You, my Lord, are faithful to all Your promises and loving toward all You have made. (Ps. 145:13)

You, my God, made the world and everything in it. You are the Lord of heaven and earth, and You do not live in temples built by hands. And You are not served by human hands, as if You needed anything, because You Yourself give all men life and breath and everything else. From one man You made every nation of men, that they should inhabit the whole earth; and You determined the times set for them and the exact places where they should live. You, my Father, did this so that men would seek You and perhaps reach out for You and find You, though You are not far from each one of us. For in You we live and move and have our being! (Acts 17:24–28)

> *Shall we still call coincidence what God calls providence?*

Many, O Lord my God, are the wonders You have done. The things You planned for us no one can recount to You; were I to speak and tell of them, they would be too many to declare. (Ps. 40:5)

How great You are, My God! You are beyond my understanding! The number of Your years is past finding out. You draw up the drops of water, which distill as rain to the streams; the clouds pour down their moisture and abundant showers fall on mankind. Who can understand how You spread out the clouds, how You thunder from Your pavilion? (Job 36:26–29)

Lord, You have been our dwelling place throughout all generations. Before the mountains were born or You brought forth the

earth and the world, from everlasting to everlasting You are God. (Ps. 90:1–2)

O Lord my God, You are very great; You are clothed with splendor and majesty. You wrap Yourself in light as with a garment; You stretch out the heavens like a tent and lay the beams of Your upper chambers on their waters. You make the clouds Your chariot and ride on the wings of the wind. You make winds Your messengers, flames of fire Your servants. (Ps. 104:1–4)

My Father, great are Your works! They are pondered by all who delight in them. Glorious and majestic are Your deeds, and Your righteousness endures forever. You have caused Your wonders to be remembered; You, Lord, are gracious and compassionate. (Ps. 111:2–4) The works of Your hands are faithful and just; all Your precepts are trustworthy. They are steadfast for ever and ever, done in faithfulness and uprightness. (Ps. 111:7–8)

Who is like You, the Lord my God, the One who sits enthroned on high, who stoops down to look on the heavens and the earth? (Ps. 113:5–6)

Oh, Father, how I thank You that my help comes from You, the Maker of heaven and earth. (Ps. 121:2)

My Lord and my God, it is You who measured the waters in the hollow of Your hand and with the breadth of Your hand marked off the heavens. (Isa. 40:12) You sit enthroned above the circle of the earth, and its people are like grasshoppers. You stretch out the heavens like a canopy, and spread them out like a tent to live in. (Isa. 40:22)

O, Lord, help me to lift my eyes and look to the heavens and acknowledge who created all these. You bring out the starry host one by one, and call each of them by name. Because of Your great power and mighty strength, not one of them is missing. (Isa. 40:26)

You, my Lord, are the everlasting God, the Creator of the ends of the earth. You will not grow tired or weary, and Your understanding no one can fathom. You give strength to the weary and increase the power of the weak. Even youths grow tired and weary, and young men stumble and fall; but when I hope in You, O, Lord, my strength will be renewed. I will soar on wings like eagles; I will run and not grow weary, I will walk and not faint. (Isa. 40:28–31)

Ah, Sovereign Lord, You have made the heavens and the earth by Your great power and outstretched arm. Nothing is too hard for You! (Jer. 32:17)

My God, since the creation of the world Your invisible qualities—Your eternal power and divine nature—have been clearly seen, being understood from what has been made, so that men are without excuse. (Rom. 1:20) O, merciful God, help us not exchange the truth of God for a lie, and worship and serve created things rather than You, our Creator—who is forever praised. Amen. (Rom. 1:25)

For me, there is but one God, the Father, from whom all things came and for whom I live; and there is but one Lord, Jesus Christ, through whom all things came and through whom we live. (1 Cor. 8:6)

You, my Christ, are the image of the invisible God, the firstborn over all creation. For by You all things were created: things in heaven and on earth, visible and invisible, whether thrones or powers or rulers or authorities; all things were created by You and for You. You are before all things, and in You all things hold together. (Col. 1:15–17)

Your love, O Lord, reaches to the heavens, Your faithfulness to the skies. Your righteousness is like the mighty mountains, Your justice like the great deep. O Lord, You preserve both man and beast. How priceless is Your unfailing love! Both high and low among men find refuge in the shadow of Your wings. I want to feast on the abundance of Your house; I want to drink from Your river of delights. For with You is the fountain of life; in Your light I want to see light. (Ps. 36:5–9)

Why does God allow us to spend so much of life in the heat of battle? Because He never meant for us to sip His Spirit like a proper cup of tea. He meant for us to hold our sweating heads over the fountain and lap up His life with unquenchable thirst.

Great are You, my Lord, and most worthy of praise. Your greatness no one can fathom. One generation will commend Your works to another; they will tell of Your mighty acts. They will speak of the glorious splendor of Your majesty, and I will meditate on Your wonderful works. They will tell of the power of Your awesome works, and I will proclaim Your great deeds. They will celebrate Your abundant goodness and joyfully sing of Your righteousness. (Ps. 145:3–7)

You, my God, have put Your words in my mouth and covered me with the shadow of Your hand—You who set the heavens in place, who laid the foundations of the earth, and who say to Zion, "You are my people." (Isa. 51:16)

You, my Father, are the One who forms the mountain, creates the wind, and reveals His thoughts to man. You are the One who turns dawn to darkness, and treads the high places of the earth—the Lord God Almighty is Your Name! (Amos 4:13)

This is what You, the Lord my God, say—You who created the heavens, You are God; You who fashioned and made the earth, You founded it; You did not create it to be empty, but formed it to be inhabited—You say: "I am the Lord, and there is no other." (Isa. 45:18)

O, Lord, You rule forever by Your power, Your eyes watch the nations—let not the rebellious rise up against You. (Ps. 66:7) The fool says in his heart, "There is no God." (Ps. 14:1)

Lord, I acknowledge that You are the "I AM." This is Your name forever, the name by which You are to be remembered from generation to generation. (Exod. 3:14–15)

O, Lord my God, help me never to worship any other god, for You, my Lord, are a jealous God. (Exod. 20:4–5)

You, my Lord, are a warrior; the Lord is Your name. (Exod. 15:3)

My Father, You are the Lord; that is Your name! You will not give Your glory to another or Your praise to idols. (Isa. 42:8)

My Father, help me to know that the Lord my God is God; You are the faithful God, keeping Your covenant of love to a thousand generations of those who love You and keep Your commands. (Deut. 7:9)

You, my God, are the Rock. Your works are perfect, and all Your ways are just. You are a faithful God who does no wrong. You are upright and just. (Deut. 32:4)

The Lord my God is God of gods and Lord of lords, the great God, mighty and awesome. You show no partiality and accept no bribes. (Deut. 10:17)

> *Psalm 31:19 reads, "How great is Your goodness, which you have stored up for those who fear you, . . . those who take refuge in you. . . ." That is what God does for those who fear Him. He sets aside and stores up goodness for His children, to be given at appropriate times in the future. What this goodness is, and when it will be bestowed, is unique to each individual according to God's plan and purpose for that person.*
>
> *Jerry Bridges,* The Joy of Fearing God

You, my Father, are my loving God and my fortress, my stronghold and my deliverer, my shield, in whom I take refuge, who subdues people under me. (Ps. 144:2)

You alone are my rock and my salvation; You are my fortress, I will not be shaken. My salvation and my honor depend on You; You are my mighty rock, my refuge. (Ps. 62:6–7)

Lord, please help me to revere Your name. You have promised that, if I do, the sun of righteousness will rise with healing in its wings and that I will go out and leap like a calf released from the stall. (Mal. 4:2)

My Father, heaven is Your throne, and the earth is Your footstool. (Isa. 66:1)

My Lord, You are slow to anger and great in power; You will not leave the guilty unpunished. Your way is in the whirlwind and the storm, and clouds are the dust of Your feet. (Nah. 1:3)

Father, those who oppose You will be shattered. You will thunder against them from heaven; You will judge the ends of the earth. (1 Sam. 2:10)

My God, whom have I in heaven but You? And earth has nothing I desire besides You. (Ps. 73:25)

Lord, to the Israelites Your glory looked like a consuming fire on top of the mountain. (Exod. 24:17) Help me to be thankful and to worship You acceptably with reverence and awe, because You, my God, are a consuming fire. (Heb. 12:28–29)

O, Father, I confess that I cannot fathom Your mysteries. I cannot probe Your limits, Almighty One. They are higher than the heavens. They are deeper than the depths of the grave. Their measure is longer than the earth and wider than the sea. (Job 11:7–9)

O, Lord, You have made everything beautiful in Your time. You have also set eternity in the hearts of men; yet we cannot fathom what You have done from beginning to end. (Eccles. 3:11)

My God, I acknowledge that Your thoughts are not my thoughts, neither are Your ways my ways. As the heavens are higher than the earth, so are Your ways higher than my ways and Your thoughts than my thoughts. (Isa. 55:8–9)

My Father and my God, You are seated on a throne, high and exalted. The train of Your robe fills the temple. Above You are seraphs, calling to one another, "Holy, holy, holy is the Lord Almighty; the whole earth is full of his glory." (Isa. 6:1–3)

> *If we have never had the experience of taking our commonplace religious shoes off our commonplace religious feet, and getting rid of all the undue familiarity with which we approach God, it is questionable whether we have ever stood in His presence. The people who are flippant and familiar are those who have never yet been introduced to Jesus Christ. After the amazing delight and liberty of realizing what Jesus Christ does, comes the impenetrable darkness of realizing Who He is.*
>
> Oswald Chambers, My Utmost for His Highest

My Father, You placed all things under the feet of my Savior, Christ, and appointed Him to be head over everything for the church, which is His body, the fullness of Him who fills everything in every way! (Eph. 1:22–23)

My Lord, where can I go from Your Spirit? Where can I flee from Your presence? If I go up to the heavens, You are there; if I make my bed in the depths, You are there. If I rise on the wings of the dawn, if I settle on the far side of the sea, even there Your hand will guide me, Your right hand will hold me fast. (Ps. 139:7–10)

My Lord and my God, You are both a God nearby and a God far away. No one can hide in secret places so that You cannot see him. You fill heaven and earth! (Jer. 23:23–24)

My Lord, Your Word is right and true; You are faithful in all You do. You love righteousness and justice. I thank You that the earth is full of Your unfailing love! (Ps. 33:4–5)

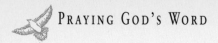

My Father and my God, You are not a man, that You should lie, not a son of man, that You should change Your mind. I thank You that when You speak, You act. And what You promise, You fulfill. (Num. 23:19)

O, Lord, You are my God; I will exalt You and praise Your name, for in perfect faithfulness You have done marvelous things, things planned long ago. (Isa. 25:1)

Now to the King eternal, immortal, invisible, the only God, be honor and glory for ever and ever. Amen. (1 Tim. 1:17)

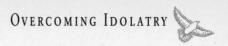

PERSONALIZING YOUR PRAYERS

Chapter 2

OVERCOMING UNBELIEF

God seems to work in themes in my life. You know what I mean. Every sermon, morning devotional, and Christian radio program all "coincidentally" speak to me about the same subject for an uncomfortable length of time. I'll even get a card in the mail from a Christian friend I haven't seen in ten years and—you guessed it—she'll share a good word on the exact "theme."

Soon after my fortieth birthday, everywhere I turned I heard a message on "belief." I'm humiliated to admit that I became somewhat annoyed not to be hearing more on the subjects I *really* needed. After all, I already was a believer, and if believers don't believe, what on earth do they do?

Several weeks passed, and I still didn't get it. Finally one morning even Oswald Chambers had the audacity to bring up the subject in that day's entry of *My Utmost for His Highest*. I looked up and exclaimed, "What is this all about?" I sensed the Holy Spirit speaking to my heart, "Beth, I want you to believe Me." I was appalled. "Lord," I answered, "Of course I believe in You. I've believed in You all my life." I felt He responded very clearly. Adamantly. "I didn't ask you to believe *in* Me. I asked you to *believe* Me."

I sat very puzzled for several moments until I was certain that the Holy Spirit had faithfully shed light on my pitifully small faith. I sensed Him saying, "My child, you believe Me for so little. Don't be so *safe* in the things you pray. Who are you trying to keep from looking foolish? Me or you?"

I don't mind telling you that my life changed dramatically after God interrupted my comfortable pace with the "theme" of belief. Some of it has been excruciating, and some of it has been the most fun I've had in my entire Christian life. I have a feeling this is one theme I probably will run into again and again in the course of my journey. Why? Because without faith it is impossible to please Him. In other words, you and I will be challenged to believe Him from one season to the next, all of our days. And if we have even half a heart for God, He's likely to shake our perimeters and stir up a little excitement.

Believing God is never more critical than when we have strongholds that need to be demolished. Believing God is also rarely more challenging. Why? Because we've battled most of our strongholds for years and perhaps tried countless remedies in an effort to be free with very little success. The enemy taunts us with whispers like, "You'll *never* be free. You've tried a hundred times. You go back every time. You're hopeless. You're weak. You're a failure. You don't have what it takes." Every one of these statements about you is a lie if you are a believer in Christ. You *do* have what it takes. You have Jesus—the Way, the Truth, and the Life. But you can't just believe *in* Him to be free from your stronghold. You must *believe Him.* Believe He can do what He says He can do. Believe *you* can do what He says you can do. Believe He is who He says He is. And believe you are who He says you are.

You may be thinking, "I *want* to believe! I just don't have enough faith!" God's Word records an encounter in Mark 9:14–24 to encourage every person who wants to believe. Christ met a man with a son who had been possessed by the enemy since childhood. No telling how many physicians, witch doctors, religious fanatics, wise men, and foolish men the father had sought to find freedom for his son. Imagine the glimmer of hope that kindled his soul when rumor circulated about the disciples of Jesus who were reputed to perform miracles. Then imagine his devastation when they too were added to the list of the failed. Jesus asked for the boy to be brought to Him. The father's desperate plea could bring an empathetic lump to the throat to any parent: "If you can do anything, take pity on us and help us." I love Jesus' powerful retort: "'*If* you can . . . ?' Everything is possible for him who believes." The father's reply comprises one of the most honest, priceless moments in the record of Christ's human encounters. "Immediately the boy's father exclaimed, 'I do believe.'" Then, as if Christ had caught his gaze eye to eye, reading his questioning mind, the father quickly restated, "Help me overcome my unbelief!"

I am convinced that God would rather hear our honest pleas for more of what we lack than a host of pious platitudes from an unbelieving heart. When I am challenged with unbelief, I have begun to make the same earnest plea to the One who would gladly supply. The following Scripture-prayers are for the purpose of fueling your faith in the One who is faithful and fueling your belief in the One who is believable. I suggest praying several of them every day. Please remember: it is *always* God's will for you to be free from strongholds. As stated in the introduction to this book, we may not always be sure God wills to heal us physically in this life of every disease or prosper us with tangible blessings, but *He always wills to free us from strongholds.* You will never have to worry about whether you are praying in God's will concerning strongholds. "It is for freedom that Christ has set us free" (Gal. 5:1).

Before you begin practicing the Scripture-prayers in this chapter, please read the following segment very carefully:

"I pray also that the eyes of your heart may be enlightened in order that you may know the hope to which he has called you, the riches of his glorious inheritance in the saints, and *his incomparably great power for us who believe.* That power is like the working of his mighty strength, *which he exerted in Christ when he raised him from the dead*" (Eph. 1:18–20, emphasis mine).

Please accept and celebrate two awesome truths derived from these Scriptures:

1. God wields incomparably great power for those who choose to believe. Read it again! *Incomparably great power!* More than enough to break the yoke of any bondage. Our belief unclogs the pipe and invites the power to flow.

2. God applies the same power to our need that He exerted when He raised Christ from the dead. Does your stronghold require more power than it takes to raise the dead? Neither does mine! God can do it, fellow believer. I know because He says so. And I know because He's done it for me. Believe Him . . . and when you don't, cry out earnestly, "Help me overcome my unbelief!"

Father God, Your Word declares that we, Your people, are Your witnesses and Your servants whom You have chosen, that we may know and *believe* You and understand that You are He. Before You no god was formed, nor will there be one after You. (Isa. 43:10) You have chosen me, God, for the express purpose of knowing and believing You. I can't really begin to know You until I choose to believe You! Make me a person of belief, Lord.

> *Second Corinthians 4:13 says, "It is written: 'I believed; therefore I have spoken.' With that same spirit of faith we also believe and therefore speak." If you are in Christ, you have been given that "same spirit of faith." The original word for spirit is literally translated "breath." When you speak God's Word out loud with confidence in Him—rather than your own ability to believe—you are breathing faith. Believing and speaking the truth of God's Word is like receiving blessed CPR from the Holy Spirit.*

Father, so often I feel like the boy's father who first exclaimed, "I do believe!" then in a flood of sincerity cried out, "Help me overcome my unbelief!" (Mark 9:24) Please help me to overcome my own unbelief, Lord, so I can start taking You at Your Word.

Father, I pray that the eyes of my heart may be enlightened in order that I may know the hope to which You have called me, the riches of Your glorious inheritance in the saints, and Your incomparably great power for us who *believe!* (Eph. 1:18–19)

Father God, according to Your Word, without faith it is impossible to please God, because anyone who comes to You must believe that You exist and that You reward those who earnestly seek You. (Heb. 11:6) Lord, I want to please You. Build faith in me so my life will honor the life of Your Son.

Father, according to Your Word, it is possible to be broken off from part of Your plan because of unbelief. Your Word says not to be arrogant but to be afraid. (Rom. 11:20) O, Father, I do not want to miss any part of Your plan because of my own unbelief! Please forgive me for any unbelief, and help me walk by faith.

> *We act out what we believe. Not what we know.*
> *Vickie Arruda*

Merciful Father, Your Word also says that if people do not persist in unbelief, they can be grafted back into the fullness of Your plan. (Rom. 11:23) Thank You, God, for so often granting the gift of second chances!

Father, I don't want to be like the ancient Israelites who were not able to enter the Promised Land "rest" because of their unbelief. (Heb. 3:19) Help me to believe You and follow You to the place of Your promised land in my own life.

Father, please help me not to be like the ancient Israelites who willfully put You to the test. (Ps. 78:18) They did not believe in You or trust in Your deliverance even after all the wonders You had shown them. (Ps. 78:22) Please swell my soul with belief and help me to trust emphatically in Your deliverance.

Father, in spite of Your chastisement, the ancient Israelites kept on sinning. In spite of Your wonders, they did not believe, so You ended their days in futility. (Ps. 78:32–33) O, Lord, I don't want my days to end in futility. I want to participate fully in what You're doing in my generation.

Lord God, teach me knowledge and good judgment, for I believe in Your commands. (Ps. 119:66)

My Savior, Christ, before You healed the blind men who cried out for Your mercy, You asked them, "Do you believe that I am able to do this?" After they replied, "Yes, Lord," You touched their eyes and said, "According to your faith will it be done to you." (Matt. 9:28–29) Father, clearly my faith impacts what You are willing to perform in my life. Please help me to believe that You are able.

Father, Your Word says that if Your disciples believe, they will receive whatever they ask for in prayer. (Matt. 21:22) Lord, as you mature my faith, also teach me how to pray and what to ask of You in prayer. I have so much to learn. Keep teaching me, Father.

> *Faith never denies reality but leaves room for God to grant a new reality.*
>
> *Jim Cymbala*

God, according to Your Word, You are not bothered by our requests. Once when others told a synagogue ruler not to bother You any more with his request, You ignored what they said and told the ruler, "Don't be afraid: just believe." (Mark 5:35–36) Help me not to be discouraged to pray and not to be afraid, but believe!

Dear Jesus, You told Your close followers, who were taught how to seek the Father's heart, that whatever they asked for in prayer they were to believe they received it and it would be theirs. (Mark 11:24) O, Father, help me to know Your heart intimately so that I'll know how to pray, what to pray, and believe in advance that I will receive it!

Father, in the parable of the sower, You teach us that the seed of Your Word that falls along the path represents the ones who hear, and then the devil comes and takes away the word from their hearts, so that they may not believe. (Luke 8:12) Lord, please help me to actively receive Your Word into my heart upon hearing it so that the devil cannot come and take it from me before it has had time to take root.

Father, I also pray that I will not be like those in the parable of the sower represented by the seed on the rock. They receive the word

> *When we become advocates of a creed, something dies; we do not believe God, we only believe our belief about Him.*
>
> Oswald Chambers, My Utmost for His Highest

with joy when they hear it, but they have no root. They believe for a while, but in the time of testing they fall away. (Luke 8:13) Help me to receive Your Word and hang on to it tightly when the time of testing comes.

Father, please help me not to be foolish and slow of heart to believe all that the prophets have spoken. (Luke 24:25)

Lord, if You speak to me regarding earthly things and I do not believe, how then will I believe when You speak of heavenly things? (John 3:12) Help me to believe You here and now and not just believe you in things concerning heaven. You are God of heaven *and* earth!

Father, according to Your Word, those who heard the testimony of the woman at the well said, "We no longer believe just because of what you said; now we have heard for ourselves, and we know that this man really is the Savior of the world." (John 4:42) Please cause my life to impact others by making them desire to meet You for themselves and believe!

God, please don't let me be the kind of person to whom You can say, "Unless you see miraculous signs and wonders, you will never believe." (John 4:48)

Lord, Your Word does not dwell in me if I don't believe the One You sent. (John 5:38)

Lord God, I acknowledge that it is by grace I have been saved, through faith—and this not from myself; it is the gift of God. (Eph. 2:8)

Father, Your Word asks, "How can you believe if you accept praise from one another, yet make no effort to obtain the praise that comes from the only God?" (John 5:44) Please help me to make every effort to obtain the praise that comes from You, Lord. I cannot obtain this praise from You without belief.

Christ Jesus, You said, "The work of God is this: to believe the one he has sent." (John 6:29) That is what You want from me more than anything in the world.

Father, help me to respond to Your Son according to Your Word: "I believe and know that You are the Holy One of God." (John 6:69)

Christ Jesus, You said that those who believe You are Your sheep. Your sheep listen to Your voice; You know them, and they follow You. You give them eternal life, and they shall never perish; no one can snatch them out of Your Father's hand. You and the Father are one. (John 10:26–30)

Dear Jesus, when I believe in You, I don't believe in You only but in the One who sent You. (John 12:44)

Father, Your Word is full of fulfilled prophecy. You told things before they happened so that when they did, people would believe. (John 14:29) Father, as surely as everything You prophesied in the past has happened, everything You prophesied for the future will happen. Help me to believe!

> *Tenacity is more than hanging on, which may be but the weakness of being too afraid to fall off. Tenacity is the supreme effort of a man refusing to believe that his hero is going to be conquered. . . . Remain spiritually tenacious.*
>
> Oswald Chambers, My Utmost for His Highest

Christ Jesus, You said to Thomas, "Put your finger here; see my hands. Reach out your hand and put it into my side. Stop doubting

and believe." (John 20:27) Lord, I cannot see Your visible hands, but if I'm willing to really look, I can see the visible evidences of Your invisible hands. Help me to stop doubting and believe!

Father, as You did for the jailer who received salvation through the witness of Paul and Silas, fill me with joy when I choose to believe. (Acts 16:34)

Father, please help me to cease being obstinate, refusing to believe. When I do this, I am maligning Your way. (Acts 19:9)

Father, a righteousness from God, apart from the law, comes through faith in Jesus Christ to all who believe. (Rom. 3:21–22)

Father, Your Word asks the question, "Does God give you His Spirit and work miracles among you because you observe the law, or because you believe what you heard?" (Gal. 3:5) The answer is because they believed what they heard. Help me to do likewise, Lord.

Lord, the Scripture declares that the whole world is a prisoner of sin, so that what was promised, being given through faith in Jesus Christ, might be given to those who believe. (Gal. 3:22)

Father, I ask You to help me to receive the Word of God not as the word of men but as it actually is, the Word of God, which is at work in me as one who believes. (1 Thess. 2:13)

Father, how I thank You that I am not of those who shrink back and are destroyed but of those who believe and are saved. (Heb. 10:39)

Father, You've told me that when I ask I am to believe and not doubt, because he who doubts is like a wave of the sea, blown and tossed by the wind. (James 1:6)

> *Faith is not believing in my own unshakable belief.*
> *Faith is believing an unshakable God when everything*
> *in me trembles and quakes.*

Lord, though I have not seen You, I want to love You deeply; and even though I do not see You now, I want to believe in You and be filled with an inexpressible and glorious joy. (1 Pet. 1:8)

Through Christ I believe in You, God, who raised Him from the dead and glorified Him, and so my faith and hope are in You! (1 Pet. 1:21)

Father, You have warned me in Your Word not to believe every spirit but to test the spirits to see whether they are from God, because many false prophets have gone out into the world. (1 John 4:1) O, God, as You increase my belief, teach me also what *not* to believe.

Father, You have written Your Word to those who believe in the name of the Son of God so that I may know I have eternal life. (1 John 5:13) Help me to know and cease doubting.

God, You said to Your children, "If you do not stand firm in your faith, you will not stand at all." (Isa. 7:9) Please teach me to stand firm, Lord.

Christ Jesus, before You rebuked the winds and the waves, You asked Your disciples, "You of little faith, why are you so afraid?" (Matt. 8:26) Help me to fully embrace that the One whom the winds and waves obey is the same One who watches over me.

Lord, You do not do many miracles where You see a lack of faith. (Matt. 13:58) Help me not to hinder Your works on my behalf over a lack of faith.

Lord, I want to be like the one to whom You said, "Woman, you have great faith! Your request is granted." (Matt. 15:28) Flourish this kind of faith in me, God!

Christ Jesus, You spoke boldly to Your disciples with the promise, "If you have faith as small as a mustard seed, you can say to this mountain, 'Move from here to there' and it will move. Nothing will be impossible for you." (Matt. 17:20) Lord, develop in me the kind of faith that moves mountains in the power of Your Holy Spirit.

Lord, You have told us in Your Word that in the last days many will turn away from the faith and will betray and hate one another. (Matt. 24:10) O, Father, please help me never to turn away and turn cold.

Lord, just as Your apostles pled and ultimately received, I ask you also to increase my faith! (Luke 17:5)

Lord, You asked in Your Word, "When the Son of Man comes, will He find faith on the earth?" (Luke 18:8) You search the world over for people with faith. Make me one of them, Lord. Find faith in me.

Christ Jesus, You said emphatically, "I tell you the truth, anyone who has faith in me will do what I have been doing." In fact, You said, "He will do even greater things than these, because I am going to the Father." (John 14:12)

Father, by faith in the name of Jesus, make me strong. Help me to realize that it is Jesus' name and the faith that comes through Him that heal me. (Acts 3:16)

Father, I want You to be able to look at my life as You did Stephen's and be able to say that I am full of the Holy Spirit and faith, and that many people were brought to the Lord through my witness. (Acts 11:24)

Lord God, just as You did through Paul and Barnabas to the early disciples, strengthen this disciple and encourage me to remain true to the faith, for Your Word says, "We must go through many hardships to enter the kingdom of God." (Acts 14:22)

Thank You, God, for purifying my heart by faith. (Acts 15:9)

Merciful God, thank You for opening my eyes and turning them from darkness to light, and from the power of Satan to God, so that I may receive forgiveness of sins and a place among those who are sanctified by faith in You. (Acts 26:18)

Lord God, help me to keep up my courage and have faith in You that things will happen just as You said. (Acts 27:25)

> *Do you see that the Lord's promises have many fulfill-*
> *ments? They are waiting now to pour their treasures into*
> *the lap of those who pray. God is willing to repeat the*
> *biographies of His saints in us. He is waiting to be gra-*
> *cious and to load us with His benefits (Ps. 68:19, KJV).*
> *Does this not lift prayer up to a high level?*
>
> Charles Spurgeon, Spurgeon on Prayer
> and Spiritual Warfare

Father, I have been called for Your name's sake to the obedience that comes from faith. (Rom. 1:5) Please help me to understand that obedience demands faith.

Father, please bring strong believers into my life so that we may be mutually encouraged by one another's faith. (Rom. 1:12)

God, in the gospel a righteousness from You is revealed, a righteousness that is by faith from first to last, just as it is written: "The righteous will live by faith." (Rom. 1:17)

O, God, how I thank You that a lack of faith will never nullify Your faithfulness. (Rom. 3:3) If I am faithless, You will remain faithful, for You cannot disown Yourself. (2 Tim. 2:13)

Lord, Your Word is clear that I cannot gain righteousness through works. I have to trust You who justifies the wicked, and my faith will be credited as righteousness. (Rom. 4:5)

Father, since I have been justified through faith, I have peace with You through my Lord Jesus Christ. (Rom. 5:1)

> *How do we find the throne of grace in our time of*
> *need? Follow the blood drops! Then come as boldly as*
> *one possibly can . . . upon his knees. The praying man*
> *is the one heaven sees with bloodstains on his knees.*

Father, thank You for helping me to understand that the access I have gained into Your grace in which I now stand has come to me by faith. Help me to rejoice in the hope of Your glory! (Rom. 5:2)

Lord, according to Scripture, the Word is near me; it is in my mouth and in my heart, and it is the word of faith I am proclaiming. (Rom. 10:8)

Father, Your Word says that faith comes from hearing the message, and the message is heard through the Word of Christ. (Rom. 10:17) Cause me to continue to listen to Your Word! Without Your Word, my faith will never grow.

Lord God, You don't want me to be persuaded just by the wise and persuasive words of men. You want me to be persuaded by the demonstration of the Spirit's power, so that my faith will not rest on men's wisdom, but on God's power. (1 Cor. 2:4–5)

Father, when all other things have passed away, three things will remain: faith, hope, and love. (1 Cor. 13:13) Help me prioritize the things that will always remain.

Christ Jesus, Your Word tells me to be on my guard, to stand firm in the faith, to be a person of courage, and to be strong. (1 Cor. 16:13)

Mighty God, help me to understand that I've been called by You to walk by faith and not by sight. (2 Cor. 5:7) Strengthen my spiritual vision, Lord!

Cause my faith to continue to grow, O Lord. (2 Cor. 10:15)

Father, please help me to examine myself to see whether I am in the faith. You instruct me to test myself and realize that Christ Jesus is in me if I have received Him as Savior. (2 Cor. 13:5)

Glorious Lord, I have been crucified with Christ and I no longer live, but Christ lives in me. The life I live in the body, I live by faith in the Son of God, who loved me and gave Himself for me. (Gal. 2:20)

Father, how I thank You for the faith You have given me. Before this faith came, I was held prisoner by the law, locked up until faith was revealed. (Gal. 3:23)

Lord God, by faith I eagerly await through the Spirit the righteousness for which I hope. (Gal. 5:5)

Christ Jesus, in You neither circumcision nor uncircumcision has any value. The only thing that counts is faith expressing itself through love. (Gal. 5:6)

How I praise You, my God, that in Christ and through faith in Him I may approach God with freedom and confidence! (Eph. 3:12) Help me to understand that the amount of faith I possess will greatly affect the freedom and confidence with which I approach You.

> *Once again today . . . God has a will for your life, Christ has a Word for your life, and the Holy Spirit has a way for your life. Nothing is impossible.*

Father God, You have warned me above all other pieces of armor to take up the shield of faith, with which I can extinguish all the fiery darts of the evil one. (Eph. 6:16, KJV)

Lord God, please place someone in my path as needed who will continue with me for my progress and joy in the faith. (Phil. 1:25)

Lord, Your Word indicates that my willingness to make sacrifices and serve You faithfully flows from faith! (Phil. 2:17) Father, please help me understand the importance of faith in my walk with You.

Father God, You want to present me holy in Your sight, without blemish and free from accusation, and You will do this if I continue in my faith, not moved from the hope held out in the gospel. (Col. 1:22–23)

Lord God, I desire that these things will be remembered before You: by my work produced by faith, my labor prompted by love, and my endurance inspired by hope in my Lord Jesus Christ. (1 Thess. 1:3)

O, God, let it be said of me that my faith is growing more and more, and the love I have for others is increasing! (2 Thess. 1:3)

O, Lord, I want others to be able to boast to You about my perseverance and faith in any persecutions and trials I endure. (2 Thess. 1:4) Help me to remember that others observe the way I handle trials. I want to have a faithful witness, Lord.

Lord God, how I pray that You may count me worthy of Your calling, and that by Your power You may fulfill every good purpose of mine and every act prompted by my faith. (2 Thess. 1:11)

O, Father, help me to fight the good fight, holding on to faith and a good conscience. Please don't let me be like some who have rejected these and so have shipwrecked their faith. (1 Tim. 1:18–19)

Lord, Your Spirit clearly says that in the later times some will abandon the faith and follow deceiving spirits and things taught by demons. (1 Tim. 4:1) Please help me to be very discerning of deceptive teaching. Help me never to abandon the faith to follow after a lie.

Father, Your Word says that the love of money is a root of all kinds of evil. Please help me not be eager for money and take the chance of wandering from the faith and piercing myself with many griefs. (1 Tim. 6:10)

Jesus, Lord and Savior, help me to fight the good fight of the faith, taking hold of the eternal life to which I was called when I made my good confession in the presence of witnesses. (1 Tim. 6:12)

Father God, like Timothy's grandmother, Lois, and his mother, Eunice, help me to pass down a heritage of faith. (2 Tim. 1:5)

Lord, please help me to flee the evil desires of youth, and pursue righteousness, faith, love, and peace, along with those who call on the

Lord out of a pure heart. (2 Tim. 2:22) You want me to pursue faith, not just sit back and wait until it develops.

O, God, more than anything, I want to finish the race one of these days and be able to say, "I have kept the faith." If I keep the faith, You will have a crown of righteousness waiting for me! (2 Tim. 4:7–8)

Father, Your Word emphatically states that You do not lie. You promised before the beginning of time that faith and knowledge rest on the hope of eternal life. (Titus 1:2) Lord, You are so trustworthy. You have given me eternal life. Please grow me in the faith and knowledge that rests upon it.

Father, I pray that I may be active in sharing my faith, so that I will have a full understanding of every good thing I have in Christ. (Philem. 6) Please help me to see that I cannot share something I don't have. I must possess faith to share it!

> *The heart of our timidity to share our faith is that we often have little to spare.*

Father God, the messages I hear from Your Word will have no value to me if I do not combine them with faith. (Heb. 4:2) Help me to combine each message I hear from Your Word with faith; then great value will result.

I praise You, my God, because I have a great high priest who has gone through the heavens, Jesus the Son of God! This allows me to hold firmly to the faith I profess! (Heb. 4:14)

Lord God, help me draw near to You with a sincere heart in full assurance of faith, having my heart sprinkled to cleanse me from a guilty conscience and having my body washed with pure water. (Heb. 10:22)

Lord God, You have said that Your righteous one will live by faith and if he shrinks back You will not be pleased with him. (Heb.

10:38) Lord, I want to live a life that is pleasing to You. The life that pleases you is also a life that You so readily bless. (Heb. 11:6) I don't want to miss the great adventures You mapped out for me by shrinking back from a walk of faith.

Father, according to Your Word, faith is being sure of what I hope for and certain of what I do not see. (Heb. 11:1) Please increase my assurance and certainty of the things You've promised but that I cannot see.

Father God, by faith I understand that the universe was formed at Your command, so that what is seen was not made out of what was visible. (Heb. 11:3)

Lord, please help me to be like Abraham who, by faith, when called to go to a place he would later receive as his inheritance, obeyed and went, even though he did not know where he was going. (Heb. 11:8) Help me not to miss future blessings because I refuse to go to a place with You that I've never been before.

Father, I desire to fix my eyes on Jesus, the author and perfector of my faith, who for the joy set before Him endured the cross, scorning its shame, and sat down at the right hand of the throne of God. (Heb. 12:2)

Father, please help me to remember leaders who spoke the Word of God to me. Help me to consider the outcome of their way of life and imitate their faith. (Heb. 13:7)

Father, You have told me that the testing of my faith develops perseverance. (James 1:3) Please help me to not refuse to be faithful in tests granted for my gain.

Lord God, You have chosen those who are poor in the eyes of the world to be rich in faith and to inherit the kingdom You promised those who love You. (James 2:5) Cause me to be rich in faith, Lord!

> *The Words of men have often exerted a wonderful and a mighty influence. But the words of God . . . they give what they speak. "He spake, and it was done."*
>
> Arthur Murray, The Holiest of All

Father, according to Your Word, a man can't accurately claim to have faith if he has no deeds. Faith by itself, if it is not accompanied by action, is dead. Faith and actions work together. (James 2:14, 17, 22) Cause my faith to be evidenced by my deeds, Lord.

Lord God, I acknowledge that my faith is made complete by what I do. (James 2:22) Faith works!

Praise be to You, my God and the Father of my Lord Jesus Christ! In Your great mercy You have given me new birth into a living hope through the resurrection of Jesus Christ from the dead, and into an inheritance that can never perish, spoil, or fade—kept in heaven for me, who through faith is shielded by God's power. (1 Pet. 1:3–5)

My wise and trustworthy God, according to Your Word, trials come to me so that my faith—of greater worth than gold, which perishes even though refined by fire—may be proved genuine and may result in praise, glory, and honor when Jesus Christ is revealed. (1 Pet. 1:7)

Lord God, I know that it was not with perishable things such as silver or gold that I was redeemed from the empty way of life handed down to me from my forefathers but with the precious blood of Christ, a lamb without blemish or defect. He was chosen before the creation of the world but was revealed in these last times for my sake. Through Him I believe in God, who raised Him from the dead and glorified Him, and so my faith and hope are in God. (1 Pet. 1:18–21)

Father God, help me to be self-controlled and alert. My enemy the devil prowls around like a roaring lion looking for someone to

devour. Help me to resist him, standing firm in the faith. I can be assured that other believers throughout the world are undergoing the same kind of sufferings. (1 Pet. 5:8–9)

Lord, according to Your wonderful Word, this is the victory that has overcome the world, even our faith. Who is it that overcomes the world? Only the one who believes that Jesus is the Son of God. (1 John 5:4–5) Help me to see that faith is crucial if I am going to be a victor and an overcomer.

O, Lord, I want You to be able to say of me, "I know your deeds, your love and faith, your service and perseverance, and that you are now doing more than you did at first." (Rev. 2:19) Cause these words to be true of my life, Father.

> *Lord in Heaven, in every faith walk I encounter, keep working with me until You can victoriously boast, "You believe at last!"*
>
> *John 16:31*

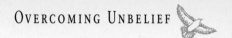

PERSONALIZING YOUR PRAYERS

Chapter 3

OVERCOMING PRIDE

Perhaps no other spiritual obstacle is quite like this one. Why? Because the challenge to overcome pride may be the only common denominator on every one of our spiritual "to do" lists. A simple reason exists for its Goliath proportions: pride is Satan's specialty. It is the characteristic that most aptly describes him. Pride is the issue that had him expelled from heaven. It is still one of Satan's most successful tools in discouraging people from accepting the gospel of Jesus Christ. Let's not fool ourselves into thinking that pride is a problem only for the lost. The most effective means the enemy has to keep believers from being full of the Spirit is to keep us full of ourselves. No wonder the Bible states and restates that God *hates* pride. It is the enemy of genuine ministry. It is the end of many homes.

Scripture exhorts believers, "Humble yourselves, therefore, under God's mighty hand" (1 Pet. 5:6). God's Word also makes that very unsettling statement in Daniel 4:37: "Those who walk in pride he is able to humble." I believe the sum total of those two verses is this: We can humble ourselves, or God can humble us. God won't put up with pride in His own children very long without dealing with it. He's much too faithful. And far too much is at stake. I know one thing from personal experience: humbling ourselves is far less painful than inviting God to humble us. He tends to make sure His lessons "take." I am absolutely convinced that the most painful season God has taken me through to date was primarily to shatter my yoke of pride. A yoke, incidentally, I didn't even recognize I had. Believe me, I'm on the lookout for it now every single day.

In some ways, Christians have to be more alert to pride than anyone. If we don't presently have an issue that is actively humbling us, we veer with disturbing velocity toward arrogance and self-righteousness. We are wise to remember that Christ never resisted the repentant sinner. He resisted the religious proud and Pharisaic. Remember, pride wears many masks. I once spoke on pride only to have someone remark afterward that she had far too little self-esteem to have pride. Pride is *not* the opposite of low self-esteem. Pride is the opposite of humility. We can have a serious pride problem that masquerades as low self-esteem. Pride is self-absorption whether we're absorbed with how miserable we are or how wonderful we are. We are wise to be on the constant lookout for pride in our lives. I believe we can safely say that if we're not deliberately taking measures to combat pride, it's probably doing something to combat humility.

If I could have addressed only a few strongholds in this book, pride would have been one of them. I'll tell you why. Pride is the welcome mat in every figurative prison cell. All we have to do to remain bound in *any area* is to refuse to take responsibility for our strongholds and repent of the sin involved. Pride is a monumental boulder in the path toward breaking free. Ironically, it probably kept a few people from taking this book to the checkout counter of a store. After all, what might the cashier think? So I'd like to brag on you a moment. You wouldn't be holding this book in your hands if you didn't have enough humility to admit to the threat of a stronghold or two. You're a step ahead, my friend. No matter what stronghold you are seeking to demolish, you might consider praying a few Scriptures out of this chapter every day, adding a few of your own on the page provided. We will never waste our time when we pray about our tendency toward pride and seek to humble ourselves before God.

I'd like to share a little added initiative to demolishing the stronghold of pride. These are some thoughts God gave me on the subject several years ago. May He use them to speak about the biggest injustice of pride: it cheats wherever it plays.

My name is Pride. I am a cheater.
I cheat you of your God-given destiny . . . because
you demand your own way.

I cheat you of contentment . . . because you
"deserve better than this."
I cheat you of knowledge . . . because you already
know it all.
I cheat you of healing . . . because you're too full of
me to forgive.
I cheat you of holiness . . . because you refuse to
admit when you're wrong.
I cheat you of vision . . . because you'd rather look
in the mirror than out a window.
I cheat you of genuine friendship . . . because
nobody's going to know the real you.
I cheat you of love . . . because real romance
demands sacrifice.
I cheat you of greatness in heaven . . . because you
refuse to wash another's feet on earth.
I cheat you of God's glory . . . because I convince
you to seek your own.
My name is Pride. I am a cheater.
You like me because you think I'm always looking
out for you. Untrue.
I'm looking to make a fool of you.
God has so much for you, I admit, but don't worry . . .
If you stick with me
You'll never know.

Father, Your Word says You will break down stubborn pride and make the sky above the proud like iron and the ground beneath him like bronze. (Lev. 26:19) Lord, Your Word is drawing a vivid picture of the arrogant life. Prayers lifted to heaven will seem to hit a ceiling of iron, and life beneath the feet will be hard. Help me to be humble before you, Lord. The life of the proud will eventually and undoubtedly become very hard.

Father, Your Word asks the questions, "Who is it you have insulted and blasphemed? Against whom have you raised your voice and lifted your eyes in pride? Against the Holy One of Israel!" (2 Kings 19:22) Please help me to have a proper respect for You, O God.

Lord, according to Your Word, after Uzziah became powerful, his pride led to his downfall. He was unfaithful to the Lord his God. (2 Chron. 26:16) Please help me to not allow pride to be my downfall.

Lord, Your Word says that Hezekiah repented of the pride of his heart, as did the people of Jerusalem; therefore the Lord's wrath did not come upon them during the days of Hezekiah. (2 Chron. 32:26) Thank You for forgiving me when I repent of the pride of my heart.

Father, according to Your Word, in his pride the wicked does not seek You; in all his thoughts there is no room for You. (Ps. 10:4) Please help me to always make room in my thoughts for You, God. Don't allow me to continue on in pride that stops me from seeking You.

Lord, Your Word speaks of the wicked wearing pride as their necklace and clothing themselves with violence. (Ps. 73:6) You indicate a link between pride and violence. Please cause my life to be void of both these evils.

Father, You've said that to fear the Lord is to hate evil; You hate pride and arrogance, evil behavior and perverse speech. (Prov. 8:13) Help me to have a healthy fear of You that abolishes pride and arrogance.

My faithful Father, You've warned me that when pride comes, then comes disgrace, but with humility comes wisdom. (Prov. 11:2)

Father, You're teaching me that pride only breeds quarrels, but wisdom is found in those who take advice. (Prov. 13:10) Help me to discern the pride that is involved when I am quarrelsome.

Lord God, Your Word clearly warns us that pride goes before destruction, a haughty spirit before a fall. (Prov. 16:18)

God, I know that a man's pride brings him low, but a man of lowly spirit gains honor. (Prov. 29:23) Help me to understand what You mean by a lowly or humble spirit. I want to be a person who gains honor in Your sight.

> *Pride is the deification of self.*
> *Oswald Chambers*, My Utmost for His Highest

Father, help me to remember in my impatience that the end of a matter is better than its beginning, and patience is better than pride. (Eccles. 7:8)

Father, a day is certainly coming when the arrogance of man will be brought low and the pride of men humbled; the Lord alone will be exalted in that day. (Isa. 2:17)

Father, Your Word clearly states that You will punish the world for its evil, the wicked for their sins. You will put an end to the arrogance of the haughty and will humble the pride of the ruthless. (Isa. 13:11)

Father, those who have been forsaken and hated by the world, You can make the everlasting pride and the joy of all generations. (Isa. 60:15) Your approval and opinion are all that really matters.

Lord, You instruct Your people to listen carefully and heed Your instruction because pride can cause the Lord's flock to be taken captive. (Jer. 13:17)

Father, help me to understand that the pride in my heart is deceiving me. (Jer. 49:16)

Father God, even mighty King Nebuchadnezzar learned to praise and exalt and glorify the King of heaven and acknowledge that everything You do is right and all Your ways are just. And those who walk in pride You are able to humble. (Dan. 4:37)

Father, Your Word says that pride hardens the heart. (Dan. 5:20) Your desire for me is that I be tenderhearted. (Eph. 4:32, KJV) Please melt any hardness in my heart.

Father, help me possess only acceptable kinds of pride such as taking pride in those who set a good example and those who encourage others by their faithful walk with You. (2 Cor. 5:12) Then, even in all our troubles, as we take godly pride in one another, our joy may know no bounds. (2 Cor. 7:4)

Father, You led Your children, the Israelites, all the way in the desert for forty years, to humble them and to test them in order to know what was in their hearts, whether or not they would keep Your commands. (Deut. 8:2) Help me to understand that sometimes You lead me on certain paths to humble me also and to see what is in my heart. Purify my heart, Lord, so that You will take joy in what You find.

Father, Your Word teaches that You humble and test Your children so that in the end it might go well with us. (Deut. 8:16) You do not humble and test us to bring us low and cause us to fail but to teach us how to succeed in You.

> *God shows us our poverty of spirit when we try, in our own strength, to walk in a way pleasing to God . . . and yet continually fail. This is the testimony the Apostle Paul gives of his own experience in Romans 7. Humility came only when the once-proud Pharisee fell on his face and cried out, "Wretched man that I am! Who will set me free from the body of this death?" (Rom. 7:24, NASB).*
>
> Kay Arthur, *Lord, Only You Can Change Me*

You, my Lord and my God, save the humble, but Your eyes are on the haughty to bring them low. (2 Sam. 22:28)

Father, You have promised that if Your people, who are called by Your name, will humble themselves and pray and seek Your face and turn from their wicked ways, then will You hear from heaven and will forgive their sin and will heal their land. (2 Chron. 7:14) Please help me to understand that corporate revival begins with personal, individual revival. Help me to humble myself and pray and seek Your face and turn from my own wicked ways. Thank You for hearing me from heaven and forgiving my sin and bringing healing to my heart.

> *No matter how perverse and wicked the world becomes, it cannot keep the church from revival. After all, even the gates of hell cannot prevail against her. The church herself is her only true foe in the war of revival. Her pride alone prevails against her. "If My people who are called by My name will humble themselves . . ."*

Wise God, You promise to guide the humble in what is right and teach them Your way. (Ps. 25:9) Give me a humble heart so I will follow You in what is right and learn Your way.

Father, You have promised to sustain the humble but cast the wicked to the ground. (Ps. 147:6)

My Father, I celebrate the fact that You, Jehovah God, take delight in Your people; You crown the humble with salvation. (Ps. 149:4)

Father God, give me courage to admit when I've entered into an unwise alliance. Help me to go and humble myself before the person and press my plea. (Prov. 6:3)

> *What blessed relief comes when we finally fall on our knees and humble ourselves before God. We suddenly realize what a heavy weight pride has been. It is exhausting to insist on thinking so highly of oneself with such mounting evidence to the contrary!*

My Father, how I thank You that the humble will rejoice in the Lord; the needy will rejoice in the Holy One of Israel. (Isa. 29:19)

Father, it is not enough for me to humble myself for one day. (Isa. 58:5) You desire humility to be a lifestyle characteristic.

Sovereign Lord, Your hand has made heaven and earth, and through You they came into being. Your Word says, "This is the one I esteem: he who is humble and contrite in spirit, and trembles at my word." (Isa. 66:2) Father, I can hardly imagine being someone You esteem, but I sincerely want to be! Make me that kind of person through the power of Your Holy Spirit, Lord.

Father God, You said to Your servant, Daniel, "Do not be afraid, Daniel. Since the first day that you set your mind to gain understanding and to humble yourself before your God, your words were heard, and I have come in response to them." (Dan. 10:12) You are my God just as You were Daniel's God. If I set my mind to gain understanding and to humble myself before You, You will hear my words and come in response to them.

> *Christ could afford to be humble as He served upon this earth. After all, He was the Son of God. He had nothing to prove. Yet does His Word not also say that we are heirs of God and joint heirs with Christ? Do you know who you are? Then go ahead and wash a few feet. God's most liberated servants are those who also know they have nothing to prove.*

My Savior and Redeemer, help me to take Your yoke upon me and learn from You, for You are gentle and humble in heart, and I will find rest for my soul. (Matt. 11:29)

Father, like Mary, help my soul to glorify You and my spirit rejoice in You my Savior, for You have been mindful of the humble state of Your servant. (Luke 1:46–48)

Lord God, Your might brings down rulers from their thrones but lifts up the humble. (Luke 1:52)

Father, You are calling upon me to be completely humble and gentle; to be patient, bearing with others in love. (Eph. 4:2) Please empower me with Your Spirit to be obedient to this command.

Faithful Father, thank You for giving us more grace. You oppose the proud but give grace to the humble. (James 4:6)

Father, I desire to humble myself before You and trust that You will lift me up. (James 4:10)

God, through the power of Your Holy Spirit, help me to live in harmony with others, be sympathetic, love as a brother or sister, be compassionate and humble. (1 Pet. 3:8)

Father, help me to clothe myself with humility toward others, because You oppose the proud but give grace to the humble. (1 Pet. 5:5) I will never live a day that I am not in need of Your grace, so please help me maintain an attitude that welcomes it.

Father, help me to humble myself under Your mighty hand, that You may lift me up in due time. (1 Pet. 5:6) You are always trustworthy and Your timing is always right. Help me to humble myself now so that You are free to do wonders later!

Glorious God, in Your majesty ride forth victoriously in behalf of truth, humility, and righteousness; let Your right hand display awesome deeds. (Ps. 45:4)

Father, according to Your Word, the fear of the Lord teaches a man wisdom, and humility comes before honor. (Prov. 15:33) Again, Your Word says, "Before his downfall a man's heart is proud, but humility comes before honor." (Prov. 18:12) I want to be a person of honor in Your sight, O, God. This goal is possible only with humility. Help me to have a humble disposition.

Father, thank You for the assurance that humility and the fear of the Lord bring wealth and honor and life. (Prov. 22:4)

> *Under conviction of worldliness, many well-meaning persons have simply transferred their huge egos from the world to the church. Beware of spiritual ambition. We are most useful to God when poured free of self and full of Christ.*

Like the apostle Paul, help me to serve You, Lord, with great humility and with tears, even when I am severely tested. (Acts 20:19)

Father, You have told me to do nothing out of selfish ambition or vain conceit but in humility consider others better than myself. (Phil. 2:3) Right this moment, I confess all selfish ambition and vain conceit to You. Forgive me for so often considering myself better than others. Help me to look not only to my own interests but also to the interests of others. Please give me an attitude the same as that of Christ Jesus. (Phil. 2:4–5)

God, in my pursuit to be free of pride, never let me delight in false humility. Help me not to be the kind of person who goes into great detail about what he has seen, and whose unspiritual mind puffs him up with idle notions. (Col. 2:18)

Father, Your Word teaches that false humility and harsh treatment of the body lack any value in restraining sensual indulgence. (Col. 2:23)

God, as one of Your chosen people, holy and dearly loved, help me to clothe myself with compassion, kindness, humility, gentleness, and patience. (Col. 3:12)

O, God, please help me to slander no one, to be peaceable and considerate, and to show true humility toward all men. (Titus 3:2)

Father, in Your Word, You define who is wise and understanding among us: The one who shows it by his good life, by deeds done in the humility that comes from wisdom. (James 3:13)

PERSONALIZING YOUR PRAYERS

Chapter 4

OVERCOMING DECEPTION

Deception is the glue that holds every stronghold together. Let's recall a concept we discussed in the introduction of the book: nothing is bigger or more powerful than God; therefore, anything other than Jesus Christ mastering the Christian's life can keep its grip only through pretension and deception. Remember, Satan is the father of lies (John 8:44). No truth is in him. However, his specialty is twisting a lie until it seems true. The list of lies we often believe when we are held in a stronghold can be unlimited. Consider just a few examples:

- I can never be victorious over this compulsion. I've had it too long.
- I can't help the mess I'm in. I'm caught, and there's nothing I can do about it.
- It may be a stronghold, but I really *need* it to get by.
- I am absolutely worthless—nothing but a failure.
- I'm in control here. This is not controlling me.
- This isn't doing me any harm. I can handle it.
- I'll know just when to stop.
- After all I've been through, I deserve this.
- There's nothing wrong with this relationship. People just don't understand us.
- Everyone thinks these kinds of thoughts most of the time. I'm only human.
- God may work for other people, but He doesn't work for me.
- I'll just have to wait until heaven to get over this. Real victory is impossible on earth.
- God can't possibly fill the void in my life. I need something more.

- I am too emotionally handicapped to ever be OK.
- It's hopeless. *I'm* hopeless.

Sometimes we're very aware of tolerating or even fueling a lie. Other times, we are caught in such a web that we can no longer see ourselves or our situations accurately. It's not always clear when we're being deceived, but one sure sign is when we begin to deceive. All you have to do to locate Satan in any situation is look for the lie. How do we recognize a lie? Anything we are believing or acting on that is contrary to what the truth of God's Word says about us is a lie. Second Corinthians 4:2 tells us how to respond to such things: "Rather, we have renounced secret and shameful ways; we do not use deception, nor do we distort the Word of God." This passage helps us identify four of Satan's specialties that must be renounced and rejected by the believer in order for him/her to walk in victory:

1. Secrecy
2. Shame
3. Deception
4. Distortion of Scripture

As you consider each one, you can readily imagine how deception permeates all four and how interrelated they are. Satan's plans toward the believer are always the antithesis of God's. Our Redeemer wants to loose us from the closets of secrecy and bring us to a spacious place of joy, freedom, authenticity, and transparency. Satan wants to keep us bound in secrecy where he can weigh us down in guilt, misery, and shame. Oh, beloved, I know from experience that so much of the shame we experience is wrapped up in the secret. In fact, the enemy knows that once we expose the secret places of our lives to the light of God's Word, we're on our way to freedom.

I am not suggesting that the only way to be free is to stand up before our congregations and tell every detail of every sin we've ever committed or considered. The King James Version translates James 5:16 far more accurately than several of the other versions: "Confess your *faults* one to another, and pray one for another, that ye may be healed" (emphasis mine). Some of the other translations say, "Confess your *sins* to each other . . ." (emphasis mine). The original word translated "faults" in the KJV and "sins" in the NIV is *paraptoma,* which means "fault, lapse, error, mistake, wrongdoing."[1] Contrast 1 John 1:9 where we are told that "If we confess our sins, he is faithful and just and will forgive us our sins and purify us from all unrighteousness." The original word for sin in this verse is *hamartia,* meaning any way in which we miss the mark and any "aberration from the truth." The word is often "spoken of particular sins. . . ."[2] James 5:16 refers to the confessions we make to others, while 1 John 1:9 refers to the confessions we make to God. Please notice the slight contrast between sharing our faults, weakness, and mistakes with others and confessing every detail of every sin to God.

A big difference exists between God and believers: He can always take it. He can always forgive it. And He can always forget it. Refreshingly, *some* believers can too. However, sometimes others can't take the gory details without stumbling over them. At times our own Christian brothers and sisters can unfortunately be some of our biggest obstacles in letting go of the devastating particulars of our past. Let's face it: some believers have the maturity to help free us from our grave clothes, and others just keep picking up anything we dare to shed and handing it back to us.

If we're going to live in freedom, we have no choice but to renounce every single secret place of sin in our lives to God, exposing even the smallest detail to the light of God's Word. This is the means by which God injects truth in the inner parts (Ps. 51:6). I have also found incalculable help and freedom in confessing details of my past sins and strongholds to a few other trustworthy, mature believers for the sake of accountability. There are a couple of people I really trust who basically know every detail of my life.

In my public ministry, whether in writing or in speaking, I make a practice of James 5:16 by sharing about my weaknesses and faults and giving a more general testimony of my past experiences in the pit of sin. I have not hidden the fact that God has delivered me from much shame and sin. I do not see, however, any way in which the body of Christ would be edified by every detail of my past. He may lead you differently, but I am at total peace in my own life with the balance of a general public confession of sin and a specific private confession of sin to God and a few others.

Living a consistently victorious life takes courage! But this courage leads to glorious, indescribable liberty! What relief awaits you if you really decide to let God's truth set you free . . . then keep you free. Be willing to ask God on a regular basis if you are overlooking or denying a stronghold in your life. Because of my past track record, I've had to learn to dialogue openly with God about areas of my life that are at risk: areas where I've been defeated before or circumstances that suddenly result in anger or insecurity. I also ask Him to help me discern the very first signs of Satan's deceptions in my life.

Let's reiterate, however, that the most effective way to veer from deception is to walk in truth. Third John 4 says, "I have no greater joy than to hear that my children are walking in the truth." The wonderful news is: the joy that results from your walk in truth won't just be God's. It will be yours too. As Christ said, "I have told you this so that my joy may be in you and that your joy may be complete."

> *Those who walk in truth will walk in liberty.*

Father, this moment I am choosing the way of truth. I want to set my heart on Your laws. (Ps. 119:30) Help me to choose the way of truth the rest of my days.

Lord God, when You asked the woman in the Garden, "What is this you have done?" her response was, "The serpent deceived me, and I ate." (Gen. 3:13) Just as Eve was deceived by the serpent's cunning, the minds of even those with a sincere and pure devotion to Christ can be led astray. (2 Cor. 11:3) Please help me always to be aware that the enemy will be up to his old tricks. Even the devout believer can be led astray if not held continually on the path by Your Word and keenly aware of Satan's schemes. Help me not to be deceived by the serpent's cunning.

Show me Your ways, O Lord, teach me Your paths; guide me in Your truth and teach me, for You are God my Savior, and my hope is in You all day long. (Ps. 25:4–5)

Test me, O Lord, and try me, examine my heart and my mind; for Your love is ever before me, and I desire to walk continually in Your truth. (Ps. 26:2–3)

Redeem me, O Lord, the God of truth. (Ps. 31:5) Help me to remember that nothing and no one can be redeemed without truth: the God of truth!

Do not withhold Your mercy from me, O Lord; may Your love and Your truth always protect me. (Ps. 40:11) Father, please help me learn how much Your truth protects me. Without it, I am vulnerable to the enemy and to my own flesh nature.

O God, send forth Your light and Your truth to my life. Let them guide me; let them bring me to Your holy mountain, to the place where You dwell. (Ps. 43:3)

> We begin to recognize lies when we know the Truth.

Glorious God, in Your majesty ride forth victoriously in behalf of truth, humility, and righteousness; let Your right hand display awesome deeds. (Ps. 45:4) I don't need to be afraid of truth. It is the key You will use to take me forth to victory.

Lord God, surely You desire truth in my inner parts; You teach me wisdom in the inmost place. (Ps. 51:6) Please expose to me the deeply embedded lies I've believed and replace them with permanently engraved truth.

Teach me Your way, O Lord, and I will walk in Your truth; give me an undivided heart, that I may fear Your name. (Ps. 86:11)

Do not allow anything to snatch the word of truth from my mouth, O Lord, for I have put my hope in Your laws. (Ps. 119:43)

Lord God, You are near to all who call on You, to all who call on You in truth. (Ps. 145:18)

Father, Your Word exhorts us to buy the truth and never sell it, and to get wisdom, discipline, and understanding. (Prov. 23:23) Help me to understand that sometimes truth is costly but not nearly as costly as deception. Truth will never fail to return enormous dividends.

Lord God, You tell us in Your Word that You have not spoken in secret, from somewhere in a land of darkness; You have not said to Jacob's descendants, "Seek me in vain." You, the Lord, speak the truth; You declare what is right. (Isa. 45:19)

Father, You have said in Your Word, "Whoever invokes a blessing in the land will do so by the God of truth; he who takes an oath in the land will swear by the God of truth. For the past troubles will be forgotten and hidden from my eyes." (Isa. 65:16) Lord, I have plenty of past troubles. They seem to continue to be right before my eyes. Please, God of truth, invoke a blessing over my life and release me from my past.

O Lord, Your Word says Your eyes constantly look for truth. When You chastised the children of Israel, You struck them, but they felt no pain; You crushed them, but they refused correction. They made their faces harder than stone and refused to repent. (Jer. 5:3) Lord God, have mercy on me. Help me not to be unresponsive to Your correction. You only chastise in love in order to bring me back to the place of safety . . . to You, Lord God. Help me not hide behind lies. When You look for truth, I pray You will find truth in me!

Lord God, I do not want You to have to say of me, "This child has not obeyed the Lord her God or responded to correction. Truth has perished; it has vanished from her lips." (Jer. 7:28) Lord, if I allow truth to perish in my life and never return to it, I will be held in bondage the rest of my days.

Merciful God, according to Your Word, everyone who does evil hates the light, and will not come into the light for fear that his deeds will be exposed. But whoever lives by the truth comes into the light, so that it may be seen plainly that what he has done has been done through God. (John 3:20–21) O, God, help me to not be afraid to let You shine Your light on my darkness. Please cause Your light to permeate, expose, and treat any darkness or deception in me so that I can live freely in Your light!

Father God, according to Your Word, if I'm really going to be one of Your disciples, I must hold to Your teaching. *Then* I will know the truth, and the truth will set me free. (John 8:31–32) Help me to see the vital link between Your truth and my liberty.

Lord God, You have told us in Your Word that the devil was a murderer from the beginning, not holding to the truth, for there is no truth in him. When he lies, he speaks his native language, for he is a liar and the father of lies. (John 8:44) Please help me discern that wherever deception exists, the devil is at work.

Christ, my Savior and Lord, You are my way. You are my truth. You are my life. You are my only means of going to the Father. (John 14:6) Thank You, Jesus, for the access You afforded me when You laid down Your life in my place.

Grace: *mercy, forgiveness, compassion, blessing, love, kindness—all personified in our Lord. Our God is boundless in grace. Before Him, we are all like the woman caught in adultery; we have all sinned. We stand accused. But God does not condemn us to death under the law. He extends His unmerited, special favor to us. His grace is even more precious because it is free to us, but supremely costly to Him. God Himself paid the price so that He could freely lavish His grace upon us.*

Cynthia Heald, A Woman's Journey
to the Heart of God

Father, You sent Your Holy Spirit to be a Counselor to me. He came straight from You to me and other believers. He is the Spirit of truth who goes out from the Father, and He faithfully testifies truth to me concerning Your Son, Jesus. (John 15:26)

Your Holy Spirit, the Spirit of truth, will guide me into all truth. He will not speak on His own; He will speak only what He hears from You. (John 16:13) As the Holy Spirit within me searches and pinpoints areas of deception in my life, give me sound discernment to understand as He guides me into all truth. Thank You, faithful Father.

Lord God, sanctify me by the truth; Your Word is truth. (John 17:17) Please help me to embrace fully what this verse is saying, Lord. I can be saved by You, but if I don't allow You to teach me and mature me through Your Word, I will never fulfill what You sanctified or set me apart in this earthly existence to do.

Lord, Your Word is clear: wickedness suppresses truth. Your wrath will be revealed from heaven against all the godlessness and wickedness of men who suppress the truth by their wickedness. (Rom. 1:18)

O Merciful Father, please help me never to exchange the truth of God for a lie. (Rom. 1:25) If any area remains in my life where I have made such a tragic exchange, reveal it and set me free.

Lord, Your Word is clear that those who are self-seeking and who reject the truth and follow evil will experience Your wrath and anger. (Rom. 2:8)

Lord Jesus, according to Your Word, love does not delight in evil but rejoices with the truth. (1 Cor. 13:6) Help me, Lord, to possess a genuine and godly love for others and to rejoice with the truth.

Father God, in all sincerity, I desire to renounce all secret and shameful ways; I want to forsake the use of all deception, and learn not to distort the Word of God. On the contrary, by setting forth the truth plainly, I desire to commend myself to every man's conscience in the sight of God. (2 Cor. 4:2)

My faithful Father, I desire to become mature, attaining to the whole measure of the fullness of Christ. Then I will no longer be an infant, tossed back and forth by the waves, and blown here and there by every wind of teaching and by the cunning and craftiness of men in their deceitful scheming. Instead, please teach me to speak the truth in love, growing up into Him who is the head, that is, Christ. (Eph. 4:13–15)

> *Sin wears a cloak of deception. Therefore, the first stage . . . involves the exposure of our hearts to truth and the cleansing of our hearts from lies. . . . Once the Spirit breaks the power of deception in our lives, He can break the power of sin.*
>
> Francis Frangipane, Holiness, Truth and the Presence of God

Father God, continue to teach me. Help me to recognize what is in accordance with the truth that is in Jesus. (Eph. 4:21)

Lord God, I was once darkness, but now I am light in You. Help me to live now as a child of light for the fruit of the light consists in all goodness, righteousness, and truth. Help me to seek You and find out what pleases You. (Eph. 5:8–10)

My all-powerful God, enable me to stand firm, with the belt of truth buckled around my waist and with the breastplate of righteousness in place. (Eph. 6:14) Help me to understand that without the girding of truth, I am defenseless against the devil. Truth is my main defense against the father of lies.

God, according to Your Word, people perish because they refuse to love the truth and so be saved. (2 Thess. 2:10) Please, Lord, give me a love for truth! Immeasurable fruit is produced by the love of truth.

Father, when I sin against You and choose to walk in deception rather than truth, please send others to gently instruct and confront me. Grant me repentance leading me to a knowledge of the truth. (2 Tim. 2:25)

Father, please never allow me to be one who is always learning but never able to acknowledge the truth. (2 Tim. 3:7)

Lord, Your inspired Word declares that the knowledge of Your truth leads to godliness. (Titus 1:1)

Father, Your Word exhorts us that if one of us should wander from the truth, someone should bring him back. (James 5:19)

Lord God, according to Your Word, we purify ourselves by obeying the truth. This purification frees us to have sincere love for our brothers, loving one another deeply, from the heart. (1 Pet. 1:22)

Lord, help me to know that I belong to the truth, and set my heart at rest in Your presence. (1 John 3:19)

Your truth lives in me, O God, and will be with me forever. (2 John 2)

My faithful God, I thank You for the grace, mercy, and peace from You the Father and from Jesus Christ, Your Son, that is with me in truth and love. (2 John 3)

> *If my Father says something about me, even if I cannot see it yet, I can rest assured it is so . . . and begin to put on that truth . . . and walk in it. I can no longer blame someone else for how I view myself. I cannot make the old excuse "that's just the way I am," because it is no longer "the way I am." I take back the stolen ground by simply being in relationship with my Father. His holy genes are now part of my inheritance from Him. I must simply stand and be who He says I am.*
>
> *Dennis Jernigan,* This Is My Destiny

Father God, help me to give You great joy by walking in the truth, just as You commanded us. (2 John 4)

Lord, I want You to have the great joy of hearing others talk about my faithfulness to the truth and how I continue to walk in the truth. (3 John 3)

Father God, You have no greater joy than to hear that Your children are walking in the truth. (3 John 4)

Lord, without You I would be foolish, disobedient, deceived, and enslaved by all kinds of passions and pleasures. I would live in malice and envy, being hated and hating others. (Titus 3:3) I don't want that kind of life, God! I want to live life in the power and fullness of Your Spirit.

Father God, You have adamantly warned Your children not to be deceived. (James 1:16) Am I presently being deceived in any way? If I am, please reveal it to me and give me the courage to cease cooperating with deceptive schemes.

God in heaven, Your Word assures us that the devil, who deceives the world, will be thrown into the lake of burning sulfur, where he will be tormented day and night forever and ever. (Rev. 20:10)

> *Each area of our lives that is controlled by sin is an aspect of our soul under deception. . . . Consequently, the more truthful one becomes with himself and God, the more He is delivered from the "deceitfulness of sin" (Heb. 3:13), allowing righteousness to come forth.*
>
> Francis Frangipane, Holiness, Truth
> and the Presence of God

Father God, like the children of Israel in the prophet Jeremiah's day, I live in the midst of deception; in their deceit many people refuse to acknowledge You. (Jer. 9:6) Father, please help me not to be taken captive by the deception that surrounds me in this society.

Father, Your Word says that when people plant wickedness they will reap evil. You diagnose the root of the problem by saying that they have eaten the fruit of deception. These same people depend on their own strength and on many warriors. (Hos. 10:13) O God, please help me not to eat the fruit of deception. Cause me to recognize the rottenness of this "fruit," refusing to partake.

Father, help me to be discerning of messengers with false visions and deceptive divinations: the ones who say, "The Lord declares," though You, the Lord, have not sent them. (Ezek. 13:6)

Father, I acknowledge that at times in my life I've fed on ashes instead of Your Word and let my deluded heart mislead me. Help me recognize when the thing I'm holding onto for security is a lie. (Isa. 44:20)

I praise You, God of heaven and Lord of earth! You are not a man, that You should lie, nor a son of man, that You should change Your mind. Do You speak and then not act? Do You promise and not fulfill? (Num. 23:19) You are always faithful, God! How grateful I am to know that You will never lie to me.

Father God, I acknowledge that the Spirit clearly says that in later times some will abandon the faith and follow deceiving spirits and things taught by demons. (1 Tim. 4:1) As the time of Your return approaches, there will be increasing deception and literally twisted doctrines taught by angels of darkness. Please develop a higher level of discernment in me, Jesus. Help me to know truth well so that I will quickly recognize the most finely crafted lie.

> *God's faithfulness cannot be fathomed by comparing Him to the noblest of men. God is not a man. He does not simply resist ignoble tendencies. He lacks them altogether. You can take Him at His Word.*

Father God, You command me for my own good not to merely listen to the Word but to do what it says. If I only listen and do not obey, I will undoubtedly deceive myself. Help me to comprehend that the Word of God is my perfect law of liberty! (James 1:22; 1:25, KJV)

My faithful God, help me to see to it that no one takes me captive through hollow and deceptive philosophy, which depends on human tradition and the basic principles of this world rather than on Christ. (Col. 2:8)

I praise You, God, and magnify Your powerful name! For Your Word is living and active. Sharper than any double-edged sword, it penetrates even to dividing soul and spirit, joints and marrow; it judges the thoughts and attitudes of the heart. Nothing in all creation is hidden from Your sight. Everything is uncovered and laid bare before You. (Heb. 4:12–13) Thank You for the assurance that if I will stay in Your Word and obey Your teaching, I will quickly discern the threat of deception and will walk in truth and liberty. Your eyes see into the inmost places of my heart and mind. Please help me to allow You to show me things I need to see and teach me how to be free.

Father, help me to encourage others daily, as long as it is called "today," so that they may not be hardened by sin's deceitfulness. (Heb. 3:13) Send me encouragers when I need them as well. Your Word clearly teaches that sin's deceitfulness hardens us. Keep me tender through Your truth.

Father God, Your Word says, "Woe to those who draw sin along with cords of deceit, and wickedness as with cart ropes." (Isa. 5:18) Please make me instantly aware the moment I am tempted to pick up a cord of deceit.

Father, You have warned me for my own good not to trust anything about my heart unless it is fully surrendered to You. My heart is deceitful above all things and beyond cure. I will never be able to understand it. You the Lord search the heart and examine the mind. (Jer. 17:9–10) Create in me a pure heart, O God, and renew a steadfast spirit within me. (Ps. 51:10) Help me, Lord, above all else to guard my heart, for it is the wellspring of life. (Prov. 4:23) Please help me to recognize that the primary target of deception is my heart. In other words, I must be careful not to trust feelings and emotions on their own. I must wear the breastplate of righteousness so that I will do the right thing even when I don't feel the right thing. In the meantime, I ask You, Lord, to knead the right kind of feelings into my heart.

Heal me, Lord, and I will be healed; save me and I will be saved, for You are the one I praise. How I celebrate the fact that You have not run away from being my shepherd; You have not desired the day of despair. (Jer. 17:14, 16)

> *True freedom will only bloom in your life when you put on the truth of who God says you are.* Knowing *who God wants you to be is not the same as* practicing *who He wants you to be. When life gets complicated and failures abound, turn your heart and mind back to the basics. Remember who you are in Christ, practice being who God says you are, and in time, you'll be walking in the . . . hall of freedom.*
>
> *Dennis Jernigan,* This Is My Destiny

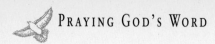

PERSONALIZING YOUR PRAYERS

_____
_____
_____
_____
_____
_____
_____
_____
_____
_____
_____
_____
_____
_____
_____
_____
_____
_____
_____
_____
_____
_____

Chapter 5

OVERCOMING THE INSECURITY OF FEELING UNLOVED

All of us have insecurities . . . even the most outwardly confident people we know. Minor insecurities can be little more than occasional challenges, but when life suddenly erupts like a volcano, insecurity turns into panic. *Want* suddenly feels like *need*. A hidden pocket of unmet needs suddenly quakes and leaves a cavern. The fear or the feeling of being unloved is probably our greatest source of insecurity, whether or not we can always articulate it.

Jehovah God, the Great Soul-ologist, identified man's chief desire in Proverbs 19:22: "What a man desires is unfailing love; better to be poor than a liar." Look at the verse carefully. What in the world does being better off "poor than a liar" have to do with a man's desiring unfailing love?

Think about it for a moment! The Holy Spirit is pinpointing the deep origin of our constant cravings to have more and more of anything. He is implying that our human tendency is to stockpile belongings or amass wealth in order to satisfy a cavernous need in our souls. He is also suggesting that we are lying if we're saying that our greatest need is anything besides unfailing love. The word *desires* in Proverbs 19:22 implies a deep craving. Each of us craves utterly unfailing love: a love that is unconditional, unwavering, radical, demonstrative, broader than the horizon, deeper than the sea. And it would be nice if that love were healthy, liberating rather than suffocating, and whole. Interestingly, the Word of God uses the phrase "unfailing love" thirty-two other times, and not one of them refers to any source other than God, Himself. You see, God had the transcendent advantage. Because He created us, God got to make us any way He wanted us. It's not His will for anyone to perish, and since the only way to have eternal life is to receive Him, God created us with a cavernous need that we would seek to fill until we found *Him*.

Searching for perfect, unfailing love in anyone else is not only fruitless, it is miserably disappointing and *destructive*. I am convinced our hearts are not healthy until they have been satisfied by the only completely healthy love that exists: the love of God, Himself. The following words by Oswald Chambers are not only written in the front of my Bible, they are engraved deeply in my mind: "No love of the natural heart is safe unless the human heart has been satisfied by God first."[1] We are not free to love in the true intent of the word until we have *found* love. All of us have looked, but the important question is *where?* In the search for unfailing love, if we unknowingly allow Satan to become our tour guide, the quest will undoubtedly lead to captivity. I know from experience.

We are not wrong to think we desperately need to be loved. We *do*. But we are wrong to think we can make anyone love us the way we need to be loved. Our need does not constitute anyone else's call but God's. Many of us have heard the devastating words, "I just don't love you anymore." Others may not have heard the words, but they have felt the feeling. The fear. Throughout life we will lose people who really loved us to death or changing circumstances. As dear and as rich as their love was, it was not *unfailing*. It moved. It died. It changed. It left wonderful memories . . . but it left a hole. Only God's love never fails. Even when 1 Corinthians 13:8 says, "Love never fails," it refers to the agape love of God given to us and exercised through us.

Several years ago when my heart desperately needed to be in God's ICU, He helped me picture something I believe all of us do virtually every day. We each have our unmet needs, and we carry them around all day long like an empty cup. In one way or another, we hold out that empty cup to the people in our lives and say, "Can somebody please fill this? Even a tablespoon would help!"

Whether we seek to have our cup filled through approval, affirmation, control, success, or immediate gratification, we are miserable until *something* is in it. I have come to dearly love and appreciate Psalm 143:8: "Let the morning bring me word of your unfailing love, / for I have put my trust in you. / Show me the way I should go, / for to you I lift up my soul." What a heavy yoke is shattered when we awaken in the morning, bring our hearts, minds, and souls and all their "needs" to the Great Soul-ologist, offer Him our empty cups, and ask Him to fill them with *Himself!* No one is more pleasurable to be around than a person who has had her cup filled by the Lord Jesus Christ. He is the only One who is never overwhelmed by the depth and *length* of our need. Imagine how different our days would be if we had our cups filled by Christ first thing in the morning. During the course of the day, anything else anyone is able to offer could just be the overflow of an already full cup. This person will never lack company or affection because she draws daily from the well of unfailing love. This blessed of all believers will know from experience what the apostle Paul meant in Colossians 2:10 (KJV): "Ye are complete in Him."

A precious friend of mine, Danice Berger, helped me compile many of the Scriptures I rewrote into prayer in the next two chapters. She was experiencing a very difficult season in which the issues of feeling unloved, insecure, and rejected were almost overwhelming. She knew the answers were right there in God's Word, but sometimes our hearts are in such pain that we are resistant to risk exposure long enough to receive them. Not only is Danice a schoolteacher, she is a serious student of God's Word. The Holy Spirit prompted me to call her and ask her to research Scripture on the topics of feeling loved and accepted by God when we are feeling unloved and rejected by others. I have known Danice a long time, and I know she loves a good challenge; so I basically dared her to do it. She took the dare. She spent hour upon hour researching security and acceptance in the love of God. The results? Not only did she equip you with many of the truths in the next two chapters, she received them herself. Danice did her homework . . . and in the midst of it, she discovered the same unfailing love that had been there all along. This time she lifted the empty cup and let Him pour.

Lord God, help me to trust in Your unfailing love; cause my heart to rejoice in Your salvation. Help me to sing to You, Lord, for You have been good to me! (Ps. 13:5–6)

I call on You, O God, for You will answer me; give ear to me and hear my prayer. Show the wonder of Your great love, You who save by Your right hand those who take refuge in You from their foes. Keep me as the apple of Your eye; hide me in the shadow of Your wings. (Ps. 17:6–8)

Show me Your ways, O Lord, teach me Your paths; guide me in Your truth and teach me, for You are God my Savior, and my hope is in You all day long. Remember, O Lord, Your great mercy and love, for they are from old. Remember not the sins of my youth and my rebellious ways; according to Your love remember me, for You are good, O Lord. (Ps. 25:4–7)

O God, help me to meditate on Your unfailing love! (Ps. 48:9) Help me not have the sin of unbelief after all You've done to tell me You love me and demonstrate Your love for me.

The earth is filled with Your love, O Lord! Teach me Your decrees. (Ps. 119:64) May Your unfailing love be my comfort, according to Your promise to Your servant! (Ps. 119:76)

I give thanks to You, Lord, for You are good: Your love endures forever. I give thanks to You, the God of gods: Your love endures forever. I give thanks to You, the Lord of lords: Your love endures forever. To You who alone does great wonders: Your love endures forever. Who by Your understanding made the heavens: Your love endures forever. Who spread out the earth upon the waters: Your love endures forever. Who made the great lights and the sun to govern the day: Your love endures forever . . . To You, Lord, the One who remembered me in my low estate and freed me from my enemies: Your love endures forever. I give thanks to the God of heaven: Indeed, Your love endures forever! (Ps. 136:1–8, 23–26)

Jesus Christ, my Kinsman Redeemer and my Bridegroom, Your banner over me is love! (Song of Songs 2:4)

O God, though the mountains be shaken and the hills be removed, yet Your unfailing love for me will not be shaken nor Your covenant of peace be removed. You are the Lord who has compassion on me. (Isa. 54:10) Thank You, God.

My faithful God, help me to call this to mind and therefore always have hope: Because of Your great love, I am not consumed, for Your compassions never fail. They are new toward me every morning; great is Your faithfulness. I will say to myself, "The Lord is my portion; therefore I will wait for Him." (Lam. 3:22–24)

How I thank You, God, that You will heal my waywardness. You love me freely. (Hos. 14:4)

Lord, like Jonah, help me to be convinced that You are slow to anger and abounding in love. (Jon. 4:2) Unlike Jonah, help me to delight in Your compassionate ways, O God, for I am such a recipient of Your grace and mercy.

> *How do we "abide" in the love of God? We dwell no further from His side than the place we are most keenly aware of His great affection. Was it not the disciple who reclined against Christ Jesus who saw himself as the "beloved disciple"? Place your ear against the chest of the Savior so that, when troubled times come, you may not know what will befall you, but you can hear the steady pulse of the boundless love of Him who holds you.*

Lord God, help me not only to fully accept how much You love me, but help me to *abide* in Your love! (John 15:9, NASB)

Glorious God, how I celebrate the fact that my eyes have never seen, my ears have never heard, and my mind has never conceived what You have prepared for me and all others who truly love You. Help me

also to understand that this awesome plan is revealed to me by Your Spirit. (1 Cor. 2:9)

Father God, thank You for telling me that You Yourself express Your love uniquely to those who have loved Christ and believe He came from God. (John 16:27)

O God, please set my heart at rest in Your presence when my heart wants to condemn me. For You, God, are greater than my heart, and You know everything. (1 John 3:19–20)

My Father, I am unspeakably grateful that You have demonstrated Your own love for me in this: while I was still a sinner, Christ died for me. (Rom. 5:8)

You, God, loved me so much that You have given Your one and only Son, and since I believe in Him, I shall not perish but have eternal life. For You, God, did not send Your Son into the world to condemn me but to save me through Him. (John 3:16–17)

My wonderful Savior, Jesus, as hard as this is for me to fathom, Your Word says that as Your Father has loved You, so You love me! You love me so much that You want me to remain in Your love. If I obey Your commands, I will remain in Your love, just as You have obeyed Your Father's commands and remain in His love. You told me this so that Your joy may be in me and that my joy may be complete. (John 15:9–11)

Because of Your great love for me, You, God, who are rich in mercy, made me alive with Christ even when I was dead in transgressions—it is by grace I have been saved. And You, God, raised me up with Christ and seated me with Him in the heavenly realms in Christ Jesus, in order that in the coming ages He might show the incomparable riches of His grace, expressed in His kindness to me in Christ Jesus. (Eph. 2:4–7)

Father God, how great is the love You have lavished on me, that I should be called a child of God! And that is what I am! (1 John 3:1)

Father, as surely as You convinced the apostle Paul, convince me thoroughly that neither death nor life, neither angels nor demons, neither the present nor the future, nor any powers, neither height nor depth, nor anything else in all creation, will be able to separate me from the love of God that is in Christ Jesus my Lord. (Rom. 8:38–39)

> *The bedrock of our Christian faith is the unmerited, fathomless marvel of the love of God exhibited on the Cross of Calvary, a love we never can and never shall merit . . . Undaunted radiance is not built on anything passing, but on the love of God that nothing can alter. The experiences of life, terrible or monotonous, are impotent to touch the love of God, which is in Christ Jesus our Lord.*
>
> *Oswald Chambers,* My Utmost for His Highest

Lord, my God, You long to be gracious to me; You rise to show me compassion. For You, the Lord, are a God of justice. Blessed are all who wait for You! We the people of God, will one day weep no more. How gracious You will be when I cry for help! As soon as You hear, You will answer me. Although You, Lord, have at times given me the bread of adversity and the water of affliction, my teachers will one day be hidden no more; with my own eyes I will see them. Whether I turn to the right or to the left, my ears will hear a voice behind me, saying, "This is the way; walk in it." (Isa. 30:18–21)

My Savior, Jesus Christ, Your Word says that greater love has no one than this, that he lay down his life for his friends. (John 15:13) You have demonstrated the greatest act of friendship in my behalf that exists. I thank You, Lord.

Lord God, I praise You and thank You for not treating me as my sins deserve or repaying me according to my iniquities. For as high as the heavens are above the earth, so great is Your love for those who fear You; as far as the east is from the west, so far have You removed my transgressions from me. (Ps. 103:10–12)

O Lord, You are good and Your love endures forever; Your faithfulness continues through all generations. (Ps. 100:5)

My Jesus, according to Your Word, whoever has Your commands and obeys them, he is the one who loves You. He who loves You will be loved by Your Father, and You too will love him and show Yourself to him. (John 14:21) O, God, please help me to live obediently and have the joy of seeing You revealed in all sorts of marvelous ways.

Lord, my God, may Your unfailing love be my comfort, according to Your promise to Your servant. (Ps. 119:76)

You, eternal God, are my refuge, and underneath are Your everlasting arms. You will drive out my enemy before me, saying, "Destroy him!" (Deut. 33:27)

Lord God, Your anger lasts only a moment, but Your favor lasts a lifetime; weeping may remain for a night, but how I thank You that rejoicing comes in the morning. (Ps. 30:5)

I will be glad and rejoice in Your love, O God, for You saw my affliction and knew the anguish of my soul. You have not handed me over to the enemy but have set my feet in a spacious place. (Ps. 31:7–8) Hallelujah!

Father God, according to Your Word, the angel of the Lord encamps around those who fear You, and You deliver them. Continually whet my appetite and woo me to taste and see that You are good; blessed am I when I take refuge in You! Lord God, please continue to develop in me the right kind of fear of You because Your Word says that those who fear You lack nothing. The lions may grow weak and hungry, but those who seek You, Lord, lack no good thing. (Ps. 34:7–10)

You, Lord, redeem Your servants; no one will be condemned who takes refuge in You. (Ps. 34:22)

When I said, "My foot is slipping," Your love, O Lord, supported me! When anxiety was great within me, Your consolation brought joy to my soul! (Ps. 94:18–19)

Lord God, I desire to bow down to You in worship. I want to kneel before the Lord my Maker; for You are my God, and I am among the sheep of Your pasture, the flock under Your care. (Ps. 95:6–7)

Though You, Lord, are on high, You look upon the lowly, but the proud You know from afar. Though I walk in the midst of trouble, You preserve my life; You stretch out Your hand against the anger of my foes, with Your right hand You save me. You, Lord, will fulfill Your purpose for me; Your love, O Lord, endures forever—do not abandon the works of Your hands. (Ps. 138:6–8)

You, my faithful Lord, are gracious and compassionate, slow to anger and rich in love. You, my Lord, are good to all; You have compassion on all You have made. All You have made will praise You, O Lord; Your saints will extol You. (Ps. 145:8–10)

Your pleasure, O God, is not in the strength of the horse, nor Your delight in the legs of a man; You, O Lord, delight in those who fear You, who put their hope in Your unfailing love. (Ps. 147:10–11) Please help me to put *my* hope unreservedly in Your unfailing love!

Lord God, I believe that Your feelings toward me are consistent with Your feelings toward Your people, Israel, for You are the same yesterday, today, and forever. Therefore I believe You will hear me and bless the praying of Your words to Israel as words over my own life too: This is what You, the Lord, say—You who created me, who formed me: "Fear not, for I have redeemed you; I have summoned you by name; you are mine. When you pass through the waters, I will be with you; and when you pass through the rivers, they will not sweep over you. When you walk through the fire, you will not be burned; the flames will not set you ablaze. For I am the Lord, your God, the Holy One of Israel, your Savior." I am precious and honored in Your sight! (Isa. 43:1–4)

My merciful Father, I claim and choose to believe Your Word that says that though You bring grief, You will show compassion, so great is Your unfailing love. According to Your Word, You do not

willingly bring affliction or grief to the children of men. (Lam. 3:31–33)

Thank You, Lord, for always being good, a refuge in times of trouble. You care for those who trust in You. (Nah. 1:7)

Lord, according to Your Word, even when five sparrows were sold for two pennies, not one of them was forgotten by You. Indeed, the very hairs of my head are all numbered. Help me never to be afraid; I am worth far more to You than many sparrows. (Luke 12:6–7)

> *God is never unbiased toward His children. He does not momentarily set aside His parenthood to discipline us objectively and unaffectionately. He never parts the sea of His fathomless love to take us across begrudgingly. The hardest decisions God ever makes in our behalf crest the highest waves of His love.*

Lord God, I have the assurance of Your Word that You, the God of all grace, who called me to Your eternal glory in Christ, after I have suffered a little while, will Yourself restore me and make me strong, firm, and steadfast. (1 Pet. 5:10)

I call to You, God, and You save me. Even if I cry out in distress evening, morning, and noon, You will never fail to hear my voice. (Ps. 55:16–17)

Lord God, it is because You love me and keep Your Word that You brought me out with a mighty hand and redeemed me from the land of slavery, from the power of the pharaoh of this world. Help me to absolutely know therefore that You, the Lord my God, are God; You are the faithful God, keeping Your covenant of love to a thousand generations of those who love You and keep Your commands. (Deut. 7:8–9)

Great is Your love toward me, O Lord. Your faithfulness endures forever. Praise You, Lord! (Ps. 117:2)

As I walk with You, Lord, You will not let my foot slip—You who watch over me will not slumber; indeed, You who watch over Your children will neither slumber nor sleep. You, the Lord, watch over me—You are my shade at my right hand; the sun will not harm me by day nor the moon by night. You, Lord God, will keep me from all harm—You will watch over my life; You will watch over my coming and going both now and forevermore. (Ps. 121:3–8)

O Lord, because You are my help, I sing in the shadow of Your wings. My soul clings to You; Your right hand upholds me. (Ps. 63:7–8)

Lord God my Savior, when Your kindness and love appeared, You saved me, not because of righteous things I had done, but because of Your mercy. You saved me through the washing of rebirth and renewal by the Holy Spirit, whom You poured out on me generously through Jesus Christ my Savior, so that, having been justified by Your grace, I would become an heir having the hope of eternal life. (Titus 3:4–7)

Lord, how I thank You for showing Your love to me by sending Your one and only Son into the world that I might live through Him. This is love: not that I loved You, but that You loved me and sent Your Son as an atoning sacrifice for my sins. (1 John 4:9–10)

> *What heartbreak we must bring to God when we continue to disbelieve His love. What more could He have said? What more could He have done? Believe even when you do not feel. Know even when you do not see. He gave the life of His Son to demonstrate His love. The time has come to believe.*

Lord God, according to Your Word, You set apart Your children from the nations to be Your own. (Lev. 20:26)

Father God, Your Word tells me to know assuredly that You, the Lord, have set apart the godly for Yourself; You, Lord, will hear when I call to You. (Ps. 4:3)

Lord God, put Your words in my mouth and cover me with the shadow of Your hand—You who set the heavens in place, who laid the foundations of the earth, and who say to Your children, "You are my people." (Isa. 51:16)

Help me to see and believe that You, the Sovereign Lord, come with power, and Your arm rules for You. Your reward is with You, and Your recompense accompanies You. You tend Your flock like a shepherd: You gather the lambs in Your arms and carry them close to Your heart; You gently lead those that have young. (Isa. 40:10–11) O, Lord, help me to realize that You love me and care so deeply for me!

Christ Jesus, long before You became flesh and dwelled among us (John 1:14), the Word of God prophesied that You would be despised and rejected by men, a man of sorrows, and familiar with suffering. Prophecy was fulfilled exactly as Isaiah said. Like one from whom men hide their faces, You were despised, and people did not esteem You. Surely You took up our infirmities and carried our sorrows, yet the people You came to save considered You stricken by God, smitten by God, and afflicted. But You were pierced for our transgressions, You were crushed for our iniquities; the punishment that brought us peace was upon You, and by Your wounds we are healed. We all, like sheep, have gone astray, each of us has turned to his own way; and the Lord has laid on You the iniquity of us all. (Isa. 53:3–6) Savior Jesus, I do not have the proper words of gratitude for all You were willing to do for me to be saved. How can I doubt Your love for me after all that You so willingly did? Help me to believe You!

Christ Jesus, You look down upon the masses of people on this earth and have compassion on them. So many are harassed and helpless, like sheep without a shepherd. (Matt. 9:36) Thank You for Your mercy, O Savior, that endures forever.

O Christ, cause Your love to absolutely compel me. Help me to be convinced that because One died for all, therefore all died. Help me to realize and fully appreciate the fact that because You died for all, we who live should no longer live for ourselves but for You who died for us and was raised again. (2 Cor. 5:14–15) Please don't let me miss the joy and fulfillment of living my life for You. Please don't let my own stubbornness of heart stand in the way of fulfilling Your plan for my life.

Lord God, help me to *know* the grace of my Lord Jesus Christ, that though He was rich, yet for my sake He became poor, so that I through His poverty might become rich. (2 Cor. 8:9) Please help me to continually discover the riches of Christ in my life, Lord.

I gratefully acknowledge that I have been crucified with You, Christ, and I no longer live, but You live in me. The life I live in the body, I live by faith in You, the Son of God; You love me and gave Yourself for me. I do not set aside the grace of God, for if righteousness could be gained through the law, You died for nothing! (Gal. 2:20–21)

God, I pray that out of Your glorious riches You will strengthen me with power through Your Spirit in my inner being, so that Christ may dwell in my heart through faith. And I pray that I, being rooted and established in love, may have power, together with all the saints, to grasp how wide and long and high and deep is the love of Christ, and to know this love that surpasses knowledge—that I may be filled to the measure of all the fullness of God. Now to You who are able to do immeasurably more than all I ask or imagine, according to Your power that is at work within me, to You be glory in the church and in Christ Jesus throughout all generations, for ever and ever! Amen. (Eph. 3:16–21)

O God, help me always to be thankful that I am loved by You, because from the beginning You chose me to be saved through the sanctifying work of the Spirit and through belief in the truth. (2 Thess. 2:13)

You are the Lord my God, who brought me out of slavery; You broke the bars of my yoke and enabled me to walk with my head held high. (Lev. 26:13) How I thank You for this, O Lord!

For surely, O Lord, You bless the righteous; You surround them with Your favor as with a shield. (Ps. 5:12) O, Father, please help me to be Your idea of righteous. I know that on my own, my righteousness is as filthy rags before You, but because I have received Christ and daily desire to walk with Him, I now stand in His righteousness. Help me to flesh out His righteousness in my life.

Father God, Your Word says for everyone who is godly to pray to You while You may be found; surely when the mighty waters rise, they will not reach me. You are my hiding place; You will protect me from trouble and surround me with songs of deliverance. (Ps. 32:6–7) O, thank You, God!

Lord, many are the woes of the wicked, but Your unfailing love surrounds the one who trusts in You. (Ps. 32:10) You are so trustworthy, God. Please help me to place my complete trust in You.

> *Although it seems safe and logical to be in charge of your life, being in charge becomes a heavy, lonely responsibility. Your Father graciously offers to take your life, protect you, strengthen you, and comfort you on your journey. You need not fear relinquishment, for it leads to freedom, security, and the real you.*
>
> Cynthia Heald, A Woman's Journey to
> the Heart of God

You, the Lord my God, are my sun and shield; You, Lord, bestow favor and honor; no good thing do You withhold from those whose walk is blameless. (Ps. 84:11) Lord, I can't claim a blameless walk, but I ask You to please empower me to walk with You faithfully and to never cease pursuing it.

Father, I thank You for the vivid picture You paint in Your Word as You promise to cover me with Your feathers and grant me refuge under Your wings; Your faithfulness will be my shield and rampart. I need not fear the terror of night, nor the arrow that flies by day, nor the pestilence that stalks in the darkness, nor the plague that destroys at midday. A thousand may fall at my side, ten thousand at my right hand, but You will keep destruction from coming near me. (Ps. 91:4–7)

Lord God, I love Your Word! You offer to rescue those who love You and protect those who acknowledge Your name. I will call upon You, and You will answer me; You will be with me in trouble, You will deliver me and honor me. Lord, I ask You to satisfy me with long life and show me Your salvation. (Ps. 91:14–16)

Father God, according to Your Word, those who trust in the Lord are like Mount Zion, which cannot be shaken but endures forever. As the mountains surround Jerusalem, so the Lord surrounds His people both now and forevermore. (Ps. 125:1–2) Hallelujah!

My God, You say to me in Your Word, "I, even I, am he who comforts you." (Isa. 51:12) Thank You, Lord! Help me to sense and respond to Your comfort.

Lord, please help me not to be like Ephraim whom You taught to walk, taking them by the arms; but they did not realize it was You who healed them. Please help me to realize without a doubt that You are the One who heals me. Like Ephraim, You have led me with cords of human kindness, with ties of love; You lifted the yoke from my neck and bent down to feed me. (Hos. 11:3–4) Help me to acknowledge You daily and never forget who teaches me how to walk.

You, the Lord my God, are with me, You are mighty to save. You will take great delight in me, You will quiet me with Your love, You will rejoice over me with singing! (Zeph. 3:17)

You, O Lord, love me with an everlasting love; You have drawn me with loving-kindness. You will build me up again and I will be rebuilt. I will take up my tambourine and go out to dance with the joyful! (Jer. 31:3–4)

Lord God, in Your love You kept me from the pit of destruction; You have put all my sins behind Your back. (Isa. 38:17) You will

never fail to forgive the truly repentant sinner, O Lord, because You love us so much.

Lord, according to Your Word, what a man desires or craves deeply is *unfailing love.* (Prov. 19:22) Every other use of the words *unfailing love* in Scripture is attributed to You alone. You are the only one capable of perpetually unfailing love. Help me to understand that my deep cravings for someone to love me with that kind of love were meant to be satisfied in You alone. Thank You, Lord.

Father God, Your Word exhorts me to sow for myself righteousness, and reap the fruit of unfailing love, and break up my unplowed ground; for it is time to seek You, Lord, until You come to shower righteousness on me! (Hos. 10:12)

You, Jesus Christ, are the faithful witness, the firstborn from the dead, the ruler of the kings of the earth. To You—who loves me and has freed me from my sins by Your blood, and has made me to be part of Your kingdom and priests to serve Your God and Father—to You be glory and power for ever and ever! Amen. (Rev. 1:5–6)

> *My whole heart has not one single grain, this moment, of thirst after approbation. I feel alone with God; He fills the void; I have not one wish, one will, one desire, but in Him; He hath set my feet in a large room. I have wondered and stood amazed that God should make a conquest of all within me by love.*
>
> *Lady Huntington,* Streams in the Desert

PERSONALIZING YOUR PRAYERS

Chapter 6

OVERCOMING FEELINGS OF REJECTION

Few of us will embrace the difficult challenge of being rejected. In Philippians 3:10, the apostle Paul stated the deepest desire of his impassioned heart: "I want to know Christ and the power of his resurrection and the fellowship of sharing in his sufferings." A vital and admittedly painful part of God's conforming process in our lives is our willingness to fellowship with Christ in His sufferings. The first suffering of Christ recorded in the Gospel of John is found in the eleventh verse of chapter one: "He came to that which was his own, but his own did not receive him." *Rejection.* Remember, these were Christ's own people. He *loved* them. His heart must have longed to be accepted by them. The Hebrew people shared a sense of community with which we have little to compare in our society. To be excluded from the fellowship and acceptance of that community was considered a fate worse than death by many. In fact, Scripture tells us that certain Pharisees who really wanted to believe were afraid to express their acceptance of Christ for fear of the same rejection. John's Gospel also tells us that Christ was rejected by His own brothers. If you've never experienced rejection, you might be wondering whether *suffering* is too strong a word for it; however, if you've been rejected by someone you love, you'll agree that few injuries are more excruciating.

Rejection in and of itself is not a stronghold. Our reaction to rejection determines whether we become bound by it. Only God knows the tragic number of His own children who have allowed themselves to be imprisoned by continuing feelings of rejection for the rest of their lives. I would never imply that getting over rejection is easy; but it is possible for every single person who puts his or her heart and *mind* to it to overcome. That's what this chapter is all about. Overcoming rejection is God's unquestionable will for your life if you belong to Him. How do you overcome rejection? By applying large doses of God's love to your wounded heart daily and by allowing Him to renew your mind until the rejected thinks like the *accepted*.

Jesus Christ will never leave you or forsake you. He will never cast you away. He is incapable of suddenly deciding He no longer wants you. If you have received God's Son as your Savior, nothing you can do will cause Him to reject you. Believe what God's Word tells you about *Him* and about *you*. You are defined by the love and acceptance of the Creator and Sustainer of the universe. He happens to think you are worth loving . . . and keeping. Find your identity in Him.

I had both the pain and the joy of watching someone deal victoriously with rejection. Both she and her husband were active members of a church in another city. They had been married twenty-five years when she learned that he was having an affair. He had no history of unfaithfulness but had allowed Satan to twist a friendship into an illicit relationship. To make matters worse, the husband confessed with tears that he was in love with the other woman. My friend was devastated—not for days or weeks but for months. Her husband agreed not to file for divorce, but he would not agree to cease all contact with the other woman. The marriage appeared to be hopeless.

My friend cast herself entirely upon Jesus Christ and His Word because it was, in her words, her only means of survival. She had been a Christian since her youth and served her church faithfully but she had never before been forced to live and breathe on God's Word. Transformation happened before my very eyes. God seemed to open His Word like the Red Sea and she walked through that flood of pain on dry land. Over the course of the next four years, this man saw such inner strength and spiritual beauty overtake his wife that he fell in love with her all over again. Either of them will tell you they have a marriage today that they never had before. I'm not suggesting that if every rejected spouse does likewise the results will always be the same. Both parties must eventually be willing and patient to allow God to perform a miracle of healing and forgiveness. I am suggesting, however, that the rejected person who turns entirely to God and His Word can find glorious restoration and acceptance in Christ no matter what happens. No matter what kind of rejection you may have suffered, may these Scripture prayers be used by God to bring you much strength.

Lord Jesus, You came and preached peace to those of us who were far away and peace to those of us who were near. For through You, Jesus, we both have access to the Father by one Spirit. Consequently, we are no longer foreigners and aliens, but fellow citizens with God's people and members of God's household, built on the foundation of the apostles and prophets, with You, Christ Jesus, Yourself as the chief cornerstone. In You the whole building is joined together and rises to become a holy temple in the Lord. And in You, we too are being built together to become a dwelling in which God lives by His Spirit. (Eph. 2:17–22)

Lord, I am so grateful to be one of Your chosen people, part of a royal priesthood, a holy nation, a people belonging to You, God, that I may declare the praises of You who called me out of darkness into Your wonderful light. (1 Pet. 2:9)

For the sake of Your great name, Lord, You will not reject Your people, because You, Lord, were pleased to make me Your own. (1 Sam. 12:22) Praise Your wonderful name!

> *God was pleased to make you His own. Pleased! He didn't just feel sorry for you. He wasn't obligated to you. He chose you because He delights in you. You were never meant to get through life by the skin of your teeth. You were meant to flourish in the love and acceptance of Almighty Jehovah. When He sings over you, dance!*

Lord God, in Your Word You pose the question, "Can a mother forget the baby at her breast and have no compassion on the child she has borne?" You assure me that though she may forget, You will absolutely never forget me! You have engraved me on the palms of Your hands. (Isa. 49:15–16)

Lord God, just as Your children the Israelites were chosen out of all the peoples on the face of the earth to be Your people, Your treasured possession, I believe that we, the body of Christ, have been too. You did not set Your affection on Your children and choose us because we were more numerous than other peoples. It was because You loved us that You redeemed us from slavery, from the power of the enemy. Help me to know with certainty that You, the Lord my God, are God. You are the faithful God, keeping Your covenant of love to a thousand generations of those who love You and keep Your commands. (Deut. 7:6–9)

I thank You, my God, who always leads me in triumphal procession in Christ and through me desires to spread everywhere the fragrance of the knowledge of Him. For You have called me to be the aroma of Christ among those who are being saved and those who are perishing. (2 Cor. 2:14–15)

Lord God, according to Your Word, Your Spirit Himself testifies with our spirit that we are Your children. Now if we are children, then we are heirs—heirs of Yours and coheirs with Christ, if indeed we share in His sufferings in order that we may also share in His glory. Help me to really embrace the truth that any present sufferings I encounter are not worth comparing with the glory that will be revealed in me. (Rom. 8:16–18)

Lord God, I thank You for Your Word that assures me that there is now no condemnation for those who are in Christ Jesus, because through Christ Jesus the law of the Spirit of life set me free from the law of sin and death. (Rom. 8:1–2)

Lord God, I revel in Your promise that You will go before me and make the rough places smooth; You will shatter the doors of bronze and cut through their iron bars. And You will give me the treasures of darkness and hidden wealth of secret places, in order that I may know that it is You, the Lord, the God of Israel, who calls me by my name. (Isa. 45:2–3, NASB)

Father God, I ask You to lead me when I'm blinded by ways I have not known, along unfamiliar paths please guide me; Lord, turn the darkness into light before me and make the rough places smooth. I pray these are the things You will do; I know You will not forsake me. (Isa. 42:16)

Even if my father and mother forsake me, You, Lord, will receive me. (Ps. 27:10)

Lord God, I desire to claim the words Moses delivered to Your ancient people: Help me not to be afraid. Enable me to stand firm so I will see the deliverance that You, the Lord, will bring me today. You, Lord, will fight for me; help me only to be still. (Exod. 14:13–14)

I praise You, Lord, with all my soul, and I desire never to forget all Your benefits—You, Lord, are the one who forgives all my sins and heals my diseases, who redeems my life from the pit and crowns me with love and compassion, who satisfies my desires with good things so that my youth is renewed like the eagle's. You, Lord, work righteousness and justice for all the oppressed. (Ps. 103:2–6)

Father God, make me strong and courageous. Help me not to be afraid or terrified because of anyone else, for You, the Lord my God, go with me; You will never leave me or forsake me. (Deut. 31:6)

Lord, how I thank You for the assurance that You will not reject Your people; You will never forsake Your inheritance. (Ps. 94:14)

My Lord, You are a refuge for the oppressed, a stronghold in times of trouble. Those who know Your name will trust in You, for You, Lord, have never forsaken those who seek You. (Ps. 9:9–10) Oh, Lord, I do know Your name. Please swell my trust in You.

> *In a sense we are all, in some way, outcasts until we meet the Lord. We are thirsty for people to love and accept us. We drink from many wells to try to satisfy our longings, but eventually, we tire of always having to draw water to get our needs met. Each of us asks, Isn't there someone who will give me water without manipulating me or requiring me to jump through hoops for it? Isn't there someone who will love me just for who I am? Then Jesus appears at high noon.*
>
> Cynthia Heald, A Woman's Journey to
> the Heart of God

But You, O God, do see trouble and grief; You consider it to take it in hand. The victim commits himself to You; You are the helper of the fatherless. (Ps. 10:14) O, God, help me to understand that I am no longer a victim of anyone else's misuse or rejection when I commit myself entirely to You. Make me a victor, Lord Jesus!

The wicked lie in wait for the righteous, seeking their very lives; but You, Lord, will not leave them in their power or let them be condemned when brought to trial. Your instruction to me is to wait for You and keep Your way. You will exalt Your own to inherit the land; when the wicked are cut off, we will see it. (Ps. 37:32–34)

Father, before Your Son was taken for trial and crucifixion, He shared His heart for us in a deep intercessory prayer. He wants those You have given Him to be with Him where He is, and to see His glory, the glory You have given Him because You loved Him before the creation of the world. Righteous Father, though the world does not know You, Jesus knows You, and we know that You sent Him. Lord God, Your Son came to make You known to me, and He will continue to make You known in order that the love You have for Him may be in us and that Jesus Himself may be in us. (John 17:24–26) Father, according to Your Word, You give the Son what He asks; therefore I thank You for making Yourself known to me and welcoming me to be in You. No matter how I may encounter rejection in the world around me, I am welcomed to abide in the Creator of heaven and earth and the perfect Son of the Most High God.

Lord God, if I feel hated by the world, You have told me to keep in mind that it hated You first. You said that if I belonged to the world, it would love me as its own. As it is, I do not belong to the world, but You, awesome and magnificent God, have chosen me out of the world. That is why the world hates me. Help me to remember the words You spoke to me: "No servant is greater than his master." If they persecuted You, they will persecute me also. If they obeyed Your teaching, they will obey the teaching of Your disciples also. (John 15:18–20)

My Savior, Jesus Christ, as unimaginable as this may seem, when I am obedient to You, You call me friend. You desire to make known to me everything You learned from Your Father! I did not choose You, but You chose me and appointed me to go and bear fruit—fruit that will last. Then the Father will give me whatever I ask in Your name. (John 15:13–16) Develop Your heart within me, Jesus, so I will know how to ask of the Father in Your great name. Help me

> "In the year that king Uzziah died, I saw also the Lord." Isaiah 6:1. *Our soul's history with God is frequently the history of the "passing of the hero." Over and over again God has to remove our friends in order to bring Himself in their place, and that is where we faint and fail and get discouraged. Take it personally: In the year that the one who stood to me for all that God was, died—I gave up everything? I became ill? I got disheartened? Or—I saw the Lord?*
>
> *Oswald Chambers,* My Utmost for His Highest

also to be perpetually aware that You chose me, so I never need to feel left out.

Lord Jesus, You said that if anyone loves You, he will obey Your teaching. You also assured that Your Father would love him and that both of You would come to him and make Your home with him. (John 14:23) O, Lord, I pray that both You and the Son would dwell in me richly and fully through Your Holy Spirit. Make my heart Your home, Lord Jesus.

Lord Jesus, You asked Your Father to give me a Counselor that would be with me forever—the Spirit of truth. The world cannot accept the Holy Spirit, because it neither sees Him nor knows Him. But I know Him, for He lives with me and is in me. You have not left me as an orphan. You came to me. Even though the world does not see You any more, I can see You through the work of Your Holy Spirit. Because You live, I also live. Help me to realize that You, Jesus, are in Your Father, and I am in You, and You are in me. (John 14:15–20)

Jesus, teach me not to let my heart be troubled. Help me to trust in Your Father and trust also in You. In Your Father's house are many rooms; if it were not so, You would have told me. You have gone there to prepare a place for me. You will most assuredly come back and take me to be with You some day so that I may also be where You are. (John 14:1–3)

Lord Jesus, You have promised that the Holy Spirit, whom the Father sent in Your name, will teach Your disciples all things and will remind those who follow You of everything You have said in Your Word. Peace You leave with me; Your peace You give me. You do not give to me as the world gives. My heart need not be troubled or afraid. (John 14:26–27)

Because You, Sovereign Lord, help me, I will not be disgraced. Therefore help me set my face like flint, and I know I will not be put to shame. He who vindicates me is near. Who then will bring charges against me? Let us face each other! Who is my accuser? Let him confront me! It is the Sovereign Lord who helps me. Who is he that will

condemn me? They will all wear out like a garment; the moths will eat them up. (Isa. 50:7–9)

Since ancient times no one has heard, no ear has perceived, no eye has seen any God besides You, who acts on behalf of those who wait for Him. You come to the aid of those who gladly do right, who remember Your ways. (Isa. 64:4–5) O, Lord, please empower me to live obediently through Your Holy Spirit so that You are fully released to act in my behalf. Do more than I can see, hear, or even imagine, Lord Jesus!

Anointed Savior Jesus, the Spirit of the Sovereign Lord is on You, because He has anointed You to preach good news to the poor. He has sent You to bind up the brokenhearted, to proclaim freedom for the captives and release from darkness for the prisoners, to proclaim the year of the Lord's favor and the day of vengeance of our God, to comfort all who mourn, and provide for those who grieve in Zion—to bestow on them a crown of beauty instead of ashes, the oil of gladness instead of mourning, and a garment of praise instead of a spirit of despair. Those who receive will be called oaks of righteousness, a planting of the Lord for the display of His splendor. We will rebuild the ancient ruins and restore the places long devastated; we will renew the ruined cities that have been devastated for generations. (Isa. 61:1–4) Lord Jesus, You are so willing and able to minister to me. Give me a humble and cooperative spirit to receive Your incomparable, liberating ministry.

Lord, I have heard the slander of many; at times there is terror on every side; I sometimes feel that others conspire against me and the enemy plots to take my life. But I trust in You, O Lord; I say, "You are my God." My times are in Your hands; deliver me from my enemies and from those who pursue me. Let Your face shine on Your servant; save me in Your unfailing love. (Ps. 31:13–16)

Merciful, compassionate God, even my close friend, whom I trusted, he who shared my bread, has lifted up his heel against me. But You, O Lord, have mercy on me; raise me up . . . Empower me to live a life pleasing to You, and my enemy will not be able to triumph over me. Lord, as a New Testament believer, uphold me in

Your integrity instead of my own and set me in Your presence forever. (Ps. 41:9–12)

You are my lamp, O Lord; the Lord turns my darkness into light. With Your help I can advance against a troop; with my God I can scale a wall. As for You, my God, Your way is perfect; the word of the Lord is flawless. You are a shield for all who take refuge in You. For who is God besides You, Lord? And who is the Rock except my God? It is You, God, who arms me with strength and makes my way perfect. You make my feet like the feet of a deer; You enable me to stand on the heights. You train my hands for battle; my arms can bend a bow of bronze. You give me Your shield of victory; You stoop down to make me great. You broaden the path beneath me so that my ankles do not turn. (2 Sam. 22:29–37)

You, Lord, are my shepherd; I shall not be in want. You make me lie down in green pastures; You lead me beside quiet waters; You restore my soul. You guide me in paths of righteousness for Your name's sake. Even though I walk through the valley of the shadow of death, I will fear no evil, for You are with me; Your rod and Your staff, they comfort me. You prepare a table before me in the presence of my enemies. You anoint my head with oil; my cup overflows. Surely goodness and love will follow me all the days of my life, and I will dwell in the house of the Lord forever. (Ps. 23:1–6)

For in the day of trouble You will keep me safe in Your dwelling; You will hide me in the shelter of Your tabernacle and set me high upon a rock. Then my head will be exalted above the enemies who surround me; at Your tabernacle will I sacrifice with shouts of joy; I will sing and make music to the Lord. (Ps. 27:5–6)

I am seeking You, Lord, and You will answer me; You will deliver me from all my fears. (Ps. 34:4)

Lord God, Your Word says that You love the just and will not forsake Your faithful ones. They will be protected forever. (Ps. 37:28) My justification is found in Your Son and my Savior, Jesus Christ. (Rom. 8:30) He is faithful even when I am not. (2 Tim. 2:13)

Thank You, Father, that I can be absolutely sure You will never leave me or forsake me because I am in Jesus. (Heb. 13:5)

Lord God, You are so tenderhearted. You set the lonely in families, You lead forth the prisoners with singing; but the rebellious live in a sun-scorched land. (Ps. 68:6)

My faithful God who is the same yesterday, today, and forever (Heb. 13:8), be to me what You were to Abram: my shield and my very great reward. (Gen. 15:1)

Lord, I believe that Your heart toward Your children today is like Your heart toward the children of Israel. I believe You also took us from the ends of the earth; from its farthest corners You called us. You said, "You are my servants; I have chosen you and have not rejected you. So do not fear, for I am with you; do not be dismayed, for I am your God. I will strengthen you and help you; I will uphold you with my righteous right hand." One day because of You, Lord, I will search for my enemies and will not find them. Those who wage war against me will be as nothing at all. For You are the Lord, my God, who takes hold of my right hand and says to me, "Do not fear; I will help you." (Isa. 41:9–13)

Merciful Savior, according to Your Word, I am blessed when men hate me, when they exclude me and insult me and reject me as evil, because of You, the Son of Man. Your Word says I have cause to rejoice in that day and leap for joy, because great is my reward in heaven. For that is how their fathers treated the prophets. (Luke 6:22–23)

Lord Jesus, just as Your sufferings flow over into our lives, so also through You our comfort overflows. (2 Cor. 1:5) You are so faithful, Jesus.

Lord God, I am hard pressed on every side, but not crushed; perplexed, but not in despair; persecuted, but not abandoned; struck down, but not destroyed. I always carry around in my body the death of Your Son, Jesus, so that the life of Jesus may also be revealed in my body. (2 Cor. 4:8–10) Lord, help me always to remember that if I am truly crucified with Christ, I am also raised to resurrection life! Help me never to forget that the purpose of crucified life is to walk in the power of Your resurrection. (Gal. 2:20)

Dear Lord, why am I always surprised at the painful trials I suffer, as though something strange were happening to me? Help me to rejoice that I participate in the sufferings of Christ, so that I may be overjoyed when Your glory is revealed. If I am insulted because of the name of Your Son, Christ, I am blessed, for the Spirit of glory and of God rests on me. (1 Pet. 4:12–14)

For You, the Lord my God, are a merciful God; You will not abandon or destroy me or forget the covenant with my spiritual forefathers, which You confirmed to them by oath. (Deut. 4:31) I belong to Christ, therefore I, too, am Abraham's seed and heir according to the promise. (Gal. 3:29) Like Isaac, I am a child of promise. (Gal. 4:28)

You, Lord, have declared that You know the plans You have for me. Your plans are to prosper me and not to harm me, plans to give me hope and a future. Because of all You've done for me through Your Son, Jesus, when I call upon You and come and pray to You, You will listen. I will seek You and find You when I seek You with all my heart. You have declared, "I will be found by you." You will bring me back from captivity. (Jer. 29:11–14)

You, Mighty Defender, defend the cause of the fatherless and the widow, and love the alien, giving him food and clothing. (Deut. 10:18)

You will not take Your love from me. You will never betray Your own faithfulness, O Lord. You will not violate Your covenant or alter what Your lips have uttered. (Ps. 89:33–34)

For my Maker is my husband—the Lord Almighty is Your name—the Holy One of Israel is my Redeemer; You are called the God of all the earth. You, Lord, will call me back as if I were a wife deserted and distressed in spirit—a wife who married young, only to be rejected. With deep compassion You will bring me back. You may chasten me, but with everlasting kindness You will also have compassion on me. (Isa. 54:5–8) Thank You, Lord.

One of us can rout a thousand, because You, the Lord our God, fights for us, just as You promised. Faithful God, help me to be very careful to love You, the Lord my God. (Josh. 23:10–11)

How I thank You, Lord, for having the power to turn any curse into a blessing for me, because You, the Lord my God, love me. (Deut. 23:5)

> *The steps of the believer are steeped in constant change. Fingers are painfully peeled away from the security of sameness one at a time. Again and again. Great wisdom lies in freeing our fellow sojourners . . . cherished though they are. With hands freshly loosed we find liberty to embrace the One who will never change, and courage to release to Him those who ever will.*

PERSONALIZING YOUR PRAYERS

Chapter 7

Overcoming Addiction

Addiction is one of the cruelest of all yokes because it deceives us unmercifully and ruthlessly. It comes to us like a friend, promising to bring comfort. It kisses us on the cheek like Judas, stealing from our treasury, then rents us for a cheap fee to the opposition. Addiction is a yoke that convinces us we must wear it to survive. Nothing makes us feel more powerless. No ungodly master is a more unyielding dictator. Countless people, even those in the family of our faith, have concluded that they are hopeless to overcome this relentless beast. After more failures than they can bear to count, many believers accept earthly defeat as compulsory and await a freedom that will only come in heaven. The accuser of the brethren chides them constantly with his tally of failures and convinces them that they are unable to derail the miserable cycle of self-loathing.

No matter whether your addictions are to substances or behaviors, God can set you free. What He requires from you is *time, trust,* and *cooperation.* The immense power of an addiction is rarely broken in a day. You see, God has as much to teach us as He has to show us. He could show us His power by instantaneously setting us free from all desire for our stronghold. Often, however, God chooses the process of teaching us to walk with Him and depend on Him daily. Few things beyond our salvation are "once and for all." If He delivered us instantly, we would see His greatness once, but we would soon forget . . . and we'd risk going back. On the other hand, if God teaches us victory in Christ Jesus day by day, we live in the constant awareness of His greatness and His sufficiency. Hard lessons are often long-lasting lessons. Never forget that God is far more interested in our getting to know the Deliverer than simply being delivered.

Begin to see yourself like the young shepherd boy, David, when he dared to take a stand against his Goliath. David wasn't blind. He was realistically aware of the mammoth size of his foe. What was the key to his courage? David knew that Goliath was not only his enemy. Far more important—he was God's enemy! Long before the apostle Paul was inspired to write Romans 8:31, David dared to believe, "If God is for us, who can be against us?" When David saw the Philistine champion from Gath step out and shout "his usual defiance," he asked, "Who is this uncircumcised Philistine that he should defy the armies of the living God?" No matter how long your addiction has shouted its usual defiance at your attempts to fight it, realize that your enemy is also God's enemy. It is a means by which Satan himself is seeking to defy the army of the living God. Call upon God to rise up in anger toward the enemy that binds you and fight him in your behalf with a holy vengeance. God could fight this one all alone. He really doesn't need your help; however, God reserves the right to involve us in our own victories, so get ready to fight. Overcoming addiction may be the battle of your life. But it will also be the most rewarding, liberating victory of your life. It will be your own Goliath story for the rest of your days.

Realize that God's unquestionable will is your freedom from this yoke, but also trust that He has written a personalized prescription for your release. Remember when King Saul offered young David his armor to wear as he opposed Goliath? "Saul dressed David in his own tunic. He put a coat of armor on him and a bronze helmet on his head. David fastened on his sword over the tunic and tried walking around, because he was not used to them. . . . So he took them off. Then he took his staff in his hand, chose five smooth stones from the stream, put them in the pouch of his shepherd's bag and, with his sling in his hand, approached the Philistine" (1 Sam. 17:38–40). God may have used a method to set someone else free that doesn't work as effectively for you. Perhaps the success of others has done little more than increase your discouragement and self-hatred. Don't let the enemy play mind games with you. God's strength is tailor-made for weakness. We are never stronger than the moment we admit we are weak. Seek God diligently and ask Him to show you the way to victory. Use these Scripture-prayers in conjunction with any plan He sets forth for you. I have a dear friend who is presently using them as part of a twelve-step program she's attending. I have another friend who is integrating them into the support group she leads. Ask God how He wants to use these Scripture-prayers in your journey to freedom. How God chooses to apply His truth is His call. Becoming legalistic about our freedom would be nothing more than an oxymoron.

Without a doubt, some of the people I respect most in the faith are those who have allowed God to set them free from the strangling stronghold of addiction. One of my heroes of the faith is an editor who was assigned to work with me on the second Bible study I wrote. I had no idea how Dale McCleskey would impact my life and how God would use him to enrich my writing. He has the unique gifting of the Holy Spirit to be both smart and wise. I have requested him for every study following our first joint venture. He has been the Grace Police in my writing ministry, swerving me away from oncoming legalism. We are partners in the cause of "grace and truth" that comes through Jesus Christ (John 1:17). Thank goodness our Savior came equipped with both, for where would we be with just one or the other?

Dale, my dear friend and colaborer in the gospel, equipped me with most of the following Scriptures I then reworded into prayer. Yes, he is what they call a "recovering alcoholic," although he has lived in victory for many years and serves His Deliverer with a passion. I, too, am in constant recovery from the ravages of my own sin nature. May God use the following Scripture-prayers dramatically in your life. May He enable you, His servant, to speak His Word "with great boldness," and may He stretch out His hand to heal and perform miraculous signs and wonders through the name of His holy servant, Jesus (Acts 4:29–30). Be tenacious and patient, child of God. If you fall, don't listen to the accusations and jeers of the evil one. Get back up and walk with God again. How many times? Until you're free.

God, I am so grateful that my own heavenly Father is the Sovereign Lord who made the heavens and the earth by His great power and outstretched arm. Nothing is too hard for you! (Jer. 32:17)

I confess to You that I am overwhelmed by the task ahead, but I am thankful that You have authority over all things. Heaven is Your throne and earth is Your footstool (Matt. 5:35); therefore, anything over my head is under Your feet!

Father, Your Word promises me that the one who conceals his sins does not prosper, but whoever confesses and renounces them finds mercy. (Prov. 28:13) Your Word also says that if we claim to be without sin we deceive ourselves and the truth is not in us. (1 John 1:8) Help me, Lord! I need Your truth in me!

Lord, I confess all the sin involved in my addiction to You, and I thank You that You are always faithful and just to forgive me of all my sin and purify me from all unrighteousness. (1 John 1:9)

Oh, Lord, You have searched me and You know me. You know when I sit and when I rise. You perceive my thoughts from afar. You discern my going out and my lying down; You are familiar with all my ways. Before a word is on my tongue, You know it completely. You hem me in—behind and before; You have laid your hand upon me. I do not need to feel shame or fear in Your intimate knowledge of every detail of my life because Your Word says that Your knowledge of me is wonderful! Thank You, Father. (Ps. 139:1–6)

O, Lord, please forgive me for my self-loathing. Help me to praise You because I am fearfully and wonderfully made; Your works are wonderful, I know that full well. (Ps. 139:14)

Search me, O God, and know my heart; test me and know my anxious thoughts. See if there is any offensive way in me, and lead me in the way everlasting. (Ps. 139:23–24)

God, according to Your steadfast Word, pride only breeds quarrels, but wisdom is found in those who take advice. (Prov. 13:10) My pride has caused such conflict, Lord! Please help me to humble myself and receive Your wisdom!

> *Although God Himself is never rushed to perform His
> will on earth, there is one thing He does rush to. He
> rushes to the aid of His children. Often He does not
> intervene, however, until that lost child cries out for
> help. He rushes to answer the appeals for mercy from
> those who have walked their own way and suddenly
> find themselves trapped in their own snares. He is not
> willing that any should perish, but He waits for us to
> use our wills to turn to him.*
>
> *Shawn Craig,* Between Sundays

Father, Your Word says that he who walks with the wise grows wise, but a companion of fools suffers harm. (Prov. 13:20) Please surround me with the right kind of companions!

Father, Your Word also says that fools mock at making amends for sin, but goodwill is found among the upright. (Prov. 14:9) Please help me to make any necessary amends for hurts I may have caused.

Lord, please help me to listen to advice and accept instruction so that in the end I will be wise. (Prov. 19:20)

Father, Your Word says that a person who lacks self-control is like a city whose walls are broken down. (Prov. 25:28) Sometimes I feel like there is so much rubble, I can't rebuild the wall. (Neh. 4:10) Your Word claims that You are the Repairer of Broken Walls, and the Restorer of Streets with Dwellings. (Isa. 58:12) Please introduce Yourself to me by these wonderful names and rebuild the rubble in my life.

Father God, please help me to forgive and release anyone who had to confront or wound my heart in an effort to help me find wholeness. Your Word says that open rebuke is better than hidden love. It also says that wounds from a friend can be trusted, but an enemy multiplies kisses. (Prov. 27:5–6)

Father, according to Your Word, he who is full loathes honey, but to the hungry even what is bitter tastes sweet. (Prov. 27:7) I am asking You in Jesus' name to make even the thought of any harmful substance on my tongue bitter. Restore in me a taste for what is good.

God, according to Your Word, blessed is the man who always fears the Lord, but he who hardens his heart falls into trouble. (Prov. 28:14) Please make and keep my heart soft toward You, Lord!

Lord, Your Word says that he who trusts in himself is a fool, but he who walks in wisdom is kept safe. (Prov. 28:26) I've come to realize that I cannot trust in myself. My safety is in learning to trust in You. Please help me!

O, Lord, cause my soul to yearn for You in the night and long for You in the morning. (Isa. 26:9) Please transfer my yearning and longing to You because I can have You to my fill! You will never be a detriment to me!

> *So how do we go from stumbling to standing? The answers will vary according to where and how we fail, but the source will always remain the same: God and His precepts of life. That's why you must be in the Word of God on a consistent basis . . . You have to determine to take advantage of what God has made available.*
>
> Kay Arthur, As Silver Refined

O Lord, our God, other lords besides You have ruled over me, but Your name alone is the one I want to honor. (Isa. 26:13) Please help me to understand that this addiction has been a terrible and destructive ruler in my life. Help me to cease to honor it.

My Father, please help me to see the object of my addiction like a bed too short to stretch out on and a blanket too narrow to wrap

around me. (Isa. 28:20) Help me to accept the truth that it's not enough!

Father, as a believer in Your Son, Jesus Christ, I am under grace, not under law (Rom. 6:14); therefore, sin does not have permission to be my master.

Lord, Your Word says that when I offer myself to someone or something to obey as a slave, I am a slave to the one whom I obey, whether I am a slave to sin, which leads to death, or to obedience, which leads to righteousness. (Rom. 6:16) O, Father, I deeply desire to be a slave to righteousness!

My Lord and my Creator, I confess to you that I, like everyone else in the human condition, am weak in my natural self. I used to offer the parts of my body in slavery to impurities. I have also personally experienced the ever-increasing nature of wickedness. (Rom. 6:19) No matter what I've tried to tell myself, my addictions will only grow worse without Your absolute intervention. Thank You, Father, that no matter how I've been enslaved, You can set me free!

Father, I thank You in advance that I am going to be set free from this sin and I can become a slave to You, reaping glorious benefits that lead to holiness! (Rom. 6:22)

God, I have died to the law through the body of Christ so that I might belong to another, to Him who was raised from the dead. You saved me in order that I might bear fruit to You. (Rom. 7:4) Thank You in advance, my Father, that You are going to use my life and cause it to bear fruit!

My merciful God, I have learned the hard way that nothing good lives in me, that is, in my sinful nature. For I have the desire to do what is good, but I cannot carry it out. (Rom. 7:18) But in You I have the power I need! You've given me the treasure of the Holy Spirit who lives in this weak jar of clay to show that this all-surpassing power is from God and not from me! (2 Cor. 4:7)

Father of mercies, no matter what I've done or how long I've done it, there is, therefore, now no condemnation for those who are in Christ Jesus, because through Christ Jesus the law of the Spirit of life set me free from the law of sin and death. (Rom. 8:1–2) Hallelujah! Help me to fully accept this truth.

Lord, because I have accepted Christ as my Savior, Your Word says that I am controlled not by the sinful nature but by the Spirit, because the Spirit of God lives in me. And if anyone does not have the Spirit of Christ, he does not belong to Christ. (Rom. 8:9)

Father, according to Your Word, since Christ is in me, my body is dead because of sin, yet my spirit is alive because of righteousness. (Rom. 8:10) And if the Spirit of Him who raised Jesus from the dead is living in me, He who raised Christ from the dead will also give life to my mortal body through His Spirit, who lives in me! (Rom. 8:11)

God, I claim Your Word that says I did not receive a spirit that makes me a slave again to fear, but I received the Spirit of sonship. And by Him I cry, "Abba, Father." (Rom. 8:15) Help me to cry out unashamedly to You, my Father, when I am gripped by fear. This kind of fear is not of You! (2 Tim. 1:7)

Lord, no matter what kind of suffering my addictions have caused me, I thank You that my present sufferings are not worth comparing with the glory that will be revealed in me. (Rom. 8:18)

Father, Your Word promises that we can know that in all things God works for the good of those who love Him, who have been called according to His purpose. (Rom. 8:28) My addictions are not exempt from this list! As hard as it may be for me to comprehend, You can and will work this terrible challenge for good if I will cooperate with You and see myself as one called according to Your purpose.

Father, what glorious news that You foreknew me and all my struggles, and yet You also predestined me to be conformed to the likeness of Your Son, that He might be the firstborn among many brothers! (Rom. 8:29)

> *If you say there's no hope, you're listening to the father of lies (John 8:44). You've encountered the thief who comes to steal, kill, and destroy (John 10:10)— the one who's determined to keep you a failure, to defeat you on every front he can. The only way you'll bring him down, the only way you'll extinguish those fiery arrows that will impale you on the stake of continuous defeat until you're consumed in its flames of destruction is through the Word. His Word is truth, and it alone can sanctify you—set you apart for victory. You may think there's no recovery from your failure. But my friend, if you have God, you have a future—and it's not a dismal one.*
>
> *Kay Arthur,* As Silver Refined

God, how I thank You that I can confidently claim that if You are for me, who can be against me? (Rom. 8:31) As Your child, help me to realize every day of my life that You are for me and never against me.

Father, who can separate me from the love of Christ? Can trouble or hardship or persecution or famine or nakedness or danger or sword? No, in all these things I am more than a conqueror through Him who loves me! (Rom. 8:35, 37)

Oh, Father, Your Word tells me that anyone who trusts in You will never be put to shame. (Rom. 10:11) How I celebrate that the time has come to put all shame behind me!

Father, You urge me in Your absolute mercy toward me to offer my body as a living sacrifice, holy and pleasing to God. This is my spiritual act of worship. You call on me not to conform any longer to the pattern of this world, but to be transformed by the renewing of my mind. Then I will be able to test and approve what Your will is. Your good, pleasing, and perfect will! (Rom. 12:1–2)

Lord, Your Word exhorts me not to be overcome by evil but to overcome evil with good. (Rom. 12:21) Help me, dear God, when I'm feeling overcome by evil!

Father, help me to clothe myself with the Lord Jesus Christ, and not to think about how to gratify the desires of the sinful nature. (Rom. 13:14) I desperately need Your help to do this, Father! Teach me and help me!

Father, according to Your Word, it is better not to eat meat or drink wine or to do anything else that will cause a brother or sister to fall. (Rom. 14:21) I pray that not only will I be mindful of this exhortation with others but that You will cause those around me not to do things that will cause me to fall!

My God of peace, I celebrate that You will soon crush Satan under Your feet. The grace of our Lord Jesus is with me! (Rom. 16:20)

Dear God, no matter what I once was, I have been washed, I have been sanctified, and I have been justified in the name of the Lord Jesus Christ and by the Spirit of our God! (1 Cor. 6:11)

O, God, I desperately need Your discernment when something may be permissible for me but not necessarily beneficial. Please empower me to resist things that are not beneficial so that I will not be mastered by anything! (1 Cor. 6:12)

Father, help me to truly embrace the fact that my body is a temple of the Holy Spirit, who is in me, whom I have received from God.

> *Knowing a truth intellectually is only half the battle. So what's to be done? I have no certain cure, certainly no quick cure, but I know it's important to rehearse the lovely, rich truths and promises that remain when other things change. Keep telling these truths, in all their many-sided glory, and one day, walls already cracked will crumble and fall.*
>
> Jim McGuiggan, Where the Spirit of the Lord Is

I am not my own. (1 Cor. 6:19) Thank You, Father! I am so much better off belonging to You than belonging to myself!

Father, You found my life worth buying at a tremendously high price. Therefore please help me honor You with my body. (1 Cor. 6:20)

Victorious God, I thank You and boldly claim that the weapons with which I fight this addiction are not the weapons of the world. On the contrary, they have divine power to demolish strongholds. I demolish arguments and every pretension that sets itself up against the knowledge of God, and I choose to take captive every thought to make it obedient to Christ! (2 Cor. 10:4–5)

Lord, You have said to me, "My grace is sufficient for you, for my power is made perfect in weakness." Therefore I will boast all the more gladly about my weaknesses, so that Christ's power may rest on me. (2 Cor. 12:9)

God, You have released me to resurrection life! For through the law I died to the law so that I might live for God. I have been crucified with Christ and I no longer live, but Christ lives in me. The life I live in the body, I live by faith in the Son of God, who loved me and gave Himself for me. (Gal. 2:19–20)

Father, Your Word says that when the time had fully come, You sent Your Son, born of a woman, born under law, to redeem those under law, that we might receive the full rights of sons. Because I am a son, You sent the Spirit of Your Son into my heart, the Spirit who calls out, "Abba, Father." (Gal. 4:4–6) I am Your child! I have the full right of a son! And it is my right to be free in You!

> *We, too, have been freed—freed to serve God without looking over our shoulders to see if He's glaring at us with suppressed hostility, freed to offer ourselves as servants, and freed to accept the commission.*
>
> Jim McGuiggan, Where the Spirit of the Lord Is

Father, I celebrate as fact that I am no longer a slave, but a child; and since I am a child, You have made me also an heir. (Gal. 4:7)

My Lord and Redeemer, formerly, when I did not know You, I was a slave to those who by nature are not gods. But now that I know You—or rather am known by You—I desperately do not want to turn back once again to those weak and miserable principles. Help me not to be enslaved by them all over again. (Gal. 4:8–9)

Father, Your Word says that it is for freedom that Christ has set us free. With all my heart I desire to stand firm, then, and not let myself be burdened again by a yoke of slavery. (Gal. 5:1) Lord, I am helpless on my own. Empower me with the strength of Your Holy Spirit. Please help me, Lord!

Father, by faith I eagerly await through the Spirit the righteousness for which I hope. (Gal. 5:5)

Father, Your Word says that I, Your child, was called to be free. Please help me not to use my freedom to indulge the sinful nature; rather, help me to use my freedom to serve others in love. (Gal. 5:13)

> *Often God seems to place His children in positions of profound difficulty, leading them into a wedge from which there is no escape; contriving a situation which no human judgment would have permitted, had it been previously consulted. . . . The issue will more than justify Him who has brought you hither. It is a platform for the display of His almighty grace and power. He will not only deliver you; but in doing so, He will give you a lesson that you will never forget, and to which, in many a psalm and song, in after days, you will revert. You will never be able to thank God enough for having done just as He has.*
>
> Mrs. Charles E. Cowman, Streams in the Desert

My Lord and Savior, you have told me that if I live by the Spirit, I will not gratify the desires of the sinful nature. (Gal. 5:16) Please teach me *how* to live by the Spirit, then empower me to follow through.

Lord, I belong to Christ Jesus, therefore I have crucified the sinful nature with its passions and desires. (Gal. 5:24) Help me to live in the reality of this liberating crucifixion.

Lord, since I live by the Spirit, help me to keep in step with the Spirit. (Gal. 5:25)

Father, according to Your Word, if someone is caught in a sin, someone who is spiritual should restore him gently. Your Word also says that even the spiritual believer must be very alert because he or she may also be tempted. (Gal. 6:1) Father, I pray for those You are putting in my path to help me. I pray for their protection as well as my own. I also pray that I will know when I am strong enough to help others. When that time comes, I pray that You will cause me to be absolutely alert so that I do not fall to temptation.

Father, Your Word promises that the one who sows to please his sinful nature, from that nature will reap destruction, but the one who sows to please the Spirit, from the Spirit will reap eternal life. (Gal. 6:8) Teach me and help me to sow to please the Spirit.

My mighty God, thank You for Your Word that exhorts me not to become weary in doing good. At the proper time I will reap a harvest if I do not give up. (Gal. 6:9) Father, this process of breaking free is hard work! Please remind me often that it is also a very good work. Help me to know without a doubt that any effort You require of me will have effect. Please help me never to give up, no matter how long it takes. I will reap a harvest, in Jesus' name!

Glorious Father, and God of our Lord Jesus Christ, please give me the Spirit of wisdom and revelation, so that I may know You better. (Eph. 1:17)

Father, I pray also that the eyes of my heart may be enlightened in order that I may know the hope to which You have called me, the riches of Your glorious inheritance in the saints. (Eph. 1:18)

Father, Your incomparably great power is available for us who believe. This power is like the working of Your mighty strength, which You exerted in Christ when You raised Him from the dead and seated Him at Your right hand in the heavenly realms. (Eph. 1:19–20) If You can raise Jesus from the dead and seat Him beside You, You can deliver me from every stronghold!

Because of Your great love for me, You, God, who are rich in mercy, made me alive with Christ even when I was dead in transgressions. It is by grace I have been saved. (Eph. 2:4–5)

My wonderful Father, You have also raised me up with Christ and seated me with Him in the heavenly realms in Christ Jesus! (Eph. 2:6)

Father, according to Your Word, at one time I was separate from Christ, excluded from citizenship in Israel and foreigner to the covenants of the promise, without hope and without God in the world. But now in Christ Jesus I who once was far away have been brought near through the blood of Christ. (Eph. 2:12–13) O, Lord, help me to sense Your nearness!

I pray that out of Your glorious riches You will strengthen me with power through Your Spirit in my inner being, so that Christ may dwell in my heart through faith. And I pray that I, being rooted and established in love, may have power, together with all the saints, to grasp how wide and long and high and deep is the love of Christ, and to know this love that surpasses knowledge—that I may be filled to the measure of all the fullness of God. (Eph. 3:16–19)

Father God, please help me to get rid of all bitterness, rage and anger, brawling and slander, along with every form of malice. (Eph. 4:31) Only with Your help is this possible.

Lord, according to Your Word, I was once darkness, but now I am light in the Lord. Help me to live as a child of light. (Eph. 5:8)

Father, Your Word instructs me to put on the full armor of God so that I can take my stand against the devil's schemes. For my struggle is not against flesh and blood, but against the rulers, against the authorities, against the powers of this dark world and against the spiritual forces of evil in the heavenly realms. Therefore, help me to put on the full armor of God, so that when the day of evil comes, I will be able to stand my ground. (Eph. 6:10–13) Don't ever let me forget that I have a very real enemy who wants me in bondage. Help me to discern his schemes and take my stand against him in the power of Your Spirit.

Father, help me to be confident of this, that He who began a good work in me will carry it on to completion until the day of Christ Jesus. (Phil. 1:6)

Father, Your Word assures me that it is God who works in me to will and to act according to His good purpose. (Phil. 2:13)

Awesome God, Your Word says that knowing Christ Jesus my Lord is so wonderful that I can consider everything a loss compared to its surpassing greatness. Help me to consider anything rubbish that I have to lay down in order to gain (more knowledge and a more abiding presence of) Christ. (Phil. 3:8)

O, Father, I thank You that my citizenship is in heaven. I eagerly await a Savior from there, the Lord Jesus Christ, who, by the power that enables Him to bring everything under His control, will transform my lowly body so that it will be like His glorious body. (Phil. 3:20–21) Lord, how I celebrate the fact that You have power to bring everything under Your control!

Lord God, I acknowledge the promise of Your Word that I can do everything through Christ who gives me strength. (Phil. 4:13)

> *Nothing lies beyond the reach of prayer except that which lies outside the will of God.*
>
> Mrs. *Charles Cowman,* Streams in the Desert

O, Lord, I earnestly pray that I may live a life worthy of You and may please You in every way: bearing fruit in every good work, growing in the knowledge of God, being strengthened with all power according to Your glorious might so that I may have great endurance and patience, and joyfully giving thanks to the Father, who has qualified me to share in the inheritance of the saints in the kingdom of light. (Col. 1:10–12)

Lord God, Your Word says that once I was alienated from God and was an enemy in my mind because of my evil behavior. But now You have reconciled me by Christ's physical body through death to present me holy in Your sight, without blemish and free from accusation. (Col. 1:21–22) O, Lord, how I celebrate being free from accusation!

Father, Your Word exhorts me to set my mind on things above, not on earthly things. (Col. 3:2) This can be such a battle, Lord! Please help me every single day to set my mind on You.

My Redeemer, I know that it was not with perishable things such as silver or gold that I was redeemed from the empty way of life handed down to me from my forefathers, but with the precious blood of Christ, a lamb without blemish or defect. (1 Pet. 1:18–19)

Father, I desperately need Your help to rid myself of all malice and all deceit, hypocrisy, envy, and slander of every kind. Like a newborn baby, help me to crave pure spiritual milk, so that by it I may grow up in my salvation. (1 Pet. 2:1–2)

God, Your Word tells me to humble myself under Your mighty hand, that You may lift me up in due time. (1 Pet. 5:6)

Father, teach me and help me to cast all my anxiety on You because You care for me. (1 Pet. 5:7)

My Shield and my Fortress, help me to be self- controlled and alert. My enemy the devil is prowling around like a roaring lion looking for someone to devour. (1 Pet. 5:8)

Thanks be to You, my God, who always leads me in triumphal procession in Christ. Through me and other believers, You desire to

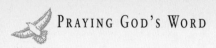

spread everywhere the fragrance of the knowledge of Him! (2 Cor. 2:14) You only lead to victory, Christ Jesus. If I will keep following You, I'll get there.

> *When fitted with the armor of God, we will not be blindsided by the fiery darts of the Enemy. Past failures lose their power, for they have been dealt with. Present thoughts will not overrun me, for I am in command of my thoughts and I make the final decision on what I believe. The opinions of others do not bombard me, for I have decided to believe what God says about who I am—regardless of what I or anyone else thinks.*
>
> *Dennis Jernigan,* This Is My Destiny

PERSONALIZING YOUR PRAYERS

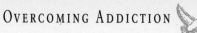

Chapter 8

OVERCOMING FOOD-
RELATED STRONGHOLDS

What a relief to know that we'll never battle anything out of God's jurisdiction. God can as easily defeat His opposition on Mt. Carmel as Mt. Zion. It's all His turf. The same is true in regard to our own battlegrounds. God created us as to be whole creatures made of three different components: body, soul, and spirit. As long as we see God as Lord of our spirits alone, we will continue to live in areas of defeat. God is as surely Lord of our souls and body as He is our spirits. It's all His turf. In fact, take a refreshing look at 1 Thessalonians 5:23–24. "May God himself, the God of peace, sanctify you through and through. May your whole spirit, soul, and body be kept blameless at the coming of our Lord Jesus Christ. The one who calls you is faithful and he will do it." First of all, please celebrate the glorious fact that God *Himself* is the One at work in you and through you. He hasn't just assigned you a mighty angel. God is thoroughly interested and involved in every single part of you: body, soul, and spirit.

Second, notice that the verse identifies God specifically as the God of peace. The Word of God is perfectly inspired; therefore, every identification of God, every name He is called, is in perfect context. In this case the inference of the title is that the believer will be awash with God's peace when every part of the life—body, soul, and spirit—is surrendered to His wise, loving, and liberating authority. I know far too well how distant the peace of God is when we refuse to bow a part of our lives to His rule. Peace is the fruit of authority. *God's* authority. As Colossians 3:15 says, "Let the peace of Christ *rule* . . ." (emphasis mine). Christ brings His peace where He is Prince. That's what the title "Prince of Peace" represents.

Third, don't miss what God *Himself* desires to do. First Thessalonians 5:23 proceeds to tell us that this glorious God of peace wants to sanctify us "through and through." The original Greek word for "sanctify" is *hagiazo,* meaning "to make clean, render pure, . . . to consecrate, devote, set apart from a common to a sacred use, . . . to regard and venerate as holy, to hallow."[1] In other words, God deeply desires for us to grant Him total access to set apart every single part of our lives—body, soul, and spirit—to His glorious work. Always keep in mind that anything to God's glory is also for our good. The two concepts are never at odds. God's inclusion of the physical body is proof among many others in Scripture that He cares deeply what happens to these tents of flesh in which we dwell. Indeed, our physical bodies are the temples of the Holy Spirit in this dispensation of God's kingdom calendar (1 Cor. 6:19).

For just a moment, let's think of ourselves like triangles. Imagine each point of the triangle being labeled as body, soul, or spirit. If the triangle is sitting on its base, only one point is "up." Imagine that point being the one in present control of us. For instance, when distinguished from the spirit as in 1 Thessalonians 5:23, the soul represents the seat of our emotions and our personality. If the "soul" is in the upward, authoritative position in our lives, then we are ruled by our feelings and our personality types. All of us know what kind of trouble results from being under that kind of authority! Our feelings and personalities are given to us by God, but they are not meant to control us. Now picture that the "body" is in the upward position and momentarily ruling over our triangular selves. We don't have to be terribly bright to imagine what can happen because we've all experienced the upheaval firsthand: our fleshly appetites and physical drives and habits take over. Our "appetites" become our masters. Certainly, our physical bodies are gifts from God "fearfully and wonderfully made," but when they control us, the result is bondage. Also understand that one area exerts tremendous influence over the others. As you know, our feelings can drive our physical appetites just as our physical appetites can drive our feelings.

By this time, you've figured out the answer. The "point" we need in the upward position to live in victory is the Spirit. All of us were born with a "spirit." When distinguished from the soul, it represents the part of us created in the image of God to know Him and enjoy His fellowship. It is the primary component in us that sets us apart from all other creatures. Until we are redeemed and inhabited by Christ (Rom. 8:9), our spirits are no better off than our souls and bodies. But, glory to God, when we receive Christ, His Spirit takes residency in ours!

First Corinthians 6:17 speaks of this supernatural consolidation: "he who unites himself with the Lord is one with him in spirit." The key to victory as we occupy this triangular temple is to bow daily, perhaps a half dozen times daily, to the control of the Holy Spirit over our lives. Our bodies and our feelings and personalities are wonderful components sanctified by God when the Spirit is in control. I am convinced that a huge part of wholeness in the life of a believer is when God has been allowed to sanctify (take over and set apart) our *whole* spirit, soul, and body.

Before we get started with our Scripture-prayers, I'd like for you to see one more very important truth encased in 1 Thessalonians 5:24. Thank goodness the Word says, "The one who calls you is faithful and he will do it." You and I *cannot* get our bodies and souls under continued control. Cease trying to "get yourself together" and be disciplined in your own strength. It is useless. We might make it work for a little while, but failure is imminent, and when it comes, it is very destructive. The King James Version offers some interesting wording in Colossians 2:20–23 that applies to our subject.

> *Wherefore if ye be dead with Christ from the rudiments of the world, why, as though living in the world, are ye subject to ordinances, (Touch not; taste not; handle not; Which all are to perish with the using;) after the commandments and doctrines of men? Which things have indeed a shew of wisdom in will worship, and humility, and neglecting of the body; not in any honour to the satisfying of the flesh.*

Notice the phrase *will worship.* You see, if man could truly subdue all his fleshly appetites by the pure power of his own determination, he would simply worship his own will. If the Word of God is about anything at all, it is about God's will rather than ours. Our liberty is paradoxically discovered through the will of God rather than our own. God will never allow us continued success through our pure fleshly determination to "touch not, taste not, handle not." He knows we would end up worshiping our own wills and methods. Through the might of His Holy Spirit released through the authority of His Word, we are empowered to say no to the things we should—to our excesses, withholdings, compulsions, and harmful consumptions—and say yes to freedom, moderation, and better health. When we bow to God's authority, we invite Him to take control, and *He* is the One who does it, as 1 Thessalonians 5:24 tells us.

The question of authority is one we are challenged to answer every single day. The concept of rededicating our lives to Christ only at infrequent revivals or conferences can prove disappointing and defeating. Joshua 24:15 suggests a far more workable approach: "Choose *this day* whom you will serve" (emphasis mine). Christ repeated the concept when He called us to take up our crosses *daily* and follow Him. Do you want to know something wonderful? A daily recommitment is not to ensure that we'll never fail, but to help us develop the mentality that every single day is a new day. A new chance to follow Christ. Obedience to God is not some diet we suddenly blow. It is something to which we recommit every single day, no matter how we blew it the day before. Victorious living is not an instant arrival. It is the pursuit of one victorious day at a time until the sun sets on enough to begin forming victorious habits.

So, are you just about to give up? Good. Give yourself up to God, to the authority of His Holy Spirit. Both Galatians 5:22 and 2 Timothy 1:7 tell us that self-discipline is a work and a quality of the fruit of the *Spirit*. Stop feeling guilty because you don't have any self-discipline on your own. Neither does that together-looking person next to you. None of us can master ourselves. Some yokes may be more obvious than others, but all of us have had them. God is the only One who can sanctify and make every part of us whole . . . "and He will do it." All He wants is our trust, our belief, and a little time.

Overeating, compulsive undereating, anorexia, and bulimia are

all food-related strongholds. No matter how long any one of these has had a believer in its grip, he or she can be free. You never have to wonder if God's will is for you to be liberated from these strongholds. The answer is yes, so begin praying His will over your life with confidence. Again, please remember that the method through which God applies His truth to set you free is up to Him. You can use these Scripture-prayers in conjunction with any method God designs for you.

I am indebted to my dear friend, Carole Lewis, and the wonderful staff at *First Place, a Christ-Centered Health Program* in Houston, Texas, for many of the Scriptures I've reworded into the following prayers. Their unwavering commitment to daily Bible study as the Holy Spirit's propelling force toward victorious living is undoubtedly the reason why God has blessed them with such an astounding success rate. For without Him, we can do nothing (John 15:5) and with Him, we can do anything (Phil. 4:13).

Lord, according to Your Word, if I wholeheartedly commit whatever I do to You, my plans will succeed. (Prov. 16:3) Lord, I acknowledge that the heart of committing any plan to You is seeking *Your* plan. Show me the right path, Father!

Lord, please help me not to merely listen to the Word, and so deceive myself. Please help me to do what it says. (James 1:22) Your Word *works,* but if I am to experience it personally, I must be obedient. I need Your help, Lord.

When Your words come to me, help me to eat them; make them my joy and my heart's delight, for I bear Your name, O Lord God Almighty. (Jer. 15:16) Increase my appetite for Your Word, my Sufficiency!

O, Lord, like David, help me to rejoice in Your strength and say of You, "How great is my joy in the victories You give!" Father, please grant me the desire of my heart to be free from this stronghold and do not withhold the request of my lips. (Ps. 21:1–2)

Through the victories You give, may Christ's glory be great! (Ps. 21:5)

For I know that my old self was crucified with You, Christ, so that this body of sin might be done away with, that I should no longer be a slave to sin—because anyone who has died has been freed from sin. (Rom. 6:6–7)

Father, the false teachers of this world promise freedom, while they themselves are slaves of depravity—for a man is a slave to whatever has mastered him. (2 Pet. 2:19) I acknowledge my slavery and deeply desire to be mastered by You alone. Only Your mastery brings liberty.

> *Satan's ultimate lie is that you are capable of being the god of your own life, and his ultimate bondage is getting you to live as though his lie is truth.*
>
> Neil Anderson, The Bondage Breaker

"Everything is permissible for me"—but not everything is beneficial. "Everything is permissible for me"—but I desire not to be mastered by anything. (1 Cor. 6:12) Lord God, help me to recognize and discern what is not beneficial for me. Help me to see that authentic liberty is being free to do certain things and free not to do others.

Lord God, I acknowledge that it is for freedom that Christ has set me free. Your desire is for me to stand firm, then, and not let myself be burdened again by the yoke of slavery. (Gal. 5:1) Help me, Lord. Empower me.

God, according to Your liberating Word, I was called to be free. Help me not to use my freedom to indulge the sinful nature; rather, I should serve others in love. (Gal. 5:13)

Help my soul to find rest in You alone; my hope comes from You. You alone are my rock and my salvation; You are my fortress,

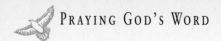

I will not be shaken. My salvation and my honor depend on You; You, God, are my mighty rock, my refuge. Help me to trust in You at all times. Remind me to pour out my heart to You, for You, God, are my refuge. (Ps. 62:5–8)

You know the plans You have for me, O Lord. You have declared that they are plans to prosper me and not to harm me, plans to give me a hope and a future. (Jer. 29:11)

You are the Lord, the God of all mankind. Nothing is too hard for You! (Jer. 32:27)

In view of Your mercy, Lord, I offer my body as a living sacrifice, holy and pleasing to You, God. This is my spiritual act of worship. I desire not to be conformed any longer to the pattern of this world, but to be transformed by the renewing of my mind. Then I will be able to test and approve what Your will is—Your good, pleasing, and perfect will. (Rom. 12:1–2)

Lord, though I live in the world, I do not wage war as the world does. The weapons I fight with are not the weapons of the world. On the contrary, they have divine power to demolish strongholds. Your power can demolish arguments and every pretension that sets itself up against the knowledge of You, God, and take captive every thought and make it obedient to Christ. (2 Cor. 10:3–5) Enable me, Lord! Help me not just to read it and say it, but to believe it and do it!

Lord, I have too long given the devil a foothold. (Eph. 4:27) Please help me to stop offering him so many opportunities to bring defeat into my life. Your plan for me is victory.

Now unto You who are able to do immeasurably more than all I ask or imagine, according to Your power that is at work within me, to You be glory in the church and in Christ Jesus throughout all generations, forever and ever! Amen. (Eph. 3:20–21)

God, I do not consider myself yet to have taken hold of it. But one thing I do: Forgetting what is behind and straining toward what is ahead, I press on toward the goal to win the prize for which You have called me heavenward in Christ Jesus. (Phil. 3:13–14) Help me to forget all past failures or even achievements and to focus on pressing forward with You now.

> *Perhaps one of the unforgivable sins is to give up on ourselves and God. Hold a cup under an opened faucet and it will quickly fill. The process is slightly more difficult if you hold your cup upside down. So, turn your cup right side up.*
>
> *Tim Hansel,* Holy Sweat

Lord Jesus, I can do everything through You because You give me strength. (Phil. 4:13)

You, Lord, will rescue me from every evil attack and will bring me safely to Your heavenly kingdom. To You be glory for ever and ever. Amen. (2 Tim. 4:18)

Lord, I can find great encouragement in knowing that many believers, weak in their natural selves, have walked faithfully and victoriously with You. (Heb. 11) Therefore, since I am surrounded by such a great cloud of witnesses, help me throw off everything that hinders and the sin that so easily entangles, and help me run with perseverance the race marked out for me. Help me fix my eyes on Jesus, the author and perfecter of my faith, who for the joy set before Him endured the cross, scorning its shame, and sat down at the right hand of Your throne, O God. (Heb. 12:1–2)

I am Your dear child, and I am from You, God, and have overcome the influences of the evil kingdom, because the One who is in me is greater than the one who is in the world. (1 John 4:4)

In a race all the runners run, but only one gets the prize. Lord, help me to run in such a way as to get the prize. (1 Cor. 9:24)

Lord, please help me not to miss the grace of God. Help me to see to it that no bitter root grows up in me to cause trouble and defile many. (Heb. 12:15)

By faith Abraham, when called to go to a place he would later receive as his inheritance, obeyed and went, even though he did not know where he was going. (Heb. 11:8) Lord, help me to be willing to follow You in obedience even when I'm not sure where I'm heading.

Lord God, help me not to allow the worries of this life, the deceitfulness of wealth, and the desires for other things to come in and choke Your Word, making it unfruitful in my life. (Mark 4:19)

Dear God, as one of Your own, please help me to flee from sin and pursue righteousness, godliness, faith, love, endurance, and gentleness. (1 Tim. 6:11)

Search me, O God, and know my heart; test me and know my anxious thoughts. See if there is any offensive way in me, and lead me in the way everlasting. (Ps. 139:23–24)

Lord God, according to Your Word, everyone born of You overcomes the world. This is the victory that has overcome the world, even our faith. Who is it that overcomes the world? I do, when I truly believe that Jesus is the Son of God. (1 John 5:4–5)

My faithful Father, whether I turn to the right or to the left, cause my ears to hear a voice behind me saying, "This is the way; walk in it." (Isa. 30:21)

Lord, help me to guard the good deposit that was entrusted to me. I must guard it with the help of the Holy Spirit who lives in me. (2 Tim. 1:14)

I am among Your chosen people, Your royal priesthood, Your holy nation. I am part of a people belonging to You, God, that I may declare the praises of You who called me out of darkness into Your wonderful light. (1 Pet. 2:9)

Lord God, according to Your Word, where there is no revelation, the people cast off restraint. (Prov. 29:18) O, Father, help me to understand that I have no power of restraint or self-control without Your Word made alive in me by Your Holy Spirit!

Lord, I pray You will give me the desire of my heart—which at this moment is to be free—and make all my plans succeed. (Ps. 20:4)

Above all else, help me to love You, the Lord my God, with all my heart and with all my soul and with all my strength. (Deut. 6:5)

Father God, help me to put on Your full armor so that I can take my stand against the devil's schemes. (Eph. 6:11)

Lord God, Your divine power has given me everything I need for life and godliness through my knowledge of You who called me by Your own glory and goodness. (2 Pet. 1:3)

> *Our hearts beat excitedly over stories of people like Abraham and Moses, yet we fail to recognize that they were as frail and nervous as we are. We stand in awe of Moses at the burning bush: "Now there is a bush that burns," we say. "I would like to be a bush like that, but I'm just a heap of ashes." And that's as far as we get. We discuss the phenomenon of what God can do in a life, tell amazing stories about it, praise it—but then resign ourselves to being nothing more than what we think we are, a mere bystander, resigned to sitting in the balcony among the spectators. But it is not the* bush *that sustains the flame. It is God in the bush, and so, any old bush will do!*
>
> *Tim Hansel,* Holy Sweat

My Father in heaven, please help me to live a life of love, just as Christ loved me and gave Himself up for me as a fragrant offering and sacrifice to You. (Eph. 5:2)

Thank You, God, for choosing me in Christ before the creation of the world to be holy and blameless in Your sight. (Eph. 1:4)

By Your grace, Lord, I have been saved, through faith—and this not from myself, it is the gift of God—not by works, so that I cannot boast. (Eph. 2:8–9) Therefore, as it is written: "Let him who boasts boast in the Lord"! (1 Cor. 1:31)

Christ Jesus, You Yourself are my peace, who has . . . destroyed the barrier, the dividing wall of hostility, by abolishing in Your flesh the law with its commandments and regulations. (Eph. 2:14–15)

Lord God, help me to know this love that surpasses knowledge—that I may be filled to the measure of all the fullness of God. (Eph. 3:19)

Lord, continue to teach me with regard to my former way of life, to put off my old self, . . . and to put on the new self, created to be like You, God, in true righteousness and holiness. (Eph. 4:22–24)

Lord, what You are commanding me today is not too difficult for me or beyond my reach. (Deut. 30:11)

Lord, according to Your Word, it is better not to make a vow than to make a vow and not fulfill it. (Eccles. 5:5) Please help me to realize that the power to be victorious does not come from my ability to make and keep a vow out of pure determination. Sooner or later, I will fail if I'm only trying to fulfill a vow. The power to be victorious comes from realizing the vow You have already made to me when You gave me Your Spirit and Your Word. As Your Word says in Zechariah 4:6, success won't come by might nor by power, but by the Spirit of the Lord Almighty!

Lord, help me to be self-controlled and alert. My enemy the devil prowls around like a roaring lion looking for someone to devour. (1 Pet. 5:8)

If I call to You, You will answer me and tell me great and unsearchable things I do not know. (Jer. 33:3)

Lord, I make it my goal to please You, whether I am at home in the body or away from it. (2 Cor. 5:9)

God, I am so thankful there is now no condemnation for those who are in Christ Jesus. (Rom. 8:1) If You do not condemn me, I have no right or place to condemn myself. Help me not to get caught up in a defeating cycle of self-condemnation.

Those who know Your name will trust in You, for You, Lord, have never forsaken those who seek You. (Ps. 9:10)

Lord, the fruit of Your Spirit is love, joy, peace, patience, kindness, goodness, faithfulness, gentleness, and self-control. Against such things there is no law. (Gal. 5:22–23) Please fill me with Your Spirit and eclipse my personality with Yours.

Father God, help me not to grieve, for Your joy, Lord, is my strength. (Neh. 8:10)

Father God, please help me to keep in mind that my struggle is not against flesh and blood, but against the rulers, against the authorities, against the powers of this dark world and against the spiritual forces of evil in the heavenly realms. (Eph. 6:12)

> *You don't have to outshout him or outmuscle him to be free of his influence. You just have to* outtruth *him.* Believe, declare, and act upon the truth of God's Word, *and you will thwart Satan's strategy.*
>
> Neil Anderson, The Bondage Breaker

Lord, I come to You in prayer, and I ask You now to let Your peace, God, which transcends all understanding, guard my heart and my mind in Christ Jesus. (Phil. 4:7)

Powerful Lord, help me not become weary in doing good, for at the proper time I will reap a harvest if I do not give up. (Gal. 6:9)

I am one of Your chosen people, O God. I acknowledge and accept as fact that I am holy and dearly loved. In response, help me to clothe myself with compassion, kindness, humility, gentleness, and patience. (Col. 3:12)

Help me, Lord, to take Your yoke upon me and learn from You, for You are gentle and humble in heart, and I will find rest for my soul. (Matt. 11:29)

Lord, according to Your Word, the key to not gratifying the desires of the sinful nature is to live by the Spirit. (Gal. 5:16) Teach me to live by the Spirit, Lord!

Lord, whatever is true, whatever is noble, whatever is right, whatever is pure, whatever is lovely, whatever is admirable—if anything is excellent or praiseworthy—help me to make the choice to think about such things. (Phil. 4:8) Lord God, help me to feed the Spirit, not the flesh! Changing the way I think will change the way I feel!

God of hope, fill me with all joy and peace as I trust in You, so that I may overflow with hope by the power of the Holy Spirit. (Rom. 15:13)

Merciful God, restore to me the joy of Your salvation and grant me a willing spirit, to sustain me. (Ps. 51:12)

Lord, help me to be very careful not to think of myself more highly than I ought, but rather think of myself with sober judgment, in accordance with the measure of faith God has given me. (Rom. 12:3) Help me also not to think of myself as anything less than a child of Yours, God, dearly loved by You. (Eph. 5:1) Your deep desire is for me to possess both humility *and* security.

Lord, I know what it is to be in need, and I know what it is to have plenty. I want to learn the secret of being content in any and every situation, whether well fed or hungry, whether living in plenty or in want. I can do everything through You, Lord, who gives me strength. (Phil. 4:12–13)

I have been crucified with You, Christ, and I no longer live, but You live in me. The life I live in the body, I live by faith in You, the Son of God, who loves me and gave Yourself for me. (Gal. 2:20)

Lord, as a member of the body of Christ, help me consider how I may spur others on toward love and good deeds. I will not give up meeting with others in Christ, as some are in the habit of doing, but I choose to encourage others—and all the more as I see the Day approaching. (Heb. 10:24–25)

Faithful, loving Lord, according to Your Word, two are better than one, because they have a good return for their work: If one falls down, his friend can help him up. But pity the man who falls and has no one to help him up! (Eccles. 4:9–10, 12) Please help me to form healthy relationships and find support in those who encourage me to get back on my feet and walk with You when I fall. Between You, me when I'm willing, and a good friend to hold me accountable, a cord of three strands is not quickly broken.

Danger: Traveling Alone

God created us all to be part of His body. We function together. Fellowship is a precious gift the Lord gives His children. To neglect fellowship or refuse to draw near those who can make our journey all that it should be is to make ourselves vulnerable to compromise. Anytime we withdraw from wise friends who will hold us accountable, we seek our own desires. We become resistant to "all sound wisdom" (Prov. 18:1)—and that is a precarious place to be. If we are committed to travel toward the heart of God, then we need to move toward the wise friend, of any age, who can help us stay on the journey.

Cynthia Heald, A Woman's Journey to the Heart of God

Lord, in Your infinite wisdom You warn us that "He who separates himself seeks his own desire, / He quarrels against all sound wisdom." (Prov. 18:1, NASB) Help me to be very careful not to isolate myself.

Lord God, Your Word tells me that one handful with tranquility is better than two handfuls with toil and chasing after the wind. (Eccles. 4:6) Please set me free from the false security that comes from having more of anything than I really need.

Jesus, according to Your Word, if I truly desire to come after You, I must deny myself and take up my cross daily and follow You. (Luke 9:23)

Lord God, You have humbled me to teach me that man does not live on bread alone but on every word that comes from the mouth of the Lord. (Deut. 8:3) Please develop in me a hunger for Your presence and Your Word that exceeds any physical cravings I could ever experience.

> *To give emotionally wounded people only a weight-loss plan is like putting a band-aid on a cancerous lesion.*
>
> *Carole Lewis,* First Place

O God, You are my God, earnestly I seek You; my soul thirsts for You, my body longs for You, in a dry and weary land where there is no water. I have seen You in the sanctuary and beheld Your power and Your glory. Because Your love is better than life, my lips will glorify You. I will praise You as long as I live, and in Your name I will lift up my hands. My soul will be satisfied as with the richest of foods! (Ps. 63:1–5)

Lord God, help me to remember You when I go to bed. Occupy my thoughts through the watches of the night. Because You are my help, I sing in the shadow of Your wings. My soul clings to You; Your right hand upholds me. (Ps. 63:6–8)

Lord God, You are the One who hears prayer. To You may all men come! When I was overwhelmed by sins, You forgave my transgressions. Blessed are those You choose and bring near to live in Your courts! I am filled with the good things of Your house, of Your holy temple. (Ps. 65:2–4)

Lord, my soul is in anguish. How long, O Lord, how long? Turn, O Lord, and deliver me; save me because of Your unfailing love. (Ps. 6:3–4)

How long will I turn Your glory into shame, O Lord? How long will I love delusions and seek false gods? (Ps. 4:2) Expose the delusions and false gods in my life, O Lord, and set me free!

Lord, You beckon me in Your Word to come to You when I'm thirsty, to come to the waters; I can come to You when I have no money. I can come, buy, and eat! Why do I spend money and labor on things that don't satisfy? Your Word tells me to listen to You and eat what is good, and my soul will delight in the richest of fare. (Isa. 55:1–2)

Lord, You fill the hungry with good things! (Luke 1:53)

Lord God, if I do away with the yoke of oppression, with the pointing finger and malicious talk, and if I spend myself in behalf of the hungry and satisfy the needs of the oppressed, then light will rise in the darkness, and my night will become like noonday. (Isa. 58:9–10)

You, Lord, will guide me always; You will satisfy my needs in a sun-scorched land and will strengthen my frame. I will be like a well-watered garden, like a spring whose waters never fail. (Isa. 58:11)

Lord God, like Your people Israel, You will ransom me from the hand of those stronger than me. I will come and shout for joy on the heights of Zion; I will rejoice in the bounty of the Lord— the grain, the new wine and the oil, the young of the flocks and

herds. I will be like a well-watered garden and I will sorrow no more. I will dance and be glad. You will turn my mourning into gladness; You will give me comfort and joy instead of sorrow. You have declared that You will satisfy Your people with abundance, and we will be filled with Your bounty. (Jer. 31:11–14)

Lord, You will refresh the weary and the faint. (Jer. 31:25)

Lord God, I acknowledge to You that like the ancient Israelites I eat but I am often not satisfied. (Lev. 26:26) Help me not to confuse the hunger of my soul with the hunger of my body. If I eat physical food and I am still not satisfied, help me discern a far greater need and bring it to You, O Lord. You are the only One who can truly satisfy the soul.

Father God, according to Your Word, if physical things were allowed to completely satisfy us, our hearts would become proud, and we would forget the Lord our God, who brought us out of the land of slavery. (Deut. 8:12–14)

Lord, when You bring this captive completely back to You, I will be like those who dream! My mouth will be filled with laughter and my tongue with songs of joy! The Lord has done great things for me, and I am filled with joy! (Ps. 126:1–3)

Lord God, I know that my body is a temple of the Holy Spirit, who is in me, whom I have received from You. I am not my own; I was bought at a price. Therefore I desire to honor You with my body. (1 Cor. 6:19–20) Since I am a temple of Your Holy Spirit, cause Your glory to fill *this* temple of God like You did in days of old! (2 Chron. 5:14)

You, O Lord, have filled my heart with greater joy than when my grain and new wine abound! (Ps. 4:7)

> *Blessed are those who hunger and thirst for righteousness, for they will be filled.*
>
> *Jesus Christ,* Matthew 5:6

OTHER SCRIPTURES YOU CAN PRAY

Romans 4:20–21
Psalm 143:8
Psalm 1:1–3
John 8:32
Colossians 3:14
Ephesians 5:8

Ephesians 4:3
Ephesians 6:18
Romans 5:8
James 1:26
Isaiah 58:6–9
Psalm 16:11

PERSONALIZING YOUR PRAYERS

Chapter 9

OVERCOMING ONGOING FEELINGS OF GUILT

Satan is the master of accusation. Revelation 12:10 identifies him as the "accuser of our brothers, who accuses them before our God day and night." Satan's primary problem is that he is eaten up with jealousy over Jesus Christ. The enemy of our souls was the "morning star" who was "cast down to the earth" for saying in his heart, "I will ascend to heaven; I will raise my throne above the stars of God; I will sit enthroned on the mount of assembly, on the utmost heights of the sacred mountain. I will ascend above the tops of the clouds; I will make myself like the Most High" (Isa. 14:12–14). I practically shudder to even write that final blasphemy. Simply said, Satan wants what Christ *has*. He knows he can't have it; therefore, he attempts to counterfeit and counteract everything Christ *does*.

In Luke 5:24, Christ announced emphatically, "The Son of Man has authority on earth to forgive sins." Indeed, the acceptance of God's forgiveness through Jesus Christ His Son swings our prison doors wide open. Satan knows that "what he [Christ] opens no one can shut." (Rev. 3:7) If he is powerless to shut prison doors Christ has opened, what is Satan's next best option? He can convince us to stay, even though we've been freed to leave. One of his primary methods of keeping freed men pinned by their own volition in their prison cells is *accusation*.

Never in all of Scripture does Christ resist the repentant sinner. He resisted the proud and the self-righteous religious but never the humble and repentant. Indeed, forgiveness is why He came. When we approach God in genuine repentance, taking full responsibility for our own sins, our prison doors swing open. Tragically, we could sit right there in our prison cells for the next five years in torment if we don't stand on God's promises and walk forward in His truth. Since

Satan knows that forgiveness leads to freedom, he takes on the role of tormentor, taunting us with guilt and condemnation. If Christ has forgiven us, he does everything he can to see to it that we don't forgive ourselves.

Picture a death-row inmate quarantined in his cramped prison cell. Evidence of who he's been is scribbled in graffiti all over the cell walls. Now picture the inmate receiving a pardon from the governor. Imagine the click of the key as it unlocks the door, then the music of the door as it swings open. Before the inmate can stand to his feet and walk out the door, the warden of the prison walks in the cell, sits beside him, and says, "You can't leave. You *know* what you've done. You know you're guilty as charged. You know you deserve this filthy, miserable cell. Read what is written all over these walls. *That's* the real you. It wouldn't matter where you went, how you dressed. No one would be fooled. You're the only fool. You're a death-row inmate. You'll never be free. Just sit right here with me, and I'll keep you company."

If this scene were in a movie, we'd be tempted to yell, "What are you doing? Are you crazy? The prison door is open! Get out of there!" Yet, you and I have reacted the same way at times in the spiritual realm. We were death-row inmates. Guilty as charged. The Governor's Son appealed to His Father on our behalf and His Father, in turn, issued us a lifetime pardon. The moment we admitted our guilt and accepted our pardon, the prison doors were opened, and as much as Satan wishes he held the keys to lock them back again, he doesn't. All he can do is try to keep us seated in an unlocked prison cell. He knows that we've been freed, but in order for us to *live* as free people, he also knows we must stand to our feet and walk out in truth. You and I both know too well what happens next. The prison warden does everything he can to convince us we belong there. Far too often, we've believed him.

Each Scripture-prayer in this chapter possesses one of two primary purposes:

1. To help ensure the presence of true repentance
2. To help the truly repentant to bask in the freedom of forgiveness

These two scriptural emphases are interwoven purposely

throughout the chapter. The reason we must make absolutely sure biblical repentance has taken place is because, if it hasn't, what we are calling "guilt" is probably the active and faithful conviction of the Holy Spirit. I remember a time in my college years when I was deeply puzzled over ongoing feelings of "guilt" deep within me over a sin for which I had asked forgiveness many times. I could not understand why I never felt out from under the weight or burden of it. Years later God pried open my eyes to 2 Corinthians 7:10: "Godly sorrow brings repentance." Suddenly I realized that I had never developed a godly sorrow over that sin. I *regretted* it because I knew it wasn't God's will for my life, but I had had no real sorrow over it. In fact, I realized I "had cherished sin in my heart" (Ps. 66:18), hanging on to it emotionally though I had let go of it physically. I had *done* the right things, but I still *felt* the wrong things.

Please let me be very clear: God's will was certainly for me to *act* in obedience immediately rather than waiting until I *felt* like it. However, I would not enjoy full freedom from the sin-burden until I let Him change my heart as well. When God opened my eyes to 2 Corinthians 7:10, I wept before the Lord and said, "I want to have godly sorrow for this sin so that I can be free . . . but I don't, Lord! What can I do? Am I stuck with it forever?" His tender response was the same one He's given virtually every time I have longed for something I lacked: "Pray for it, My child." I began to pray for godly sorrow to come to me over that cherished sin. It came at first like the gentle morning tide, but ultimately it hit me like a tidal wave. I did not realize until then how different the concepts of regret and repentance are.

Does my story happen to ring a bell with you? Have you ever physically turned from a sin and ceased the activity, yet continued to cherish it to some degree in your heart? If so, we're not alone. I cannot count the times believers have come to me in the last decade and told me that they had turned from a sinful relationship, for example, but could not seem to let go of the emotional tie. Although our circumstances may be different, like us, they were still "cherishing the sin in their hearts." Godly sorrow is not defined by tears or outward displays of contrition. Godly sorrow is a change of heart resulting in complete agreement with God over the matter. You may say, "But,

Beth, I can't change the way I feel." I understand. I've been there too. But that's why it's called "godly sorrow." *It's a work of God:* He can change our hearts. The change in our feelings will come from a change in our hearts. I particularly love the NIV rendition of 1 John 3:19–20 in reference to this subject: "God is greater than our hearts, and he knows everything."

When we are challenged to repent of cherished sin, all God is waiting for us to do is invite Him to change our hearts and bring about the supernatural work of true repentance. He's looking for our willingness to let go of the sin, both physically and emotionally. You see, God will not let the issue rest until repentance takes up full residency in the heart. Why? Because until the heart change comes, we will continue to be at an overwhelming risk of returning to sinful actions.

Now let's briefly turn our attentions to the second purpose of this chapter: to help the truly repentant bask in the freedom of forgiveness. Some issues are more gray than others, but we've now arrived at a place we can get black and white: once true repentance has taken place, any accusation and guilt we continue to feel is the enemy. In the life of a believer, "guilt" experienced before repentance is the conviction of the Holy Spirit. "Guilt" experienced after repentance is the condemnation of the evil one. My prayer is that some of these Scripture-prayers will help you begin standing firmly against your accuser by walking steadfastly in God's truth. Please hear this with your heart: If you have truly repented of sin, you are forgiven no matter how you happen to "feel." Remember, Christ boldly proclaimed that He has "authority on earth to forgive sins." What are we implying when we repent of sin but let the evil one convince us to refuse to accept it? Are we saying that we can do our part (in repenting) but Christ can't do His part (in forgiving)? I finally realized that my unwillingness to accept Christ's complete forgiveness after my genuine repentance was an *authority* problem. I was in effect saying Christ couldn't do His job. I found myself having to repent for refusing to receive forgiveness!

Please trust me when I say that I know about this guilt issue. Satan has used guilt, condemnation, and accusation to nearly be the death of me at times. You see, I was a young child when I received Christ, and yet I have sinned and failed miserably in my life. I nearly have to fight not to be jealous over the testimonies of those who only knew the real pit of sin prior to their salvation and have walked faithfully since. Every horrible sin I've ever committed has been with the Holy Spirit intact; I was as saved as could be. Oh, what grief strikes my heart again even as I share this testimony. As I grow to love Christ more, every now and then a wave of grief will come over me concerning my past sin, and I will cry to myself, "How could you have done such a thing to Him?" If I do not stop and pray immediately—restating His love for me and my righteousness in Him—Satan will take my wave of sorrow as a vulnerability to accusation, and he will proceed with a hurricane of condemnation. I have had to become extremely proactive against his accusations in order to fight the good fight of faith. You must, too. Incidentally, I learned how to get back at Satan for tempting me to sin then reveling in my failure: let God plunder the enemy by bringing so much good from the bad that Satan will regret ever taking me to that wilderness of sin. What divine vengeance occurs when we let God use our past failures to humble us, to refine us, and to use us all the more effectively!

You and I are about to cease cooperating with Satan's schemes. Amen? If we are in Christ, we are not hopeless no matter which side of true repentance we're on. As we pray the following Scriptures, if we realize we've never developed godly sorrow over certain sin, let's ask Him for it! Then hang on, because He will be faithful to do it! If we *have* repented of sin and yet guilt keeps assailing us, let's start refusing to absorb the accuser's attacks any more, fighting back with prayer and God's Word. Have we been sitting in unlocked prison cells? Is the door wide open? It's time to stand in God's promises and walk out in His truth.

———— ❧ ————

Father, I thank You that if my heart has been responsive and I humbled myself before You, . . . and if I have had a heart like those who tore their robes and wept in Your presence, that You heard me. (2 Kings 22:19)

See, O Lord, how distressed I am! I am in torment within, and in my heart I am disturbed, for I have been most rebellious. Outside, the sword bereaves; inside, there is only death. (Lam. 1:20) Thank You, Lord, that I can be assured You will never forsake one of Your children crying out in agony over sin.

Lord God, I count on You not to withhold Your mercy from me; may Your love and Your truth always protect me. Father, troubles without number surround me; my sins have overtaken me, and I cannot see. They are more than the hairs of my head, and my heart fails within me. (Ps. 40:11–12)

O Lord, have mercy on me; heal me, for I have sinned against You. (Ps. 41:4)

Lord God, lift me out of the slimy pit, out of the mud and mire. Set my feet on a rock and give me a firm place to stand. Put a new song in my mouth, a hymn of praise to my God! Blessed is the one who makes the Lord his trust. (Ps. 40:2–4)

Lord, I acknowledged my sin to You and did not cover up my iniquity. I said, "I will confess my transgressions to the Lord"—and You forgave the guilt of my sin. (Ps. 32:5)

Father, I praise You with my whole heart that when the wicked forsakes his ways and the evil man his thoughts and turns to You, You will have mercy on him, for You will freely pardon! (Isa. 55:7)

Father, I thank You that You've had mercy on me according to Your unfailing love; according to Your great compassion You blot out my transgressions. You can wash away all my iniquity and cleanse me from my sin . . . You can create in me a pure heart, O God, and renew a steadfast spirit within me. (Ps. 51:1, 2, 10)

My faithful God, sorrow has led me to repentance. I pray that I have become sorrowful as You intended and was helped rather than hurt by the confrontation of my sin. Thank You for the godly sorrow that brings repentance leading to salvation and leaving no regret. (2 Cor. 7:9–10)

O, merciful God, when a prayer or plea is made by any of your people—each one aware of his afflictions and pains, and spreading out his hands toward this temple—then hear from heaven, Your dwelling place. Forgive, and deal with each man according to all he does, since you know his heart (for you alone know the hearts of men), so that they will fear you and walk in your ways all the time they live in the land you gave our fathers. (2 Chron. 6:29–31)

O, *Lord,* I have examined my ways and tested them, and returned wholeheartedly to You. (Lam. 3:40) Search me, O God, and know my heart; test me and know my anxious thoughts. See if there is any offensive way in me and lead me in the way everlasting. (Ps. 139:23–24) Lord, if in examining myself, I have overlooked sin, please show me and lead me to full repentance and restoration!

Father, Your Word says that if Your people will turn now, each of us, from our evil practices, we can stay in the land You have given us. (Jer. 25:5)

Lord, you have heard my cry for mercy; You, the Lord, accept my prayer. (Ps. 6:9)

Father, You looked down from Your sanctuary on high, from heaven You viewed the earth, to hear the groans of the prisoners and release those condemned to death. (Ps. 102:19–20)

> *Our Lord Jesus does not flatter us. He lets us see our cases as they are. His searching eye perceives the bare truth of things. He is* "the faithful and true witness" *(Rev. 3:14) who deals with us according to the rule of uprightness. Oh, seeking soul, Jesus loves you too much to flatter you. Therefore, I ask you to have such confidence in Him that, however much He may rebuke . . . you by His Word and Spirit, you may without hesitation reply,* "Truth, Lord."
>
> *Charles Spurgeon,* Spurgeon on Prayer and
> Spiritual Warfare

Father, You have promised that those who sow in tears will reap with songs of joy. Those who go out weeping, carrying seed to sow, will return with songs of joy, carrying sheaves with them. (Ps. 126:5–6)

Lord, I have come with weeping: I have prayed as You brought me back. You will lead me beside streams of water on a level path where I will not stumble, because You are my Father. (Jer. 31:9)

In tears I have sought You, the Lord my God. I desire to come and bind myself to You in an everlasting covenant that will not be forgotten. (Jer. 50:4–5)

Father, give me a heart to know You, that You are the Lord. I am Yours and You are mine, for I have returned to You with all my heart. (Jer. 24:7) You have said that if I will return to You, You, the Lord Almighty, will return to me. (Mal. 3:7)

Father, how I praise You for exalting Christ to Your own right hand as Prince and Savior that He might give repentance and forgiveness of sins to Your people! (Acts 5:31)

O, God, never let me show contempt for the riches of Your kindness, tolerance, and patience, not realizing that Your kindness leads me toward repentance. (Rom. 2:4)

My Father and my God, thank You for granting me repentance leading me to a knowledge of the truth! Thank You for causing me to come to my senses and escape from the trap of the devil, who had taken me captive to do His will. (2 Tim. 2:25–26)

God, thank You for disciplining me for my good, that I may share in Your holiness. (Heb. 12:10)

Lord, I remember the height from which I have fallen. I repent and deeply desire to do the things I did at first. I know that if I do not repent, You will come to me and remove any light my life has in this dark world. (Rev. 2:5)

Father, thank You for assuring me in Your Word that the ones You rebuke and discipline are the ones You love. To the best of my knowledge, I have been earnest and repentant. (Rev. 3:19)

> *Do you groan, "I know I must repent, but I am so unfeeling that I cannot reach the right measure of tenderness"? This is true; therefore, the Lord Jesus is exalted on high to give repentance. You will not more repent in your own power than you will go to heaven in your own merit. But the Lord will grant you "repentance unto life" (Acts 11:18). For repentance, also, is a fruit of the Spirit.*
>
> *Charles Spurgeon,* Spurgeon on Prayer and Spiritual Warfare

Father, my guilt has overwhelmed me like a burden too heavy to bear . . . I am bowed down and brought very low; all day long I go about mourning. . . . I am feeble and utterly crushed; I groan in anguish of heart. All my longings lie open before You, O Lord; my sighing is not hidden from You. My heart pounds, my strength fails me; even the light has gone from my eyes . . . I confess my iniquity; I am troubled by my sin . . . O Lord, do not forsake me; be not far from me, O my God. Come quickly to help me, O Lord my Savior. (Ps. 38:4, 6, 8–10, 18, 21–22) Father, You never reject the truly repentant. Thank You, Lord.

Wash me, Lord, and I will be whiter than snow. Let me hear joy and gladness; let the bones You have crushed rejoice! (Ps. 51:7–8) Break this bondage, Lord, that seems to keep me from sensing or believing Your forgiveness. Help me to rejoice that the only thing whiter than snow is a repentant sinner!

My merciful Father, I thank You for the assurance that You will not despise a broken and contrite heart. Indeed, the sacrifices of God are a broken spirit. (Ps. 51:17)

Father God, thank You for having no condemnation for those who are in Christ Jesus, because through Christ Jesus the law of the

Spirit of life set me free from the law of sin and death. For what the law was powerless to do in that it was weakened by the sinful nature, You did by sending Your own Son in the likeness of sinful man to be a sin offering. (Rom. 8:1–3) Help me to understand that the loving chastisement that might come to me after I have rebelled against You is only in the purest Father's love and is never to be confused with condemnation. (Heb. 12:6)

> *The primary means Satan employs to put volume to his accusing voice is by using no small list of willing humans. We are by nature a merciless, condemning lot. Far more would burn in eternal flames under our judgment than under that of a holy and righteous God. Know the truth so thoroughly and respond to conviction so readily that when accusations come, you can resist the devil, no matter whose voice grants him volume.*

My faithful God, if I claim to be without sin, I deceive myself and the truth is not in me. But if I confess my sins, You are faithful and just and will forgive me my sins and purify me from all unrighteousness. If any of us claim we have not sinned, we make You out to be a liar and Your word has no place in our lives. (1 John 1:8–10)

Lord, apart from You, there is no one righteous, not even one; there is no one who understands, no one who seeks You, God. All have turned away. We have together become worthless; there is no one who does good, not even one. (Rom. 3:10–12) God, the righteousness that comes from You comes through faith in Jesus Christ to all who believe. There is no difference, for all have sinned and fall short of the glory of You, God, and are justified freely by Your grace through the redemption that came by Your Son, Christ Jesus. (Rom. 3:22–23) Help me to accept that Your gift of grace has never and will never be relegated by my ability to be good and righteous. Freedom from the burden of my own sin accompanies true repentance and acceptance that Your Son's death fully pardoned me.

Blessed am I, God, because my transgressions are forgiven. My sins are covered. Blessed am I because You, Lord, will never count my sins against me. (Rom. 4:7–8)

Father, how I thank You that Your servants were also sinners saved by grace. The apostle Paul said, "I thank Christ Jesus our Lord, who has given me strength, that he considered me faithful, appointing me to his service." Even though he was once a blasphemer and a persecutor and a violent man, he was shown mercy. Like him, Lord, Your grace has been poured out on me abundantly, along with the faith and love that are in Christ Jesus. (1 Tim. 1:12–14)

Merciful Lord, I echo the words of the apostle Paul who said, "Here is a trustworthy saying that deserves full acceptance: Christ Jesus came into the world to save sinners—of whom I am the worst. But for that very reason I was shown mercy so that in me, the worst of sinners, Christ Jesus might display his unlimited patience as an example for those who would believe on him and receive eternal life. Now to the King eternal, immortal, invisible, the only God, be honor and glory for ever and ever. Amen." (1 Tim. 1:15–17) Lord, even if I were the very worst of sinners as sometimes I feel I am, You still forgive and are willing to use those who put their trust in You! Thank You, God!

Lord, I have no reason to be ashamed, because I know whom I have believed, and am convinced that You are able to guard what I have entrusted to You for that day. (2 Tim. 1:12)

Lord, even when I've been faithless, You've been faithful, for You cannot disown Yourself. (2 Tim. 2:13)

Lord God, help me not to fall victim to the accusations of Satan, the accuser of believers. He is furious because he knows his time is short. I have received Your salvation and I am in Your kingdom, O

God, and under the authority of Your Son, Jesus Christ. The enemy is overcome by the blood of the Lamb and by the word of our testimonies. (Rev. 12:10–11) Help me never to cease testifying of Your mighty work in my behalf.

If You, O Lord, kept a record of sins, O Lord, who could stand? But with You there is forgiveness; therefore You are feared. I wait for You, Lord. My soul waits, and in Your Word I put my hope. My soul waits for You, Lord, more than watchmen wait for the morning. With You, Lord, is unfailing love and with You, Lord, is *full* redemption. You Yourself will redeem me from all my sins. (Ps. 130:3–8)

O, how I praise You that *everyone* who believes in You, Jesus, receives forgiveness of sins through Your name! (Acts 10:43) There are no exceptions!

> *One reliable rod for measuring closeness to God would be the time that lapses between sin and repentance. The spiritual man still sins, but he cannot bear to resist immediate repentance. His overwhelming sensitivity results in a holier life because he repents in the early stages of what otherwise would become a contagion of sin. Indeed, those who walk closely with God frustrate the efforts of the accuser; by the time he arrives in the heavenlies to register his accusations, God can say with pleasure, "I have no memory of that sin."*

Lord Jesus, I acknowledge that You, the Son of Man, have authority on earth to forgive sins! (Luke 5:24) Please help me to understand that when I doubt Your forgiveness after my own repentance, in effect, I'm saying I can do my part but You cannot do Yours. Forgive me, Jesus, and help me not to minimize Your sovereign authority to complete this awesome, redemptive work.

Lord Jesus, help me to accept and internalize that if God is for me, who can be against me? (Rom. 8:31) It is You, God, who justifies. (Rom. 8:33) Who is he that condemns? Christ Jesus, who died—more than that, who was raised to life—is at Your right hand, O God, and is also interceding for me. (Rom. 8:34)

In all these things I am more than a conqueror through You who love me, Sovereign Lord. (Rom. 8:37)

> *He who is unconvinced of God's forgiving love is unconvinced he is more than a conqueror.*

Lord God, one reason You inspired Your Word to be written was so that I, Your dear child, could know that my sins are forgiven on account of *Your* good name. (1 John 2:12) I can be strong because the word of God lives in me, and in You I have overcome the evil one. (1 John 2:14)

Father God, You made my Savior's life a guilt offering for me. (Isa. 53:10) His death was enough to handle my guilt.

Lord, according to Your Word, he who conceals his sins does not prosper, but whoever confesses and renounces them finds mercy. (Prov. 28:13)

Although my sins testify against me, O Lord, do something for the sake of Your name. For my backsliding is great; I have sinned against You. (Jer. 14:7) O Lord, I acknowledge my wickedness and guilt. I have indeed sinned against You. (Jer. 14:20)

Wonderful Savior, Jesus, how I thank You for telling us that there will be more rejoicing in heaven over one sinner who repents than over ninety-nine righteous persons who do not need to repent! (Luke 15:7)

Father, I have been like the prodigal son, squandering my inheritance on worthless living. While I was still a long way off, You saw me and were filled with compassion for me. You ran to receive me back into Your arms. I have come to You to confess my sin against heaven and against You. I have felt unworthy to be called Your son. But You celebrated my return to You and desired to put Your best robe around me and Your ring on my finger. Because of Your great mercy, You've received me back as a child, not a servant. I felt dead, but now I feel alive again! (Luke 15:13, 20–23, 32)

Lord Jesus, in Your name and Your authority, I say to the devil, "Do not gloat over me, my enemy! Though I have fallen, I will rise. Though I sit in darkness, the Lord will be my light. I have sinned, but Christ bore my wrath on the cross. He pleads my case and established my right. He will bring me out into the light, and I will see His righteousness. Then you, my enemy, will see it and be covered with shame." (Mic. 7:8–10)

> *I wish I had a dollar for every time I heard a counselee say, "Oh, I confessed that sin a year ago—a thousand times." First, that is 999 times too many. Second, each subsequent time that sin is confessed, rather than the confession bringing relief, it only reinforces the false belief that it has not been forgiven. Double, or reconfession, only deepens the false belief that we have not been forgiven.*
>
> Dr. Chuck Lynch, I Should Forgive, but . . .

PERSONALIZING YOUR PRAYERS

Chapter 10

Overcoming Despair Resulting from Loss

I approach this chapter with tenderness of heart because those who will turn to this page are more than likely *devastated*. This chapter is written for people who have lost loved ones and either found themselves in a stronghold of ongoing despair or are trying desperately to avoid one. You will quickly notice that this section of commentary is much longer than those in the other chapters. People who are suffering terribly from a loss can use all the encouragement they can get to survive.

Please allow me to say from the beginning that nothing is more normal and appropriate than grief in response to the death of someone dear. In fact, the absence of appropriate grief after loss may be an indicator of another kind of serious stronghold. While grief is most assuredly not a stronghold, lengthy life-draining despair *is*. Blocking the healing, restorative power of God places a believer in a painful, literally debilitating, yoke of bondage.

After traveling and talking to so many believers in various crises and strongholds, I am convinced that we are giving Satan far too much credit for having some semblance of heart. Please understand, Satan has no heart. We find a strange and deceptive comfort in imagining that Satan would draw the line at certain limits and act appropriately. For instance, we mistakenly assume that surely Satan would leave us alone in our heart-rending grief because, after all, he knows we're defenseless and weak. *Wrong.* Where was Satan when Christ was in the wilderness of temptation, starving and alone? Right there with Him. Luke 4:13 concludes the record of Christ's temptation with the harrowing words: "When the devil had finished all this tempting, he left him until an *opportune* time" (emphasis mine). Where was the devil when Christ was in Gethsemane, grieving and pouring sweat-drops of blood? Putting his final touches on the trap he had set up through his puppet, Judas. Luke 22:3–6 says, "Then Satan entered Judas, called Iscariot, one of the Twelve. And Judas went to the chief priests and the officers of the temple guard and discussed with them how he might betray Jesus. They were delighted and agreed to give him money. He consented, and watched for an *opportunity* to hand Jesus over to them when no crowd was present" (emphasis mine).

Satan is an opportunist. Would he come after you while you are down? In a heartbeat . . . if he had a heart. Let's wake up from our deceptive slumber and open our eyes to the fact that Satan is the one behind every childhood victimization, every suicide, and every scandalous fall of a righteous man. The word *appropriate* isn't in his vocabulary. He's not polite, and he doesn't give us room to grieve and wait until we're on our feet again so we can have a fair fight. Satan fights dirty. Please believe it. I know that most of us would rather not have to think about warfare when we are grieving the death of a loved one but—somehow, some way—we are very wise to muster the energy to take these protective measures:

- pray for protection through our season of grief
- pray for healthy grief
- surrender our grief to God so Satan can't get a foothold
- call on warring intercessors to pray for us in our weakness
- keep lines of communication open with God even when all we can say is "Help!" or "Why?"
- believe God's Word that tells us He can and will restore abundant life . . . if we'll let Him

I have absolutely no right to talk about insurmountable, earth-shattering grief over the loss of a loved one at this point in my life. I have not yet had to face that kind of loss. My precious mother died last year. Although she can never be replaced and we miss her very much, I had already accepted that her death was imminent, and I am certain she now resides, alive and kicking, in heaven. Many adult children realize they will probably bury their senior adult parents at some point. As my mom always said, "Better you bury me than I bury you." I know exactly what she meant because

I have children of my own. Burying our aging parents is a more natural, normal kind of process and, although I have grieved, the grief has not been unmanageable for me. Let me interject immediately that although my mother's death did not happen to turn into a stronghold for me, a similar loss might turn into a stronghold for someone else. No loss is created equal, and no mourner is exactly the same.

This chapter is for anyone in a stronghold of despair after loss, no matter who the loved one and what the circumstances. If you're having great difficulty moving on after a death, you qualify! It doesn't matter one iota if anyone else understands the depth or length of your mourning. This chapter is for the mother who miscarried a precious little one and the father abandoned by his wife and children. The latter may not seem to apply, but the death of a marriage or the death of a dream can cause debilitating grief. Whatever the reason for your grief, if you're feeling paralyzed or hung up on it, this chapter is for you.

I hear numerous heartbreaking stories as I minister around the country, and I assure you, many have suffered far more devastating losses than I have so far; therefore, the words I offer you in this chapter are not based on my experience. Rather, they are based on two reliable sources:

1. the Word of God, which is truth whether or not it has yet been applied
2. the very vivid experiences of a few others who have taken God at His Word

Based on these two sources, I believe I can confidently but reverently say to you that God can put any broken person back together again no matter what he or she has suffered. I'm not just saying that God can cause a person to maintain his or her physical existence after tragedy. Many people *live* through tragedy. I'll never forget my mother-in-law's response when I asked her how she survived the death of her beloved, blonde-headed three-year-old after a house fire. She answered, "I just kept waking up. I didn't want to live. I simply didn't have much choice." Many of you know exactly what she meant. My heart still breaks for her. I am thankful I can tell you that she is no longer simply breathing. She is living once again.

Physical existence is not what Christ died to bring us. He came that we might have life and have it more abundantly. As impossible and unreachable as this truth may seem, *God can restore abundant life.* For our present purposes, we'll define a stronghold after loss as the *continued* unwillingness or presumed inability to *let Him do so.*

It is my great honor to introduce you to three of my heroes: Joy Conaway, Alison Shanklin, and Jeanine Dooley. All three of them have discovered abundant life in Christ after devastating loss. With their permission, I'd like to share their stories. First of all, please meet my friend, Joy. She and her husband, Jack, were in two separate cars, filled to the brim with furnishings for their new hill-country home where they would soon retire . . . when life crashed.

> *My son, Jay, walked out to meet me and Jeff, my other son, in the parking lot of his apartment that summer afternoon of June 28, 1994. He told me that he had just received a phone call and Jack, his father and my mate of many years, was dead. It felt as though someone reached into my body and ripped out half my heart. Every nerve, feeling, emotion, and fear rose up like a tidal wave engulfing my very being. My mind could not grasp the truth of it. My body rejected it as I stood shaking in the parking lot.*
>
> *Something, actually Someone, my precious Lord, took control and I began to do what had to be done. First I had to know where Jack was, then what arrangements had to be made, notify our families, and hold myself together for my sons. My physical body did the things that had to be done, but emotionally and spiritually it was as if I were watching . . . not participating. As my sons and I were driven from San Marcos to College Station to claim the body, the thought that came blasting into my head was, "Now what do you believe?" And then like a rushing waterfall all the things I believed about God began to pour forth. In my mind the answers were, "I*

believe You are sovereign. I believe You are love. I believe all things are possible with You. I believe You are merciful. . . ." As the characteristics of God flooded my mind, a peace that passes all understanding filled my being. To this day when everyday life seems to overtake me I begin to praise God for Who He is and life settles back into place.

As I lay in bed that night, a childhood song ran through my mind continually: "Jesus loves me this I know because the Bible tells me so." Over and over those words so simple and yet so profoundly true soothed my soul. Today when I feel that my life cannot go forward because the dreams were shattered and the one man who made me feel whole was gone, I turn to the One God who restores me. The Psalms have never been sweeter and God's promises more real. I found that praising God each day for who He is raises me above my circumstances. I knew that Jesus Christ was greater than my pain, that He promised in His Word to be the Husband of the widow and the Father to the fatherless, and that He promised His grace would be sufficient. I have learned firsthand that His words are true and they endure forever.

I will be eternally grateful for the fact that God led me to Bible Study Fellowship where, through the study of His Word, I gave my life to Him. He prepared me in so many areas for what He knew was to come. After all the ways He had gone before me, I could not doubt His precious love. I don't even want to imagine what my life would be like now if I had not known Jesus Christ personally and so intimately before Jack was taken. As it is, God is more real and more precious to me today than even the first time I knew Him. With God all things are possible: Even contentment as you face life without your life partner . . . for the One who promises to never leave us stays eternally. May His name be praised!

Now meet my friend, Alison. She and her husband Steve had only been married a short time when he was instantly swept from her life by a car accident. She was left alone . . . a child on the way. Unlike Joy, she could not draw water from the well of a long-time relationship with Jesus Christ. Still faithful, He graciously placed a young man by the name of Duncan Shanklin in her life. They were married, and he became a wonderful father to her child. Soon they were blessed with another child. Her name was Megan. When she was about a year old, Alison and Duncan were at the mortgage company signing papers for their brand-new home. Life seemed destined for happily ever after. Then tragedy struck.

> After I lost my first husband, God was in my life but only at a distance. I knew of His sovereignty but did not know Him personally. He certainly performed a miracle in my life bringing Duncan and me together, but I was only in the beginning stages of finding Him. Sadly enough, I did not even have a Scripture to cling to, but He certainly was there. Two years later when Megan had her accident was the turning point in our lives. I distinctly remember seeing such a huge difference in the people with whom God surrounded us in the hospital. The believers were full of hope and had something I desperately wanted.
>
> The night Megan died, I remember coming home and praying, "Lord, I can't take or handle my life anymore. It is Yours to take control over." Three hours later, we got a phone call to get back to the hospital. Megan had developed a temperature for some unknown reason and the Lord took her home. This is when the light went on. I realized God was the only One who truly knew how I felt. He had watched His Son suffer and die. I remember telling Him, "I don't know how a person is supposed to do this. How can I ever be happy again?" I also thought about my vow hours earlier and said, "I have trusted You, and I know You must be faithful." He seemed to

respond simply by saying, "Trust Me. I will be there."

I did not know the words of Isaiah 43:1–2 (NASB) at the time but they sprang to life for me: "Do not fear, for I have redeemed you; I have called you by name; you are Mine! When you pass through the waters, I will be with you; And through the rivers, they will not overflow you. When you walk through the fire, you will not be scorched, Nor will the flame burn you." Psalm 34:18 (NASB) also became so real to me: "The LORD is near to the brokenhearted, and saves those who are crushed in spirit." I was so brokenhearted at that time, but He showed me how to look for Him, and I saw Him at every turn. He was there, as He had promised. I also had a hope: "And we know that God causes all things to work together for those who love God, to those who are called according to His purpose." Almost to the date of Megan's accident we had our son, Brooks. What a blessing and continuation of God's faithfulness.

That year He taught me to wait on Him and never give up. He applied Psalm 27:13–14 (NASB) to my life: "I would have despaired unless I had believed that I would see the goodness of the LORD in the land of the living. Wait for the LORD; Be strong, and let your heart take courage; Yes, wait for the LORD." Later, God also blessed us with another daughter. We were so convinced we were having another boy that I didn't even have a name for her. Someone suggested "Kendall" and I looked up the name in my book. It is derived from Psalm 126:3 (NASB): "The LORD has done great things for us; We are glad." I read two verses further and God's Word said, "Those who sow in tears shall reap with joyful shouting. He who goes to and fro weeping, carrying his bag of seed, shall indeed come again with a shout of joy, bringing his sheaves with him." We cried,

"Amen, that's our life!" and we signed the birth cer-
tificate.

The Lord truly brought us full circle in that time
and restored my soul and gave me a joy I never
dreamed possible. He has since given me a ministry of
giving hope to women who have lost a husband or a
child. It is a miracle that I can truly say that I am
thankful, not for the losses, but for all God brought me
through, because I am positive I wouldn't otherwise
know Him like I do.

Alison is far too modest and humble to tell you how many people she and Duncan have led to Christ since the reality of Jesus
Christ became so vivid in their loss. You see, they don't just *believe*
God is real. They *know* He is . . . because they know they would
never have survived if He weren't. Because they are so convinced,
they share their faith constantly. They simply have plenty to share.
One night I attended a large gathering that the Shanklins, our family friends, had prepared for the express purpose of sharing Jesus
Christ. The invitation to know Him was preceded by a brief film.
While those attending were watching the film, I was standing in the
back and saw Alison go over and embrace her husband, Duncan.
They both began to cry . . . as did I. Alison pointed to the crowd riv-
eted to the message about Jesus, then whispered through smiling
tears, "All because of Megan."

Allow me to introduce you to Jeanine Dooley. Brace yourself—her story is staggering. Our relationship began years ago
when I was a mom of two young children and in my late twenties.
One of the members of our Sunday school class brought an urgent
prayer request to our attention one Sunday. A mother in a nearby
town had two young children, a toddler and a baby, who were
gravely ill. These were her only children. The doctors were mysti-
fied by the cause of their matching illnesses, but the prognosis for
both looked dim. Because most of us were mothers about her
same age with children similar ages, we were devastated for her.
We fell on our faces before God in prayer, interceding as hard as
we could. The thought that God might take those two children

home, as the doctors feared, was inconceivable . . . until it happened.

We were overcome with grief for a precious set of parents we had never even met. All of us prayed fervently for God to give them a reason to live. Because God had indelibly engraved this Christian couple on our hearts, we were filled with great rejoicing over a year later when we heard the news that God had given them a brand-new bouncing baby. I cannot explain our shock and grief months later when we learned that this little one had taken on the same symptoms as the siblings. A few days later, we received word that the third child of Steve and Jeanine Dooley had toddled through the gates of heaven.

We were wrought with confusion and questions, and our young faith rocked like a rickety boat in a winter storm. My class and I could not begin to imagine the suffering of this heartbroken couple. Jeanine was thirty-one, had buried all three of her children to a rare genetic problem, and would never be able to have any more. Having still never met them or corresponded with them personally, we all vowed to intercede as long as God left the burden on our hearts. A short while later, I took a different Sunday school class, and most of us went our separate directions in church life.

For several years, this couple came to my mind almost daily. Over the next decade, I still thought of them often. I had no idea what had happened to them or whether their marriage had survived such unimaginable tragedy. Several years ago, I received a letter at my home address. It began,

> *Dear Beth,*
>
> *You do not know me but I feel as if I know you. I have become familiar with you through your Bible studies. Recently I learned of the loss of your adopted son and his return to his birth mother. I am heartbroken for you, and I am writing to tell you that I am committing to pray you through your loss. I know that right now you might not think you will ever find joy in life again, but I am writing to encourage you that God*

*is faithful. I know because years ago, I lost three chil-
dren. . . .*

My eyes fastened to those four words as a shock wave went
through me. I had only known of one couple who had ever lost all
three of their children. I flipped the letter over to see the signature. I
cannot describe all the feelings that surged through my soul when I
saw the closing:

> *With love and prayers,*
> *Jeanine Dooley*

I burst into tears and called directory assistance in that small
city. I shook all over as I phoned her immediately. I sobbed as I said,
"Jeanine, I prayed for you on my face before God over and over
when you lost those precious children! And now you are praying for
me!" I insisted then as I still insist now that our losses could not possibly be compared. Michael is still very much alive. My name
doesn't even belong in the same paragraph as hers. In no way was
our suffering similar. What *was* similar, however, was our resolve to
make it in Christ, no matter what came our way. We have built a
long-distance friendship on that similarity. Neither one of us could
fathom how the Lord had woven our lives together through praying
for absolute strangers . . . yet sisters in the body of Christ. When I
began this book and planned this chapter, I knew I couldn't do it
without Jeanine. She is proof positive that we can survive any loss
and trust God to sustain us, restore us, and eventually even grant us
joy, purpose, and abundant life. When I asked if I could use her tender story and the Scriptures to which she cleaved in her devastation,
she wrote:

> *I consider this a joyous occasion to be able to
> share the Scriptures that God has used to bring about
> healing. . . . I asked God many years ago to please use
> me in any way that might glorify His name and in a
> way that would bring comfort to those in pain. At this
> point in my life, I feel that God has brought me to a
> place where 2 Corinthians 1:3–4 is very real and a part
> of who I am: "Praise be to the God and Father of our*

*Lord Jesus Christ, the Father of compassion and the
God of all comfort, who comforts us in all our troubles, so that we can comfort those in any trouble with
the comfort we ourselves have received." That's part of
what my ministry on this earth is all about. I can never
say that I am glad to have lost my children or even that
I think God planned it this way. But I can say that my
losses have turned out as strengths in my life and I do
consider it a privilege to serve God in the matter He
has seen fit in my life.*

*What I want more than anything is to know God
in an intimate way, and to serve Him and to share with
everyone I possibly can that Jesus Christ is Lord and
that this can be a wonderful life on earth, but nothing
compared to what is ahead for us in glory.*

This time the letter was signed, not by a stranger and not just by
a friend. But by a hero.

Love,
Jeanine

Most of the Scriptures that I rewrote into prayers in this chapter
were supplied by Joy, Alison, and Jeanine. I give you their names so
that you won't be tempted to spiritualize or compartmentalize them.
Their stories are not fables. They themselves are not angels. They're
not superhumans. They are real, live flesh-and-blood people with
real, live emotions who not only survived real, live suffering, but lived
long enough to discover a real, live Redeemer who *works . . . just as
He says He does.* I also strongly suggest the Scripture-prayers in the
chapter "Overcoming Depression." Many of those Scripture-prayers
will also apply and bring nourishment to your soul even if your present challenges don't necessarily fall under the umbrella of depression.

I have no idea what brought you to this page. But I know by faith
that whatever it is, God yearns to minister to you, comfort you,
restore you, and give you a life of abundance you never could otherwise have known. Sometimes we hang on to our despair as a way of

hanging on to the loved one. Other times, we wrestle with an unshak-
able feeling that we will betray our loved one if we ever dare to be
happy again. Please know that God has a plan for you. A plan to give
you a hope and a future (Jer. 29:11). Satan also has a plan for you. A
plan to give you hopelessness and steal your future. The quality of
your life hangs in the balance. Only you can decide. Oh, sister . . .
brother. Choose Christ.

Merciful and faithful Lord, because of Your great love I am not
consumed, for Your compassions never fail. They are new every
morning; great is Your faithfulness. I say to myself, "The LORD is my
portion; therefore I will wait for him." Lord, You are good to those
whose hope is in You, to the one who seeks You. (Lam. 3:22–25)

Though the fig tree does not bud and there are no grapes on the
vines, though the olive crop fails and the fields produce no food,
though there are no sheep in the pen and no cattle in the stalls, yet I
will rejoice in You, my Lord, I will be joyful in God my Savior. You,
Sovereign Lord, are my strength; You make my feet like the feet of a
deer, You enable me to go on the heights. (Hab. 3:17–19) Father, how
inconceivable but true that you can take me to heights far exceeding
the depths which I've known.

Even to my old age and gray hair You are He. You are the One
who will sustain me. You made me and You will carry me; You will
sustain me and You will rescue me . . . I will remember the former
things, those of long ago; You are God, and there is no other; You are
God, and there is none like You. (Isa. 46:4, 9)

As a bridegroom rejoices over his bride, so will You, my God,
rejoice over me. (Isa. 62:5b)

Surely You, Jesus, took up my infirmities and carried my sorrows, yet we considered You stricken by God, smitten by Him, and
afflicted. But You were pierced for my transgressions; You were
crushed for my iniquities; the punishment that brought me peace was
upon You, and by Your wounds I am healed. (Isa. 53:4–5)

For You know the plans You have for me, Lord. Plans to prosper me and not to harm me, plans to give me a hope and a future. (Jer. 29:11)

Lord, I don't want to waver through unbelief regarding Your promises, but I desire to be strengthened in my faith and give glory to You, God, being fully persuaded that You have power to do what You promise. You credit this kind of faith to Your children as righteousness! (Rom. 4:20–22)

Father, continue to bring me along so that I can also rejoice in my sufferings because I know that suffering produces perseverance. (Rom. 5:3)

Oh, the depth of the riches of Your wisdom and knowledge, O God! How unsearchable Your judgments, and Your paths beyond tracing out! Who has known the mind of You, Lord? Or who has been Your counselor? Who has ever given to You, God, that You should repay him? For from You and through You and to You are all things. To You be the glory forever! Amen. (Rom. 11:33–36)

Lord, as I consider what You do, I find myself feeling at times like the writer of Ecclesiastes: Who can straighten what You have made crooked? When times are good, I am to be happy: but when times are bad, consider: You have made the one as well as the other. (Eccles. 7:13–14)

Lord God, according to Your Word, there is a time for everything, and a season for every activity under heaven: a time to be born and a time to die, a time to plant and a time to uproot . . . a time to weep and a time to laugh, a time to mourn and a time to dance. (Eccles. 3:1–2, 4) You are the Creator and Sustainer of time. Nothing is "untimely" to You.

Lord, in my heart I plan my course, but You determine my steps. (Prov. 16:9) Life is not going as I planned. I am so grateful that You are not caught off guard. You knew everything that would befall me. Please direct my steps as You determine. I need You, Lord. Carry me when I cannot walk.

I want to trust in You, Lord, with all my heart and lean not on my own understanding; in all my ways I will acknowledge You, and You will make my paths straight. (Prov. 3:5–6)

Though I walk in the midst of trouble, You preserve my life; You stretch out Your hand against the anger of my foes, with Your right hand You save me. You, Lord, will fulfill Your purpose for me; Your love, O Lord, endures forever—do not abandon the works of Your hands. (Ps. 138:7–8)

> *Thou, O Lord, canst transform my thorn into a flower. And I want my thorn transformed into a flower. Job got the sunshine after the rain, but has the rain been all waste? Job wants to know, I want to know, if the shower had nothing to do with the shining. And Thou canst tell me—Thy cross can tell me. Thou hast crowned Thy sorrow. Be this my crown, O Lord. I only triumph in Thee when I have learned the radiance of the rain.*
>
> *George Matheson,* Streams in the Desert

Father, under the inspiration of Your Holy Spirit, the writer of Psalm 119 said, "It was good for me to be afflicted / so that I might learn your decrees. / The law from your mouth is more precious to me / than thousands of pieces of silver and gold. / Your hand made me and formed me; / give me understanding to learn your commands. / May those who fear you rejoice when they see me, / for I have put my hope in your word." (Ps. 119:71–74) I am only beginning to understand what he meant. We never know what You and Your Word can mean and do until we are so afflicted that we cannot live without You. Please grant me an abundance of You and teach me Your powerful Word so that meaning can come forth from this tragedy.

May Your unfailing love be my comfort, according to Your promise to Your servant. Let Your compassion come to me that I may live, for Your law is my delight. . . . My soul faints with long-ing for Your salvation, but I have put my hope in Your Word. (Ps. 119:76–77, 81)

I love You, Lord, for You heard my voice; You heard my cry for mercy. Because You turned Your ear to me, I will call on You as long as I live. The cords of death entangled me, the anguish of the grave came upon me; I was overcome by trouble and sorrow. Then I called on the name of the Lord: O Lord, save me! You, Lord, are gracious and righteous; my God is full of compassion. You, Lord, protect the simple-hearted; when I was in great need, You saved me. Be at rest once more, O my soul, for the Lord has been good to you. (Ps. 116:1–7)

My God is in heaven; He does whatever pleases Him. (Ps. 115:3) Lord, sometimes my only answer will be that You are sovereign. Your Word says that the death of Your saints is absolutely precious to You. (Ps. 116:15) One day I will have all the answers. Until then, I must trust that You have power and dominion over all things and that You know best. Help me to *believe* this even when I don't *feel* this.

I cry to You, Lord, in my trouble. Save me from my distress. (Ps. 107:13)

I desire to dwell in the shelter of You, the Most High. I will rest in the shadow of the Almighty. I will say of You, Lord, "You are my refuge and my fortress, my God, in whom I trust." (Ps. 91:1–2)

You are forgiving and good, O Lord, abounding in love to all who call to You. Hear my prayer, O Lord; listen to my cry for mercy. In the day of my trouble I will call to You, for You will answer me. (Ps. 86:5–7)

Yet You are always with me; You hold me by my right hand. You guide me with Your counsel, and afterward You will take me into glory. Whom have I in heaven but You? And earth has nothing I desire besides You. My flesh and my heart may fail, but You, God, are the strength of my heart and my portion for-ever. . . . But as for me, it is good to be near You, my God. I have made You, Sovereign Lord, my refuge; I will tell of all Your deeds. (Ps. 73:23–26, 28)

Mighty God, be my rock of refuge, to which I can always go; give the command to save me, for You are my rock and my fortress. (Ps. 71:3)

A father to the fatherless, a defender of widows, are You, God, in Your holy dwelling. (Ps. 68:5)

Lord, because You are my help, I sing in the shadow of Your wings. My soul clings to You; Your right hand upholds me. (Ps. 63:7–8)

Help me trust in You at all times; help me to pour out my heart to You, God, for You are my refuge. (Ps. 62:8) O Lord, help me not be afraid to speak to You what's on my heart. Your Word says You know my thoughts and my actions, and You know what I'm going to say before a word forms on my tongue. (Ps. 139:1–4) You will never be offended when I pour out the earnest despair and bitterness that wells in my heart. You desire for me to cry out in my agony, and You can take my feelings of anger, dismay, and confusion. In pouring my heart out to You, I rid myself of soul-cancerous bitterness. I also make room for You to pour in Your healing.

I cry out to You, God Most High, to You who fulfills Your purpose for me. You send from heaven and save me, rebuking those who hotly pursue me. You send Your love and Your faithfulness. (Ps. 57:2–3)

I choose to cast my cares on You, Lord, and You will sustain me. (Ps. 55:22)

God, You are my refuge and strength, an ever-present help in trouble. Therefore I will not fear, though the earth give way and the mountains fall into the heart of the sea, though its waters roar and foam and the mountains quake with their surging. . . . I will be still and know You are God. You, Lord Almighty, are with me. You, God of Jacob, are my fortress. (Ps. 46:1–2, 10–11)

> *We often see ourselves as fragile, breakable souls. We live in fear of that which we are certain we can't survive. As children of God, we are only as fragile as our unwillingness to turn and hide our face in Him. Our pride alone is fragile. Once its shell is broken and the heart is laid bare, we can sense the caress of God's tender care. Until then, He holds us just the same.*

O Lord, how priceless is Your unfailing love! Both high and low among men find refuge in the shadow of Your wings. They feast on the abundance of Your house; You give them drink from Your river of delights. For with You is the fountain of life; in Your light we see light. Continue Your love to those who know You, Your righteousness to the upright in heart. (Ps. 36:7–10)

I commit my way to You, Lord; I trust in You and You will do this: You will make my righteousness shine like the dawn, the justice of my cause like the noonday sun. (Ps. 37:5–6)

Praise be to You, Lord, for You showed Your wonderful love to me when I was in a besieged city. (Ps. 31:21)

One thing I ask of You, Lord, this is what I seek: that I may dwell in the house of the Lord all the days of my life, to gaze upon Your beauty and to seek You in Your temple. For in the day of trouble You will keep me safe in Your dwelling; You will hide me in the shelter of Your tabernacle and set me high upon a rock. (Ps. 27:4–5)

You, Lord, are my Shepherd. I shall not be in want. You make me lie down in green pastures, You lead me beside quiet waters, You restore my soul. You guide me in paths of righteousness for Your name's sake. Even though I walk through the valley of the shadow of death, I will fear no evil, for You are with me; Your rod and Your staff, they comfort me. You prepare a table before me in the presence of my enemies. You anoint my head with oil; my cup overflows.

Surely goodness and love will follow me all the days of my life, and I will dwell in Your house, my Lord, forever. (Ps. 23)

Lord God, according to Your Word, my "light and momentary" troubles (in relation to eternity) are achieving for me an eternal glory that far outweighs them all. So I fix my eyes not on what is seen, but on what is unseen. For what is seen is temporary, but what is unseen is eternal. (2 Cor. 4:17–18)

You say to me, Lord, "My grace is sufficient for you, for my power is made perfect in weakness." Therefore I will boast all the more gladly about my weaknesses, so that Your power may rest on me. (2 Cor. 12:9)

Help me, Lord, not to become weary in doing good, for at the proper time I will reap a harvest if I do not give up. (Gal. 6:9)

You, O God, will never leave me. Never will You forsake me. (Heb. 13:5) You are the only absolute guarantee I have in all of life. Help me cling to the one thing I can never lose.

Help me, Lord, to finally comprehend what it means to consider it pure joy whenever I face trials of many kinds. Help me to know that the testing of my faith develops perseverance. Perseverance must finish its work in me so that I may be mature and complete, lacking nothing. (James 1:2–4) Lord, You are not asking me to rejoice that I have lost someone or something precious, but You know that, in my

> *Joy sometimes needs pain to give it birth. Fanny Crosby could never have written her beautiful hymn, "I shall see Him face-to-face," were it not for the fact that she had never looked upon the green fields nor the evening sunset nor the kindly twinkle in her mother's eye. It was the loss of her own vision that helped her to gain her remarkable spiritual discernment.*
>
> Mrs. Charles E. Cowman, Streams in the Desert

loss I can rejoice in all I have to gain if I'm willing. Never must my suffering be in vain.

Help me, Lord, to know beyond a shadow of a doubt that in all things You work for the good of those who love You, who have been called according to Your purpose. (Rom. 8:28) Please help me to see the condition in that promise. You are not obligated to work all things together for good for those who neither love You nor are called according to Your purpose. You obligate Yourself to this awesome promise when I offer You my aching heart and commit myself and my suffering to Your good purposes. If I do, You will do more with my life than I could ever conceive. (1 Cor. 2:9)

Merciful Lord, restore to me the joy of Your salvation and grant me a willing spirit, to sustain me. (Ps. 51:12)

Help me, Lord, not to be anxious about anything, but in everything, by prayer and petition, with thanksgiving, present my requests to You. And Your peace, O God, which transcends all understanding, will guard my heart and my mind in Christ Jesus. (Phil. 4:6–7)

Lord, after this suffering, let it be said that what has happened to me has really served to advance the gospel. As a result, make my Savior clear to all those around me. Because of my suffering and willing perseverance, cause others to be encouraged to speak the Word of God more courageously and fearlessly. (Phil. 1:12–14)

Lord, I pray that one day I will begin to consider my precious losses gains for the sake of Christ as You use my suffering, my life, and my testimony. Whatever was to my profit I now consider loss for the sake of Christ. What is more, I consider everything a loss compared to the surpassing greatness of knowing Christ Jesus my Lord, for whose sake I have lost all things. I want to gain You, Christ, and be found in You, not having a righteousness of my own that comes from the law, but that which is through faith in You—the righteousness that comes from God and is by faith. I want to know You, Jesus, and the power of Your resurrection and fellowship of sharing in Your sufferings, becoming like You in Your death. Not that I have already obtained all this, or have already been made perfect, but I press on to take hold of that for which You, Christ Jesus, took hold of me. I do not consider myself yet to have taken hold of it. But one thing I do: Forgetting what is behind and straining toward what is ahead, I press on toward the goal to win the prize for which God has called me heavenward in You, Christ Jesus. (Phil. 3:7–14) Lord, You do not expect or want me to forget my loved one. Your Word is simply telling me not to live in the past and fail to embrace the future You have for me.

But now, this is what You, the Lord, say—You who created me, You who formed me: "Fear not, for I have redeemed you; / I have summoned you by name, you are mine. / When you pass through the waters, / I will be with you; / and when you pass through the rivers, / they will not sweep over you. / When you walk through the fire, / you will not be burned; / the flames will not set you ablaze." (Isa. 43:1–2)

You, Lord, are close to the brokenhearted and save those who are crushed in spirit. (Ps. 34:18) You are surely so close to me, Lord. Help me to sense Your presence in my life. I need You more than I need the next breath.

I am still confident of this: I will see Your goodness, Lord, in the land of the living. I will wait for You, Lord. I will be strong and take heart and wait for You. (Ps. 27:13–14)

Please teach me to delight myself in You, Lord, and You will give me the desires of my heart. (Ps. 37:4)

The Lord will do great things for me, and I will be filled with joy. I will sow in tears, then I will reap with songs of joy. If I go out weeping, carrying seed to sow, I will return with songs of joy, carrying sheaves with me. (Ps. 126:3, 5–6) O God, please help me to be willing to sow the seed of Your Word and water it with my tears, believing You even in the midst of this terrible pain. If I do, You will be faithful to fill me with joy again. You will faithfully bring a harvest forth from my life. My suffering will not be in vain.

You, the God of all grace, who called me to Your eternal glory in Christ, after I have suffered a little while, will Yourself restore me and make me strong, firm, and steadfast. (1 Pet. 5:10)

> *Have you waited long upon the Lord? For His Word? For His hand? Until He speaks—until He acts . . . and He surely will—you need not wait upon His love. Patience to wait does not come from suffering long for what we lack but from sitting long in what we have.*

Lord God, help me presently believe, then one day see, that my present sufferings cannot be compared to the glory that You will reveal in me. (Rom. 8:18)

Lord God, Your Holy Spirit helps me in my weakness. I do not know what I ought to pray for, but the Spirit Himself intercedes for me with groans that words cannot express. And He who searches my heart knows the mind of the Spirit, because Your Spirit intercedes for me in accordance with Your will. (Rom. 8:26–27)

I am convinced that neither death nor life, neither angels nor demons, neither the present nor the future, nor any powers, neither height nor depth, nor anything else in all creation, will be able to separate me from Your love, O God, that is in Christ Jesus my Lord. (Rom. 8:38–39)

Lord God, I know that when the earthly tents we live in are destroyed, we who are believers have a building from You, an eternal house in heaven, not built by human hands. Meanwhile I groan, longing to be clothed with my heavenly dwelling. For while in this tent, I groan and am burdened, because I do not wish to be unclothed but clothed with my heavenly dwelling, so that what is mortal may be swallowed up by life. Now it is You, God, who have made me for this very purpose and have given me the Spirit as a deposit, guaranteeing what is to come. Therefore, I am always confident and know that as long as I am at home in the body I am away from the Lord. I live by faith, not by sight. I am confident, I say, and would prefer to be away from the body and at home with You, Lord. So I make it my goal to please You, whether I am at home in the body or away from it. (2 Cor. 5:1–9) Lord, help me to be confident in the reality of heaven and the vivid life that my loved one is enjoying. One day I will be with my loved one, and we will enjoy You together for all eternity. Until then, help me to allow You to live through me so that I might be faithful.

Lord Jesus, I don't need to let my heart be troubled. I can trust in God, and I can trust also in You. In the Father's house are many rooms; if it were not so, You would have told me. You went to prepare a place for us. And if You went to prepare a place for us, You will come back and take us to be with You that we also may be where You are. (John 14:1–3)

Lord Jesus, I eagerly expect and hope that I will in no way be ashamed, but will have sufficient courage so that now as always Christ will be exalted . . . whether by life or by death. (Phil. 1:20)

I am suffering, but I am not ashamed. For I know whom I have believed, and am convinced that You are able to guard what I have entrusted to You for that day. (2 Tim. 1:12)

Father God, I commit myself and my suffering to You, my faithful Creator, and I will continue to do good. (1 Pet. 4:19)

Oh, that my words were recorded, that they were written on a scroll, that they were inscribed with an iron tool on lead, or engraved in rock forever! I know that You, my Redeemer, live, and that in the end You will stand upon the earth. And after my skin has been destroyed, yet in my flesh I will see You, God. I myself will see You with my own eyes. . . . How my heart yearns within me! (Job 19:23–27)

You, God, know the way that I take; when You have tested me, I will come forth as gold. My feet will closely follow Your steps; I desire to keep to Your way without turning aside. I desire never to depart from the commands of Your lips. Cause me to treasure the words of Your mouth more than my daily bread. (Job 23:10–12)

Glorious Lord God, one day I will hear a loud voice from Your throne saying, "Now the dwelling of God is with men, and he will live with them." We will be Your people, and You Yourself will be with us and be our God. You will wipe every tear from our eyes. There will be no more death or mourning or crying or pain, for the old order of things will pass away. You who are seated on the throne will say, "I am making everything new!" These words are trustworthy and true! (Rev. 21:3–5)

God, for now I know in part and I prophesy in part, but when perfection comes, the imperfect disappears. When I was a child, I talked like a child, I thought like a child, I reasoned like a child. I now desire to put my childish ways behind me. Now I see but a poor reflection as in a mirror; then I will see face-to-face. Now I know in part; then I shall know fully, Lord, even as I am fully known. And now these three remain: faith, hope, and love. But the greatest of these is love. (1 Cor. 13:9–13) Faith lives in all the places I wait to know fully.

Yes, You are coming soon! Amen. Come, Lord Jesus! Until then, Your grace is with Your people. (Rev. 22:20–21)

Praise be to You, the God and Father of my Lord Jesus Christ, the Father of compassion and the God of all comfort, who comforts me in all my troubles, so that I can comfort those in any trouble with the comfort I myself have received from God. (2 Cor. 1:3–4) You, Lord, are the only One who can turn misery into ministry.

Life is a steep climb, and it does the heart good to have somebody "call back" and cheerily beckon us on up the high hill. We are all climbers together, and we must help one another. This mountain climbing is serious business, but glorious. It takes strength and steady step to find the summits. The outlook widens with the altitude. If anyone among us has found anything worthwhile, we ought to "call back."

If you have gone a little way ahead of me, call back— 'Twill cheer my heart and help my feet along the stony track; And if, perchance, Faith's light is dim, because the oil is low, Your call will guide my lagging course as wearily I go.

Call back, and tell me that He went with you into the storm; Call back, and say He kept you when the forest's roots were torn; That, when the heavens thunder and the earthquake shook the hill, He bore you up and held you where the very air was still.

Oh, friend, call back, and tell me for I cannot see your face; They say it glows with triumph, and your feet bound in the race; But there are mists between us and my spirit eyes are dim, And I cannot see the glory, though I long for word of Him.

But if you'll say He heard you when your prayer was but a cry, And if you'll say He saw you through the night's sin-darkened sky—If you have gone a little way ahead, oh, friend, call back—'Twill cheer my heart and help my feet along the stony track.

Mrs. Charles E. Cowman,
Streams in the Desert

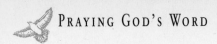

PERSONALIZING YOUR PRAYERS

Chapter 11

OVERCOMING
UNFORGIVENESS

No matter how different the rest of our challenges may be, every believer can count on a multitude of challenges to *forgive*. Remember, God's primary agenda in the life of a believer is to conform the child into the likeness of His Son, Jesus Christ. No other word sums up His character in relationship to us like the word *forgiving*. We never look more like Christ than when we forgive; since that's God's goal, we're destined for plenty of opportunities!

I believe we can safely say that we, as ambassadors of Christ in this generation, have literally been called to a ministry of forgiveness. So . . . how is your ministry going? Have you had lots of ups and downs? A few successes and a few too many failures? Me too! But I pray that God has been as unrelenting in His insistence upon your willingness to forgive as He has mine. The longer I've walked with God in prayer and His Word and come to love Him, the less I want Him to let me off easy. I'm learning that a believer's willingness to do "the hard thing" is what sets him or her apart for the extraordinary in Christ. I'm beginning to learn to say, "Lord, my flesh is so resistant to what You want right now that I can hardly stand it. But don't stop! *Insist* upon my best. *Insist* upon Your glory. Take me to the line on this, God. Don't let up on me until we've gone every inch of the distance." I remember when I used to complain, "What do You *expect* out of me?" Now, I find myself wanting God to be able to expect much from me. I don't want to occupy this small space in time in mediocrity. Do you feel the same way?

Unparalleled joy and victory come from allowing Christ to do "the hard thing" with us. Perhaps nothing is harder than forgiveness. Let's face it. Each of us has been confronted by some pretty overwhelming challenges to forgive. Some seem . . . well, *unforgivable*. We argue with God that all inflicted hurts are not created equally. For instance, sometimes the person who hurt us isn't sorry. Or won't take responsibility. Or is in the grave. Or the person might be sorry but refuses to recompense. Perhaps the person simply doesn't deserve our forgiveness. After all, forgiveness would make everything OK, and we want the record to show: we're not OK! Then, if we let it, truth begins to eclipse our mound of excuses: *we won't be OK until we forgive.* If only we could understand that God's unrelenting insistence on our forgiveness is for our own sakes, not the sake of the one who hurt us. God *is* faithful. He will plead our case and take up our cause . . . but only when we make a deliberate decision to cease representing ourselves in the matter.

Innumerable strongholds are connected to an unwillingness to forgive. Left untreated, unforgiveness becomes spiritual cancer. Bitterness takes root, and since the root feeds the rest of the tree, every branch of our lives and every fruit on each limb ultimately become poisoned. Beloved sister or brother, the bottom line is . . . unforgiveness makes us sick. Always spiritually. Often emotionally. And, surprisingly often, physically.

Please keep in mind that forgiveness is not defined by a feeling, although it will ultimately change our feelings. The Greek word most often translated "forgiveness" in New Testament Scripture is *aphiemi,* meaning "to send forth or away, let go from oneself. To let go from one's power, possession. To let go from one's further . . . attendance, occupancy."[1] Forgiveness is our determined and deliberate willingness to let something go. To release it from our possession. To be willing and ready for it to no longer occupy us. God is not asking us to let "it" go haphazardly into the black hole of nonexistence. Forgiveness means letting it go *to God.* Letting it go from our power to *His.* Forgiveness is the *ongoing* act by which we agree with God over the matter, practice the mercy He's extended to us, and surrender the situation, the repercussions, and the hurtful person to Him.

Don't expect Satan to let you off the hook of unforgiveness easily. Be prepared to recommit to forgiveness every single day until you're free. Second Corinthians 2:11 warns us to forgive "in order that Satan might not outwit us. For we are not unaware of his schemes." The King James Version says we must forgive "lest Satan should get an advantage of us." The Word of God clearly teaches that Satan takes tremendous advantage of any unforgiveness in our lives. Unforgiveness qualifies as one of the most powerfully effective forms of bondage in any believer's life. We cannot tolerate it. Yes, this stronghold demands serious demolition, but the liberty you will feel when you finally let go is inexpressible! Forgiveness is the ultimate "weight loss"!

This important chapter includes three segments. The first section below is a list of Scripture-prayers resembling those of the other chapters. Following these Scripture-prayers, you will find a segment explaining the importance of praying specifically *about* the person you're struggling to forgive. And, finally, you will find an explanation and approach for learning to pray *for* the person you're struggling to forgive. Each segment is vital in breaking the horrible bondage of unforgiveness. Please consider reading the commentary in the additional segments in this chapter before proceeding in your Scripture-prayers. I believe you'll benefit from grasping the overall goal in advance. Be strong and courageous, believer! Whatever it is . . . we *can* forgive.

Lord, as hard as this may be for me to comprehend or rationalize, Your Word is clear: if I forgive others when they sin against me, You, my heavenly Father will also forgive me. (Matt. 6:14)

Lord God, if I do not forgive others their sins, You, my Father, will not forgive my sins. (Matt. 6:15)

Father, according to Your Word, if I judge others, I too will be judged, and with the same measure I use, it will be measured to me. (Matt. 7:1–2)

Christ Jesus, when I want so badly to judge, condemn, or refuse forgiveness to another person, I can hear Your Word speak to my heart saying, "If you are without sin, be the first to throw a stone at

them." (John 8:7) I am *not* without sin. If I claim to be without sin, I deceive myself and the truth is not in me. (1 John 1:8)

Lord, at whatever point I judge another person, Your Word says I am condemning myself, because those of us who pass judgment do the same things. Now I know that Your judgment against those who do such things is based on *truth.* So when I, a mere human, pass judgment on others and yet do the same things, do I think I will escape Your judgment? (Rom. 2:1–2)

Lord, I must ask myself why I look at the speck of sawdust in another person's eye and pay no attention to the plank in my own eye. How can I say to my brother, "Let me take the speck out of your eye," when all the time there is a plank in my own eye? O God, rescue me from being a hypocrite! Give me the honesty and courage to first take the plank out of my own eye, and then I may see clearly to remove the speck from another person's eye. (Matt. 7:3–5)

Jesus, when Peter asked You, "Lord, how many times shall I forgive my brother when he sins against me? Up to seven times?" You responded, "I tell you, not seven times, but seventy-seven times." (Matt. 18:21–22)

Lord, in the parable of the unmerciful servant, the only person in the end who was imprisoned and tortured was the one who would not forgive. (Matt. 18:33–34) Help me to see the monumental price of unforgiveness. It is so enslaving and torturous. According to Matthew 18:35, You may allow me to suffer the same kind of repercussions if I refuse to forgive from my heart someone who has sinned against me.

> *Bitterness is like a rock thrown into a placid pond; after its initial splash, it sends out concentric circles that disturb the whole pond. It starts with ourselves, expands to our spouse, then to our children, friends and colleagues.*
>
> Dr. Chuck Lynch, I Should Forgive, but . . .

Lord, Your Word tells me that when I stand praying, if I hold anything against anyone, I am to forgive him or her, so that You, my Father in heaven, may forgive me my sins. (Mark 11:25)

God, if I am offering my gifts to You through worship or service and remember that my brother has something against me, I am to leave my gift there in front of the altar. I am to first go and be reconciled to my brother, then I am to come and offer my gift. (Matt. 5:23–24) Help me to be obedient to Your will, God.

Your Word asks me why I judge or look down on my brother. I acknowledge to You today, Lord, that we will all stand before Your judgment seat. It is written: "As surely as I live," says the Lord, "every knee will bow before me; every tongue will confess to God." So then, each of us will give an account of himself to God. Therefore help me stop passing judgment on others. Instead, I make up my mind not to put any stumbling block or obstacle in my brother's way. (Rom. 14:10–13)

Lord, my conscience is clear, but that does not make me innocent. It is You who judges me. Therefore I am to judge nothing before the appointed time; Your Word tells me to wait until You come. You will bring to light what is hidden in darkness and will expose the motives of men's hearts. At that time each will receive his praise from God. (1 Cor. 4:4–5)

Lord God, help me to speak and act as those who are going to be judged by the law that gives freedom, because judgment without mercy will be shown to anyone who has not been merciful. Mercy triumphs over judgment! (James 2:12–13)

If I do not judge, I will not be judged. If I do not condemn, I will not be condemned. If I forgive, I will be forgiven. (Luke 6:37) Help me, Lord, to extend more grace, and I will continue to receive more grace!

Lord God, forgive me my sins, for I also forgive everyone who sins against me. And lead me not into temptation. (Luke 11:4) Lord, I confess to You that one of my greatest temptations is to refuse for-

giveness to others. Please help me see the sober reality of Your will on this matter.

Father God, Your Word says that if someone sins against me seven times in a day, and seven times comes back to me and says, "I repent," then I am to forgive him or her. (Luke 17:4) I desire to be obedient to You. Empower me, Lord.

Lord Jesus, when You were being led out to be executed, after being beaten, ridiculed, and spit upon, You said, "Father, forgive them, for they do not know what they are doing." (Luke 23:34) If You can forgive those kinds of things and You were totally innocent, by Your strength and power, I can forgive the things that have been done to me. I also acknowledge that people who hurt me haven't always known what they were doing or what repercussions their actions would have.

Forgive me my debts, Lord, as I also have forgiven my debtors. (Matt. 6:12)

Father, help me to understand that the punishment and repercussions that come to people when they have done wrong is often sufficient for them. Instead of causing more grief, Your Word says I ought to forgive and comfort the person, so that he or she will not be overwhelmed by excessive sorrow. (2 Cor. 2:7) Lord, help me to be the kind of person I'd want ministering to me after I had failed.

> *Withholding forgiveness until an offender understands or acknowledges the emotional pain they have inflicted is a subtle form of revenge. Why? Because it's hoping that the offender would hurt a little too, in order to understand. But this type of revenge robs you of your freedom and allows the offender to keep control of you.*
>
> Dr. Chuck Lynch, I Should Forgive, but . . .

Lord, You tell me to forgive others in the sight of Christ in order that Satan might not outwit me. Help me never to be unaware of his schemes. (2 Cor. 2:11) Please help me to see how much the enemy takes advantage of unforgiveness. I offer him a foothold any time I refuse to forgive.

Lord God, empower me to bear with others and forgive whatever grievances I may have against another. Help me to forgive as You, Lord, have forgiven me. (Col. 3:13)

Your ways are not my ways, Lord God. As the heavens are higher than the earth, so are Your ways higher than mine. (Isa. 55:8–9) I may not always understand Your ways, Lord, but they are always prosperous. (Ps. 10:5) Your ways are always righteous. (Ps. 145:17) Your ways, O God, are holy. (Ps. 77:13) Your ways are loving and faithful. (Ps. 25:10) I have considered my ways, Lord. (Ps. 119:59) I choose Yours instead. Keep me from deceitful ways. (Ps. 119:29) Lord God, help me to walk in Your ways. (Ps. 119:3)

Lord, You have extended such grace to me. You have forgiven my wickedness and remembered my sins no more. (Heb. 8:12) Help me to demonstrate my gratitude by forgiving others!

Lord, I have heard that it was said, "Love your neighbor and hate your enemy." But You tell me to love my enemies and pray for those who persecute me, that I might be a child of my Father in heaven. (Matt. 5:43–44)

Father God, if I love those who love me, what reward will I get? Are not even the godless doing that? And if I greet only those to whom I am close, what am I doing more than others? Do not even pagans do that? (Matt. 5:46–47) You have called me to be different, Lord! You have called me to go far beyond the actions of even the noblest pagan.

If You, O Lord, kept a record of sin, who could stand? But with You there is forgiveness; therefore You are feared. (Ps. 130:4) Lord, after all You've done for me and after all the sin You've forgiven in my life, help me to have so much fear and reverence for You that I will not withhold forgiveness from others.

Lord, I will not say to a person who has hurt me, "I'll pay you back for this wrong!" I will wait for You, Lord, and You will deliver me. (Prov. 20:22) I will not say of someone who has wronged me, "I'll do to him as he has done to me; I'll pay that man back for what he did." (Prov. 24:29)

O Lord, You will take up my case; You will redeem my life. You have seen, O Lord, the wrong done to me. Uphold my cause! (Lam. 3:58–59) Lord, help me to see that when You are upholding my cause, I don't have to. Help me to lay this burden down and let You carry it instead.

Lord, help me to obey You and not repay anyone evil for evil. Help me to be careful to do what is right in the eyes of everybody. If it is possible, as far as it depends on me, I want to live at peace with everyone. Help me not to take revenge but leave room for Your wrath, for You have written: "It is mine to avenge; I will repay." On the contrary: If my enemy is hungry, help me to feed him; if he is thirsty, help me to give him something to drink. In doing this, I will heap burning coals on his head. (Rom. 12:17–20)

Lord God, help me not to be overcome by evil but to overcome evil with good. (Rom. 12:21)

Lord Jesus, Your precious blood of the covenant was poured out for many for the forgiveness of sins. (Matt. 26:28) After You poured out Your own blood for my forgiveness, help me not respond with a heart too hard to forgive others.

In You, Jesus, I have redemption through Your blood, the forgiveness of sins, in accordance with the riches of God's grace. (Eph. 1:7) I possess the riches of Your grace so that I will always be able to extend forgiveness to those who have hurt me.

Blessed am I because my transgressions are forgiven. Blessed am I because my sins are covered. (Ps. 32:1) May my deep gratitude be evident in the way I relate to others, O Lord.

Lord, I want it to be said of me that my many sins have been forgiven—for I have loved much. The person who has forgiven little loves little. (Luke 7:47) You have forgiven me for so much, Lord. Make it evident in the way I love You and love others.

You, the Lord my God, are merciful and forgiving, even though I have rebelled against You. (Dan. 9:9) Help me also to be merciful and forgiving to others.

> No *physical or emotional pain happens in a purpose-less vacuum. One of the purposes is to prepare us to help others.*
>
> Dr. Chuck Lynch, I Should Forgive, but . . .

O Lord, I desire not to grieve the Holy Spirit of God, with whom I was sealed for the day of redemption. By the power of Your Spirit, help me to get rid of all bitterness, rage and anger, brawling and slander, along with every form of malice. I desire to be kind and compassionate to others, forgiving others, just as in Christ You forgave me. (Eph. 4:30–32)

Lord, please help me to live in harmony with others and be sympathetic, loving as a sister or a brother, being compassionate and humble. Help me never to repay evil with evil or insult with insult, but with blessing, because to this I was called so that I may inherit a blessing. (1 Pet. 3:8–9)

At one time I too was foolish, disobedient, deceived and enslaved by all kinds of passions and pleasures. I lived in malice and envy, being hated and hating others. (Titus 3:3) I acknowledge the misery of living outside of You, Lord.

According to Your Word, blessed am I when men hate me, when they exclude me and insult me and reject my name as evil, because of the Son of Man. I am to rejoice in that day and leap for joy, because great is my reward in heaven. (Luke 6:22–23)

Wise God, according to Your Word, love is the most excellent way to deal with anything. (1 Cor. 12:31)

If I speak in the tongues of men and of angels but have not love, I am only a resounding gong or a clanging cymbal. If I have the gift of prophecy and can fathom all mysteries and all knowledge, and if I have a faith that can move mountains, but have not love, I am nothing. If I give all I possess to the poor and surrender my body to the flames, but have not love, I gain nothing. (1 Cor. 13:1–3)

Lord, according to Your Word, love is patient, love is kind. It does not envy, it does not boast, it is not proud. It is not rude, it is not self-seeking, it is not easily angered, it keeps no record of wrongs. Love does not delight in evil but rejoices with the truth. It always protects, always trusts, always hopes, always perseveres. Love never fails. (1 Cor. 13:4–8) Father, I acknowledge to You that I don't begin to possess this kind of love on my own. The only way I can experience and express love like this is to surrender my heart to You, and ask You to empty it of all its fleshly contents and make it a vessel of *Your* love. Use my heart to love the unlovely and those who have hurt me, dear Lord. I am desperate for You to work a miracle in and through my heart.

O Father, Your Word calls me to the high pursuit of being an imitator of You, God. Therefore, as a dearly loved child, I am freed to live a life of love, just as Christ loved me and gave Himself up for me as a fragrant offering and sacrifice to You. (Eph. 5:1)

I know whom I have believed, and am convinced that You, Lord, are able to guard what I have entrusted to You. (2 Tim. 1:12) I entrust this situation to You, Lord.

I humble myself, therefore, under Your mighty hand, God, that You may lift me up in due time. I cast all this anxiety on You because You care for me. (1 Pet. 5:6–7)

O Father, please cause the love of Christ to compel me to do what is right in this challenging situation. (2 Cor. 5:14)

You have shown me what is good. And what do You, Lord, require of me? To act justly and to love mercy and to walk humbly with my God. (Mic. 6:8)

Not by might nor by power, but by Your Spirit, Lord Almighty (Zech. 4:6), I will be able to forgive.

This is what You, the Lord Almighty, say: "Show mercy and compassion to one another." You have told me in my heart not to think evil of others. (Zech. 7:9–10)

Lord, I do not want to be like those who refuse to pay attention to You. Please help me not to turn my back in stubbornness and stop up my ears just because Your will is hard at times. Help me not to make my heart as hard as flint and refuse to listen to the words that You, Lord Almighty, have sent by Your Spirit. (Zech. 7:11–12)

I can do all things through You, Jesus, who gives me strength. (Phil. 4:13) What You are commanding me is not too difficult for me or beyond my reach. It is not up in heaven, so that I have to ask, "Who will ascend into heaven to get it and proclaim it to me so I may obey it?" Nor is it beyond the sea, so that I have to ask, "Who will cross the sea to get it and proclaim it to me so I may obey it?" No, the Word is very near me; it is in my mouth and in my heart so I may obey it. (Deut. 30:11–14)

Lord God, give me *more* grace (James 4:6) so that I may increasingly extend it to others.

Lord God, empower me to make every effort to live in peace with all men and to be holy; without holiness no one will see the Lord. Help me to see to it that I don't miss the grace of God and that no bitter root grows up to cause trouble and defile many. (Heb. 12:14–15)

> *Unforgiveness is not a self-contained disease. It defiles many. When life heats . . . its acid boils forth, burning everyone it touches. Neither is forgiveness self-contained. It heals many. When life heats . . . its living waters overflow—refreshing everyone it touches.*

Lord, if being obedient to You causes me to suffer, I should commit myself to my faithful Creator and continue to do good. (1 Pet. 4:19) You are honorable and always faithful. You will always cause obedience to bear fruit. Please help me to understand that the suffering caused by disobedience is far more devastating and long-lasting than any suffering I may do according to Your will.

Lord, I have the treasure of Your Holy Spirit in me, a simple jar of clay, to show that this all-surpassing power is from God and not from me. (2 Cor. 4:7) Lord, forgiving someone who has hurt me deeply is sometimes the way the power of the Holy Spirit is made most conspicuous in me. Forgive *through* me, Jesus. I am powerless without You. Show what You can do through my vessel. I offer myself to You for this authentic God-work.

PRAYING ABOUT THE PERSON YOU NEED TO FORGIVE

If our unforgiveness is toward an individual, a very important part of breaking free is learning to pray *about* the person and also *for* him or her, if the person is still living. (We'd all be shocked to know how many people are in bondage to a corpse!) Let's clarify the difference between praying *about* a person and praying *for* a person. Keep in mind that both kinds of prayer are intended by God to change our own hearts. My experience has been that praying *about* the person who has hurt us is necessary before we find any real measure of freedom to sincerely pray *for* the person. What do I mean by praying *about* them? I mean learning to tell on them to God. Yes, I'm talking about tattling. Learning to tell God what they've done to you and how upset you are. Learning to tell Him all the things you feel and how unfair you believe someone has been to you.

You might be thinking, "How irreverent!" Or you might fear being hit by a bolt of lightning if you spoke harshly about someone to God. Our wise God, Creator of the human heart, purposely picked out the heart of David as an example to us. Not coincidentally, David was the one God inspired to pen the liberating words of

Psalm 62:8, which says, "Trust in him at all times, O people; / pour out your hearts to him, / for God is our refuge." One psalm after another proves David practiced what he preached. David, the man after God's own heart, is the very one who spoke of those who had hurt or offended him by saying things like these:

- "Not a word from their mouth can be trusted; / their heart is filled with destruction. / Their throat is an open grave; / with their tongue they speak deceit" (Ps. 5:9).
- "They close up their callous hearts, / and their mouths speak with arrogance. / They have tracked me down, they now surround me, / with eyes alert, to throw me to the ground. . . . Rise up, O LORD, confront them, bring them down; / rescue me" (Ps. 17:10–11, 13).
- "But I am a worm and not a man, scorned by men and despised by the people" (Ps. 22:6).
- "I am a dread to my friends— / those who see me on the street flee from me. / I am forgotten by them as though I were dead" (Ps. 31:11–12).
- " 'Oh, that I had the wings of a dove! / I would fly away and be at rest— / I would flee far away / and stay in the desert; / I would hurry to my place of shelter, / far from the tempest and storm'. . . . If an enemy were insulting me, / I could endure it; / if a foe were raising himself against me, / I could hide from him. / But it is you, a man like myself, / my companion, my close friend" (Ps. 55:6–8, 12–13).

Does it sound like vented anger, whining, complaining, and tattling to you? It is! And we, too, are invited to bring our complaints to God when we are overwhelmed. In Psalm 64:1, David said, "Hear me, O God, as I voice my *complaint*" (emphasis mine). In Psalm 142:1–2, David wrote, "I cry aloud to the LORD; / I lift up my voice to the LORD for mercy. / I pour out my complaint before him; / before him I tell my trouble." See what I mean? David practiced what he preached in Psalm 62:8! The Holy Spirit, who inspired the blessed invitation of Psalm 62:8, did not qualify it with the words, "Pour out your heart to God if what's inside is nice and sweet." The concept of "pouring out" suggests that some of the contents in our hearts need to *go*—like hurt, anger, despair, doubt, bitterness, unforgiveness, and confusion. The idea is to pour out the bitter waters that well up in our hearts so that God can pour wellsprings of living, sweet waters back in.

Intimacy with God means sharing the depths of our hearts with Him. If what is in the depths is great joy and celebration, then share it with Him. And if what is in the depths is anger, hurt, and all sorts of injury, tell Him that too! Oh, what healing we would find if we only understood that God is about real living. We leave Him out of feelings, emotions, temptations, and situations He made Himself totally available to treat! God desires our *whole* hearts . . . whatever they encase.

One reason I think David was a man after God's own heart was because he poured his heart out to God instead of spewing his acidic feelings on everyone else. One of the wonderful things about God's immutable character is that we're not going to tempt Him to sin when we take our negative feelings to Him. He can take our frustrations without being harmed by them.

Two important things happen when we learn to pray honestly about the person who has hurt us:

1. *We pour the hurt out rather than allowing it to remain and turn bitter.* I'm certainly no counselor, but I've lived enough of life to know that anything hurtful we do not deal with will sooner or later deal with us! Pouring whatever is in our hearts out to God dramatically decreases our tendency to grow bitter.

2. *We articulate our own feelings, thereby placing them in view before our own eyes as well as God's.* This way, we also get a chance to see if something seems ridiculous, out of proportion, or right on target. Our prayers can sometimes help us gain a little insight into our own hearts.

    Remember when Jesus found Mary Magdalene at the empty tomb and He asked her, "Woman, why are you crying?" (John 20:15). Scripture clearly tells us that Christ looked straight upon the heart of everyone He met and knew all they were thinking. Jesus *knew* why Mary was crying, so why did He ask her the question? I believe one reason Christ asked was to invite her to think about the answer and articulate it for herself.

When I pour out my heart to God over an injury I feel I've received from someone, first of all, I almost always feel better. Just getting it off my chest helps immensely. And if I've been particularly hard on someone in my prayer, I often end up reconsidering my real feelings and telling God that I really didn't mean it. As I talk it out with God, I am often able to separate truth from fiction and the difference between my perceptions and reality. Other times, the exact opposite occurs. The more I talk about it with God, the more aware I become of how truly upset I am. The good news is, I'm already a step ahead in restoration because I'm dealing with it exactly where I should be.

Again, let me remind you that I am not your example. *Scripture* is. And in this subject matter, *David* is. My only contribution is to tell you that I've been a far healthier person spiritually, emotionally, mentally, and probably physically since I started practicing some of David's approaches to intimacy with God. Remember, these approaches are biblical! David wasn't the only one in Scripture who felt the freedom to pour out his heart to God. Take a look at Job's words in Job 23:1–5, 8–10:

> *Even today my complaint is bitter;*
> *his hand is heavy in spite of my groaning.*
> *If only I knew where to find him;*
> *if only I could go to his dwelling!*
> *I would state my case before him*
> *and fill my mouth with arguments.*
> *I would find out what he would answer me,*
> *and consider what he would say*
>
> . . .
>
> *But if I go to the east, he is not there;*
> *if I go to the west, I do not find him.*
> *When he is at work in the north, I do not see him;*
> *when he turns to the south, I catch no glimpse of him.*
> *But he knows the way that I take;*
> *when he has tested me, I will come forth as gold.*

Right about now, we're likely to get into subject matter some might consider heretical. Job was certainly pouring out his complaint, but notice whom this particular complaint involved: *God Himself.* You may be ducking your head at this point trying to dodge lightning, but hang on a second! This is not some secular psychology book. This is the Word of God! Job's God did not strike him dead. In fact, He scolded Job's friends for not speaking of God what was right "as my servant Job has" (Job 42:7). He also prospered Job twice as much as before. When all was said and done, Job passed the test.

Don't misunderstand me. I am *not* condoning irreverence to God. I believe the reason David's and Job's complaints were acceptable is because they were registered with hearts that truly loved and revered God. Remember, God looks upon the heart as He hears the words from our mouths. Irreverent hearts speaking pious words bring far more displeasure to God than reverent hearts speaking honest words. Look at the last two verses in the same chapter of Job we cited above:

> God has made my heart faint;
> the Almighty has terrified me.
> Yet I am not silenced by the darkness. *(Job 23:16–17)*

These verses suggest that Job had plenty of reverence for God, and yet in his horrible plight, God had not shut his mouth by the darkness. In other words, God continued to allow him to speak. God is not so cruel as to forbid us to say a single word to Him in our deep darkness. He knows what we're thinking anyway. Remember, *God is far more interested in relationship than rules.* We are allowed and even invited to speak our hearts to God—even if our complaint involves *Him*—but we might also want to be ready in case He has a few things to say in response. Listen to the way God began His retort to Job: "Brace yourself like a man; / I will question you, / and you shall answer me. Do you have an arm like God's, / and can your voice thunder like his? Then adorn yourself with glory and splendor, and clothe yourself in honor and majesty" (Job 40:7, 9–10).

God Almighty, the One who is adorned with glory and splendor and clothed in honor and majesty, invites us to pour out anything that is in our *hearts* as long as we retain an appropriate measure of reverence in our *minds*. I'd like to show you one reason why. Take a closer look at Job 23:1–5, 8–10. Do you see a progression of emotions in Job as he continues to pour out his heart? He began the brief discourse with angry, gutsy words that implied, "I demand five minutes with God! I want some answers!" As he continued to pour out his heart, however, you can see his anger begin to dissolve and his innermost feelings emerge: "When he is at work in the north, I do not see him; when he turns to the south, I catch no glimpse of him." What was Job *really* saying? He was saying that, for the life of him, he couldn't seem to find God in his situation. You see, once he poured out the anger, he got down to the real issue: his feelings were badly hurt at God. You, then, can see Job remind himself of truth: "But he knows the way that I take; when he has tested me, I will come forth as gold." In essence, he was saying, "I might not be able to find God in all this, but He hasn't lost me . . . and somehow—some way—He will work this whole miserable thing out." I'd like to suggest that Job might never have gotten to the point of uncovering his true hurt and reminding himself of God's faithful promises, had he not vented his frustration.

David and Job weren't alone in their heartfelt approaches to God. Abraham and Moses, two men who were called "friends" of God, also apparently felt they could trust God with some of the negative contents out of their hearts at times. You see, all four of these men had one thing in common: real, live, meaty *relationships* with God. They shared their joys, frustrations, celebrations, and pains with Him. You can too. That's what intimate relationships are all about.

This is the only segment of the book where I will not be supplying you with certain Scriptures to pray. This kind of prayer necessitates the sharing of your own very personal feelings. I wanted to make sure we addressed the importance of praying *about* someone who has hurt you because it is such a vital part of breaking free. Be honest with God. Pour your heart out to Him. Tell Him the things that hurt you. Tell on the one who injured you. Search the psalms to receive further permission to speak your heart, then *practice it—from your own heart with your own words!* "How often and for how long?" you might ask. As often as

you need . . . and don't stop until all the bitter waters have been poured out before God, and He's had a chance to begin pouring living water back in. "Trust in Him at all times!"

PRAYING FOR THE PERSON YOU NEED TO FORGIVE

For just a moment, envision your heart like a pitcher. When we've been hurt by another person, the habit we still retain from our old nature is to feed the heart-injury with incessant meditation. The water in the pitcher soon becomes cloudy, even contaminated. Praying *about* the person we need to forgive is the means by which we tip that pitcher heavenward and slowly begin to pour our negative feelings and frustrations out to God. As we *pour out,* a wonderful thing happens: we make room for God to *pour in.* Our omniscient God knows that a heart heals when a heart changes. Until we make room for fresh contents that change our hearts, we will never be healed from the injury and subsequent feelings of unforgiveness.

After we've practiced pouring our hearts out to God through praying *about* the person, it's time to additionally begin praying *for* the person. I already know what you may be thinking because I used to feel the same way. "Why should I pray *for* a person who has hurt me so badly?" God's ways are not our ways. He created our psyches, and He alone knows how they operate. He created our hearts so uniquely, so in His image, that they are forced to forgive in order to be free. God greatly honors our willingness to bless others when our human reaction would be to curse them. First Peter 3:9 says it all: "Do not repay evil with evil or insult with insult, but with blessing, because to this you were called, so that you may inherit a blessing." Don't miss the phrase "to this you were called." I've heard many people say, "God could never expect me to forgive or pray for blessing for that person after all she/he has done." Oh, yes, He could. In fact, to this we were called! The invitation to bless when the rest of the world would curse is one of the very characteristics that sets us apart and causes people to take note of our faith. What have we gained if we do it our way? An ulcer? A bad heart? Unending depression? Such bitterness that no one wants to be around us? God knows what He's doing. He created the rules of the heart. When we choose to go against everything our own humanity would tell us and, instead, approach our struggle God's way, we are shocked once again to see that He was right.

Let's take another look at our old friend, Job. In Job 42, God stated that He was angry with Job's friends because they had not counseled their suffering friend God's way. After confronting them with His displeasure, God said, "So now take seven bulls and seven rams and go to my servant Job and sacrifice a burnt offering for yourselves. My servant Job will pray for you, and I will accept his prayer and not deal with you according to your folly" (Job 42:8). A few verses later, Scripture says, "*After Job had prayed for his friends,* the LORD made him prosperous again and gave him twice as much as he had before. . . . The LORD blessed the latter part of Job's life more than the first" (vv. 10, 12, emphasis mine). Because Job was willing to bless those who hurt them when his human nature would have been to curse them, God was liberated to open the floodgates of heaven and pour out blessing on his life. He will undoubtedly do the same thing for us. No matter what form our blessings take, God will prosper us when we're willing to put our human inclinations on the altar and respond His way instead. Let's not be afraid to do the hard thing. To this we were called! And we *will* inherit a blessing.

The following brief addendum to the prayers toward forgiveness is to help you get started praying Scripture *for* the person who hurt you. This approach works! Not only have I practiced it personally when my heart wanted to harbor unforgiveness toward someone, but I've also stood by and watched others as they were transformed by their willingness to obey God.

One has graciously given me permission to use her testimony. She married at a time of deep rebellion against God and her parents. I don't think I could overestimate the high cost of her decision. The marriage has lasted nearly twenty *hard* years. Her husband so far has not surrendered his life to Christ. Just as all of ours have, his strongholds have enormously impacted the entire household. My friend has never sensed the release to divorce her husband. She does not have biblical grounds and, although she knows God would have mercy on her and certainly forgive her, she is committed to doing the *hard thing*. She is in no physical danger, and she simply feels she lacks grounds for severance. I can tell you that I've stood by her side through some difficult times in which I truly wondered what I would do in her position. I've watched her make some very tough decisions, but I've also witnessed the making of a godly young woman.

Many of the following Scriptures are those she contributed. You may be wondering whether the Scriptures she has prayed for her husband have all been answered. I could have supplied you with many testimonies where I might have answered, "Yes!" Instead, I chose to share a testimony of someone who is still "pressing on" faithfully. Have the Scriptures had an effect? In ways you can hardly imagine! Although her husband has not given his life to Christ, his behavior has been altered in several unique ways. More than any other effect, the most remarkable one has been in her own heart. God has performed a pure, unadulterated miracle in her heart.

Will the person you're praying for change? Will they receive the blessing you've mustered all the courage to ask God for? Maybe. Maybe *not*. That's up to them. But will *your* heart change, will you find freedom to forgive, and will you receive blessing? Absolutely! Take God at His Word and find out. Please use the Scriptures that apply to your situation, then seek out your own from God's Word and pray earnestly! I'm not sure God ever honors a prayer more than the one that was hardest for us to pray.

I pray for _____ that you would give him/her the Spirit of wisdom and revelation, so that he/she may know You better. I pray also that the eyes of his/her heart may be enlightened in order that he/she may know the hope to which You have called him/her, the riches of Your glorious inheritance in the saints, and Your incomparably great power for those who believe. (Eph. 1:17–19)

I pray for _____ that wisdom will enter his/her heart, and knowledge will be pleasant to his/her soul. I pray that discretion will protect him/her, understanding will guard him/her, and that wisdom will save him/her from the ways of wicked men. (Prov. 2:10–12)

I pray that _____'s love may abound more and more in knowledge and depth of insight, so that he/she may be able to discern what is best and may be pure and blameless until the day of Christ, filled with the fruit of righteousness that comes through Jesus Christ—to the glory and praise of God. (Phil. 1:9–11)

I pray for _____ that he/she will trust in You with all his/her heart and lean not on his/her own understanding; if in all of his/her ways he/she acknowledges You, You will make his/her paths straight. (Prov. 3:5–6)

I pray for _____ that he/she not be carnally minded, which is death, but may he/she be spiritually minded, which is life and peace. (Rom. 8:6)

I pray that _____ will be patient and not be quick-tempered. (Prov. 14:29)

I pray that _____'s tongue will bring healing . . . and that he/she will guard his/her mouth. (Prov. 15:4; 21:23)

I pray, Lord, that You will show _____ Your ways, and teach him/her Your paths; guide him/her in Your truth and teach him/her, for You are God. (Ps. 25:4–5)

Father, I pray that You will enable _____ to obey Your command to love You with all his/her heart and with all his/her soul and with all his/her strength. (Deut. 6:5)

Father, my heart's desire and my prayer is for _____'s salvation. (Rom. 10:1)

I pray that You, the God of hope, will fill _____ with all joy and peace in trusting You, that he/she may abound in hope by the power of the Holy Spirit. (Rom. 15:13)

Let _____ not deceive himself/herself. If he/she thinks he/she is wise in this age, let him/her become foolish that he/she may become wise. For the wisdom of this world is foolishness in Your sight, God. (1 Cor. 3:18–19)

Father, I pray You will love _____ through me with agape love . . . love that is patient, love that is kind. Love that does not envy, does not boast, and is not proud. Love that is not rude, and is not self-seeking, love that is not easily angered, and keeps no record of wrongs. Love that does not delight in evil but rejoices with the truth. Love that always protects, always trusts, always hopes, and always perseveres. Father, Your love through me for _____ never fails. (1 Cor. 13:4–8)

Father, I pray you will help _____ to be quick to listen, slow to speak, and slow to become angry, for man's anger does not bring about the righteous life that God desires. (James 1:19–20)

I pray for _____ to hold to Your teaching and truly be one of Your disciples. Then he/she will know the truth and the truth will set him/her free. (John 8:31–32)

I pray for _____ to abide in You and You in him/her so that he/she may bear much fruit; apart from you we can do nothing. (John 15:5, NASB)

As the Father has loved You, Jesus, You love _____. I pray that _____ will abide in Your love. I pray this so that Your joy may be in him/her and that his/her joy may be made full. (John 15:9, 11, NASB)

Father God, please let the peace of Christ rule in _____'s and my heart, since as members of one body we were called to peace. And help us be thankful. Let the word of Christ dwell in _____ and me richly. Let both of us sing psalms, hymns, and spiritual songs with gratitude in our hearts to God. (Col. 3:15–16)

Father, I pray _____ will dedicate himself/herself to You, the Lord, today—and that You may bestow a blessing upon _____ today. (Exod. 32:29)

I pray _____ will know Your name and will trust in You, for You, Lord, have never forsaken those who seek You. (Ps. 9:10)

Keep _____ as the apple of Your eye. (Ps. 17:8)

May You, Lord, answer _____ when he/she is in distress; may You protect _____. May You send _____ help from the sanctuary and grant him/her support. (Ps. 20:1–2)

Turn to _____ and be gracious to him/her. (Ps. 25:16)

Let integrity and uprightness protect _____, because his/her hope is in You. (Ps. 25:21)

Redeem _____ and be gracious to him/her. (Ps. 26:11)

Surround _____ with songs of deliverance. (Ps. 32:7)

I pray _____ will commit his/her way to You, Lord; and he/she will trust in You and You will do this: You will make Your righteousness shine like the dawn. (Ps. 37:5–6)

I pray that You, God, will be _____'s refuge and strength, an ever-present help in trouble. (Ps. 46:1)

Lord, I pray that _____ will cast his/her cares on You, and You will sustain him/her. (Ps. 55:22)

May _____'s soul find rest in You alone; his/her salvation comes from You. (Ps. 62:1)

I pray _____ will be wise about what is good, and innocent about what is evil. (Rom. 16:19)

Father, I pray that _____ will forget what is behind and strain toward what is ahead, that he/she will press on toward the goal to win the prize for which You have called him/her heavenward in Christ Jesus. (Phil. 3:13–14)

I pray, Lord, that _____ will set his/her mind on things above, not on earthly things. (Col. 3:2)

Now to You, Father, who is able to do immeasurably more than all I ask or could imagine for _____, . . . to You be glory . . . for ever and ever. Amen. (Eph. 3:20–21)

Other Scriptures You Can Pray

Romans 14:4

Luke 9:54–55

Psalm 86:5

1 Thessalonians 5:15

Romans 8:32

Romans 13:10

1 Thessalonians 5:28

2 Thessalonians 2:16–17

2 Peter 3:18

1 Peter 1:14–15

Psalm 5:12

Isaiah 40:31

Colossians 2:2–4, 8

Ephesians 5:23, 25, 28

2 Peter 3:9

2 Peter 3:18

Psalm 6:4

Psalm 30:11

Romans 15:5–6

PERSONALIZING YOUR PRAYERS

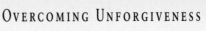

Chapter 12

OVERCOMING DEPRESSION

I desire to approach our present subject very carefully and with somewhat of a disclaimer: I am light years away from being an expert on depression. I am neither a doctor nor a professional counselor. According to those who are, feelings of depression can stem from any number of causes, whether psychological, physiological, or spiritual in nature. I am convinced, however, that God's degree in medicine extends to any specialty. He is the Great Physician over every intricate detail of our hearts, minds, souls, and bodies. No matter what significant inroads scientific research forges, we lack the omniscient vehicle necessary to travel the complex paths of the human vessel. We are far too "fearfully and wonderfully made" to comprehend. Philippians 4:6 exhorts us to "pray about everything"; therefore, "everything" has the capacity to be affected by prayer. This "permission"—indeed, *commission*—for prayer concerning all things means that no matter what the origin of depression, prayer is an important part of God's prescription. My intention, therefore, in this chapter is to equip the willing reader with Scripture-prayers whatever the cause of the downcast soul. Please use them in conjunction with any treatment God ordains for your wellness and restoration.

Feeling down for a few days does not constitute depression. Occasionally feeling depressed and battling chronic depression are two different things. Ongoing depression becomes a stronghold because its very nature is to eclipse a sense of well-being and hopefulness, strangling abundant life. All forms and origins of depression in a Christian fall under God's category of expertise. We must soberly realize that they also fall under Satan's counterfeit of expertise. In other words, it makes no difference to the devil where depression

208

originates; he will gladly take advantage of it. In fact, I believe it's one of his specialties because his fingerprints are all over it. In what way? Ask ten people to describe their depression with one word only, and overwhelmingly the common response will be "darkness." Satan is undoubtedly the prince of darkness. He is the antithesis of our God, in whom is no darkness at all (1 John 1:5). He is darkness and in him is no light at all. The best he can do is masquerade as an angel of light.

Interestingly, while believers debate whether Christians can experience depression, our ranks are nonetheless experiencing depression in record numbers. Obviously, we *can* and *have*. What injury we bring to the hurting when we become both judge and jury, misapplying Scripture to the depth of another person's pain! First John 1:6 has been used injuriously against believers suffering from depression. It says, "If we claim to have fellowship with him yet walk in the darkness, we lie and do not live by the truth." This Scripture has been wrongfully interpreted to mean that true believers do not experience seasons of darkness. Believers are most assuredly people of light, but sometimes the darkness around us can be so oppressive that we "feel it." No, we are not "of" the darkness. But sometimes we "feel" the darkness. The most wonderful insight 1 John 1:6 offers to the depressed is that our willingness to fellowship with God in the midst of our difficulty will usher forth the rays of His wonderful light.

Throughout this chapter, we will refer to the darkness believers can sense and feel through difficult seasons in their lives. God is always shining in our darkness, but sometimes "the darkness has not understood it" (John 1:5). Sometimes believers are caught off guard, experiencing feelings of depression and despair they never expected, swore they wouldn't, and do not understand. I believe the Bible suggests that our battles with depression can potentially be more painful and debilitating than the unbeliever's. The truths Christ taught in the Sermon on the Mount (Matt. 5–7) were issued to His own disciples. In Matthew 6:23, Christ said, "If then the light within you is darkness, how great is that darkness!" I believe this verse can relate to the believer's battle with depression. We are people of light; therefore, when darkness seems to invade our

hearts and minds through depression . . . how great is that darkness!

Although other strongholds have challenged me more often, God allowed me enough experience with depression to have great compassion on those who battle it. The most I have ever been defeated by darkness was years ago after I wrote the Bible study on the Old Testament tabernacle. I never had any idea at the time that the study would later be published as *A Woman's Heart: God's Dwelling Place.*

I was teaching a midweek Bible study to a group of women who asked me to start writing homework. I naively agreed. God purposefully led me to the topic of the Old Testament tabernacle, and I dove into the study with the confidence of an Olympic diver and the experience of a wet cat. By the time I realized what I had "gotten myself into," I was already committed. I had no choice but to fall on my face before Jehovah God and ask Him to teach me and show me the wonders of His Word. Indeed He did. Never in all my life had I entered the Holy of Holies with God in such a powerful and sustained way. For months I met with Him from the time my children went to school until they walked back through the door. I didn't answer the phone. I didn't go to lunch. I met with God day in and day out. He revealed treasures to me that I could never have articulated in words in a mere ten-week study. At times I literally moved to the floor to record His revelations because I was so overwhelmed by His Holy Presence.

As high as I ascended in intimacy with God throughout those months, I descended into darkness when it was complete. I had never written a Bible study before, nor had I ever spent such depth of time with God. Nothing could have prepared me for life when I departed "the Holy of Holies." Satan could not get to me while I was enclosed in that blessed sanctuary of study with God, but he was waiting right outside the door for my departure. In order not to be redundant, I will wait until the chapter on "Overcoming the Enemy" to share in greater detail about that terrible season of my life. Its relevance in this chapter is simply that Satan took advantage of a time when I dove off a cliff of closeness with God to coax me into a pit of despair, confusion, and depression.

Glory to God, I learned volumes from my experience in the wilderness following my time in the "Holy of Holies." I learned how powerless I am on my own. How weak and foolish. I learned by pure necessity how to guard my heart and mind. How to stay alert. How to fight back. I also learned to have a group of intercessors praying against any form of depression or defeat in me every time I finish writing an in-depth Bible study. Since that dreadful season, I've never again been so defeated by the darkness. But, while I was there, "how great was that darkness!" God used that period of my life not only to humble me, teach me, and train me, but also to equip me with compassion for every believer who suffers from depression.

> *Take heart! Men and women of the faith far more godly and effective than I will ever be also fought depression: Martin Luther and Charles Spurgeon are just two. Remember, the defeat is not in fighting depression . . . but in giving in.*

Why are you downcast, O my soul? Why so disturbed within me? I choose to put my hope in You, God, for I will yet praise You, my Savior and my God. My soul is downcast within me; therefore I will remember You! (Ps. 42:5–6)

My soul is downcast within me. Yet this I call to mind and therefore I have hope: Because of Your great love I am not consumed, for Your compassions never fail. They are new every morning. Great is Your faithfulness! (Lam. 3:21–23)

Lord, I don't want to be like those on the road to Emmaus, who stood still with their faces downcast when You asked, "What are you discussing together as you walk along?" They responded, "We had hoped that he was the one who was going to redeem Israel." (Luke 24:17, 21) They did not understand that the cross had to come before the kingdom. How foolish they were! The very death they had responded to with hopelessness represented the greatest hope of all time! God, I ask for forgiveness for every single time I have blamed my hopelessness on You. You are the God of hope. The Blessed Hope, Himself.

God, You who comfort the downcast, please comfort me by sending one of Your own to minister to me (2 Cor. 7:6), if indeed I will not become more dependent on him/her than You.

The Spirit of the Sovereign Lord is on You, Christ, because the Lord has anointed You to preach good news to the poor. He has sent You to bind up the brokenhearted, to proclaim freedom for the captives and release from darkness for the prisoners, to proclaim the year of the Lord's favor and the day of vengeance of our God, to comfort all who mourn, and provide for those who grieve in Zion—to bestow on us a crown of beauty instead of ashes, the oil of gladness instead of mourning, and a garment of praise instead of a spirit of despair. We will be called oaks of righteousness, a planting of the Lord for the display of His splendor. We will rebuild the ancient ruins and restore the places long devastated; we will renew the ruined cities that have been devastated for generations. (Isa. 61:1–4) Lord, pour upon me the oil of gladness and cover me with a garment of praise!

Lord God, I cry out to You. My spirit grows faint within me; my heart within me is dismayed. (Ps. 143:4)

> *God never misses a single tear of the oppressed. He sees our suffering and knows the depth of our need. He anguishes yet He waits . . . until the tears that have fallen on dry ground or upon the shoulders of others equally frail are poured instead before His throne. He waits—not until the oppressed cry out—but until we cry out to Him. Only then will we know the One and Only who redeems us.*

Lord, help me not to fear, for You are with me; I need not be dismayed, for You are my God. You will strengthen me and help me; You will uphold me with Your righteous right hand. (Isa. 41:10)

Answer me when I call to you, O my righteous God. Give me relief from my distress; be merciful to me and hear my prayer. (Ps. 4:1)

In my distress I call to You, Lord; I cry to my God for help. From Your temple You hear my voice; my cry comes before You, into Your ears. (Ps. 18:6)

God, You will give me the treasures of darkness, riches stored in secret places, so that I may know that You are the Lord, the God of Israel, who summons me by name. (Isa. 45:3) Lord, even in this difficult place, You have treasures for me here. You want me to discover the riches of relationship with You that will set me free from this place.

Lord God, in all my distress You too are distressed, and the angel of Your presence saves me. In Your love and mercy You redeem me; You lift me up and carry me all the days of old. (Isa. 63:9)

My Lord, hear me and answer me. My thoughts trouble me and I am distraught. (Ps. 55:2)

Father, like the Israelites, sometimes You speak to me through one of Your servants, but I do not listen because of my discouragement and cruel bondage. (Exod. 6:9) O, Lord, help me to listen to You, or I will never be free! Open my spiritual eyes and ears to see and hear the way to freedom.

Hope does not disappoint me, because You, God, have poured out Your love into my heart by the Holy Spirit, whom You have given me. (Rom. 5:5)

You, my God, have not run away from being my Shepherd; I know You have not desired the day of despair. What passes my lips is open before You. (Jer. 17:16)

> *Oh, dear heart, what is your condition? Are you torn with anguish? Are you sorely distressed? Are you lonely? Are you pushed aside? Then cry to God. No one else can help you. He is your only hope. Wonderful hope! Cry to Him, for He can help you. I tell you, in that cry of yours will be the pure and true worship that God desires. He desires a sincere cry far more than the slaughter of ten thousand rams or the pouring out of rivers of oil (Mic. 6:7). . . . See then, poor, weeping, and distracted ones, that it is not ritualism, it is not the performance of pompous ceremonies, it is not bowing and struggling, it is not using sacred words, but it is crying to God in the hour of trouble that is the most acceptable sacrifice your spirit can bring before the throne of God.*
>
> *Charles Spurgeon,* Spurgeon on Prayer and Spiritual Warfare

Father, even the great apostle Paul did not want us to be uninformed about the hardships he suffered in the province of Asia. He, too, was under great pressure, far beyond his ability to endure, so that he despaired even of life. (2 Cor. 1:8) Even many of Your mightiest servants have despaired of life. Like them, however, I must stand once again in Your strength and courage and allow You to pour Your life back into me.

Lord God, I am hard pressed on every side, but I don't have to be crushed; I am perplexed, but I do not have to be in despair. (2 Cor. 4:8)

Listen to my cry, for I am in desperate need; rescue me from those who pursue me, for they are too strong for me. (Ps. 142:6) Lord, an important part of my victory will be admitting that without Your complete intervention, my oppressor is too strong for me.

214

I am unable to be victorious without You. Come and rescue me with Your mighty hand.

Blessed am I, Lord, because You are faithful to correct me. I will not despise the discipline of the Almighty. I have despised my life. I have wanted people to leave me alone because I've felt my days had no meaning. (Job 5:17; 7:16) Lord, You would not leave me here on this earth a single day that was not meant to have meaning. My life does have meaning. Please help me not to despise it or isolate others from it.

You, Christ, were despised and rejected by men, a man of sorrows, and familiar with suffering. You were like one from whom men hide their faces. You were despised, and we did not esteem You. (Isa. 53:3) You know exactly how I feel, Lord. I will put my trust in You.

The thief comes only to steal and kill and destroy; You have come that I may have life, and have it to the full. (John 10:10) I acknowledge, O my God, that Your will for me is abundant life. Full life! Satan, the thief, has come to steal, kill, and destroy all things concerning my life. I stand against him in Your name and desire to accept the abundant life You came to bring me.

Victorious Lord, how I thank You that the oppressor will come to an end and destruction will cease; the aggressor will vanish from the land. (Isa. 16:4)

Lord, according to Your Word, if my eyes are bad, my whole body will be full of darkness. If then the light within me is darkness, how great is that darkness! (Matt. 6:23) Lord, this verse tells me that the focus of my gaze, where my eyes are fixed, has a monumental impact on whether light or darkness will be prevalent in my life. Please, Lord, heal my eyes—my sight!—that I might look to You, my Hope and my Redeemer.

Mighty Redeemer, the cords of death have entangled me; the torrents of destruction have overwhelmed me. The cords of the grave have coiled around me; the snares of death have confronted me. (Ps. 18:4–5)

Lord God, the cords of death have entangled Your child, the anguish of the grave has come upon me; I have been overcome by trou-

ble and sorrow. . . . But now, O Lord, You will deliver my soul from death, my eyes from tears, my feet from stumbling. (Ps. 116:3, 8)

> *People who have a seeking heart still make mistakes. But their reaction to rebuke and correction shows the condition of that heart. It determines what God is able to do with them in the future.*
>
> *Jim Cymbala,* Fresh Wind, Fresh Fire

Lord God, Your Word says, "The people walking in darkness have seen a great light; on those living in the land of the shadow of death a light has dawned." (Isa. 9:2) I, too, have been walking in darkness. Please cause Your great light to dawn in my darkness, glorious God, You who live in unapproachable light! (1 Tim. 6:16)

See, O Lord, how distressed I am! I am in torment within, and in my heart I am disturbed, for I have been most rebellious. Outside, the sword bereaves; inside, there is only death. (Lam. 1:20) God, please help me to admit the part of my torment that has come from rebellion. Show me my rebellious ways, not so that I will feel condemned and judged, but that I can confess, begin to walk in Your ways, and be free.

Even though I walk through the valley of the shadow of death, I will fear no evil, for You are with me; Your rod and Your staff, they comfort me. (Ps. 23:4)

According to Your Word, God, there is no dark place, no deep shadow, where evildoers can hide. (Job 34:22) Lord, if I have done evil in dark places, I must confess it to You. You already know and now You want to set me free. It is time for me to bring all my baggage to You and allow You to heal me, restore me, and free me from this oppressive weight.

Lord, even though I may feel covered in darkness, even the darkness will not be dark to You; the night will shine like the day, for darkness is as light to You. (Ps. 139:12) Cloak me in Your presence, God, for in You is no darkness at all.

> *I discovered an astonishing truth: God is attracted to weakness. He can't resist those who humbly and honestly admit how desperately they need Him.*
>
> *Jim Cymbala,* Fresh Wind, Fresh Fire

Lord, Your Word asks, "Who among you fears the LORD / and obeys the word of his servant?" Your Word then exhorts, "Let him who walks in the dark, / who has no light, / trust in the name of the LORD / and rely on his God." (Isa. 50:10) Father, I desire to trust in the name of my Lord and rely on You, my God, especially as I walk through this dark time.

My struggle is not against flesh and blood but against the rulers, against the authorities, against the powers of this dark world, and against the spiritual forces of evil in the heavenly realms. (Eph. 6:12) I acknowledge to You, Lord, that Satan is always at work in the darkness. I must not be naïve and deny how much he desires to take control of this season of my life. Help me to stand firm against attacks!

Lord, according to Your Word, when the Israelites heard Your voice out of the darkness, while the mountain was ablaze with fire, all the leading men of their tribes and their elders came forward. (Deut. 5:23) Please help me to hear Your voice out of my darkness and come to You, Lord.

You are my lamp, O Lord; You, the Lord, turn my darkness into light. (2 Sam. 22:29) You, O Lord, keep my lamp burning; my God turns my darkness into light. (Ps. 18:28)

Lord, Your servant Job felt he was in the land of deepest night, of deep shadow and disorder, where even the light is like darkness.

217

(Job 10:22) You restored someone who knew a much bleaker darkness than mine. You will restore me, too, if I will let You.

Lord, if the only home I hope for is the grave, if I spread out my bed in darkness, . . . where then is my hope? (Job 17:13, 15) Please help me not to see the grave as my only hope. I am one of Your children, Lord! How foolish for the grave to be my hope, for I will never live in a grave. I will be with You in glory.

Victorious Lord, I am not silenced by the darkness, by the thick darkness that covers my face. (Job 23:17) I will cry out to You and I will rebuke the enemy that seeks to devour me.

Lord, when I hoped for good, evil came; when I looked for light, then came darkness. (Job 30:26) Help me, Lord, for hope deferred has made my heart sick. (Prov. 13:12) Help me to put my hope in You.

Father, I am struggling. I feel that You have taken my companions and loved ones from me; the darkness is my closest friend. Lord, show me wonders in this place of darkness and reveal to me Your righteousness in this land of oblivion. Let them draw me to your light. (Ps. 88:12, 18) Please come and rescue me. Be my closest companion and my dearest loved one.

Lord God, help me to be obedient to You even in this difficult season. Your Word says that even in darkness light dawns for the upright, for the gracious and compassionate and righteous man. (Ps. 112:4)

Lord God, say to this captive, "Come out," and to this child in darkness, "Be free!" Good Shepherd, cause me to find pasture even on every barren hill. (Isa. 49:9)

Do not gloat over me, my enemy! Though I have fallen, I will rise. Though I sit in darkness, the Lord will be my light. (Mic. 7:8)

Lord, according to Your Word, the light shines in the darkness, but the darkness has not understood it. (John 1:5) Help me to understand that, because I'm Yours, light is shining in my darkness whether I can behold it or understand it.

> *The first "degree" of depression is* dejection—*a low-ness of spirit, a feeling of spiritual and emotional fatigue. If not reversed this dejection takes us down even further, plunging us into* despair *and finally into utter* demoralization. *At this stage of descent, hope is entirely abandoned and is replaced by apathy and numbness. . . . My goal is that no matter how fierce or long the battles we face, you and I together will be able to say, "But in all these things we overwhelmingly conquer through Him who loved us" (Rom. 8:37, NASB).*
>
> Kay Arthur, As Silver Refined

O, God, of all things help me never to be guilty of this verdict: Light has come into the world, but men loved darkness instead of light because their deeds were evil. (John 3:19) Lord, please help me not to love the darkness instead of the light! Help me not to prefer my depression because it has become comfortable and makes excuses for me. Free me!

Lord, You have come into the world as a light, so that no one who believes in You should stay in darkness. (John 12:46)

For, You, God, who said, "Let light shine out of darkness," made Your light shine in my heart to give me the light of the knowledge of the glory of God in the face of Christ. (2 Cor. 4:6)

I am a chosen person, part of a royal priesthood, a holy nation, a people belonging to You, God, that I may declare the praises of You who called me out of darkness into Your wonderful light. (1 Pet. 2:9)

You, O Lord, are like the light of morning at sunrise on a cloudless morning, like the brightness after rain that brings the grass from the earth. (2 Sam. 23:4)

Send forth Your light and Your truth, let them guide me; let them bring me to Your holy mountain, to the place where You dwell. (Ps. 43:3)

Faithful and merciful God, You have set my iniquities before You, my secret sins in the light of Your presence. (Ps. 90:8) Help me not be afraid of letting You all the way into the secret places of my heart and mind . . . for You, Lord, are already there!

You wrap Yourself in light as with a garment; You stretch out the heavens like a tent. (Ps. 104:2) Take Your garment and wrap it around me, O Lord.

Your Word is a lamp to my feet and a light for my path. (Ps. 119:105) Please help me to take this verse literally, Lord! Your Word will bring light to me during this dark season. Satan wants me to resist the very thing I need the most. Woo me to Your Word, O God!

Lord, the unfolding of Your words gives light; it gives understanding to the simple. (Ps. 119:130)

O Lord, You have searched me and You know me. You know when I sit and when I rise; You perceive my thoughts from afar. You discern my going out and my lying down; You are familiar with all my ways. Before a word is on my tongue, You know it completely, O Lord. (Ps. 139:1–4)

Lord, the night is nearly over; the day is almost here. Help me to put aside the deeds of darkness and put on the armor of light. (Rom. 13:12)

Your eyes, Lord, are on those who fear You, on those whose hope is in Your unfailing love, to deliver them from death and keep them alive in famine. I wait in hope for You, Lord; You are my help and my shield. In You my heart rejoices, for I trust in Your holy name. May Your unfailing love rest upon me, O Lord, even as I put my hope in You. (Ps. 33:18–22)

But as for me, O God, I will always have hope; I will praise You more and more. (Ps. 71:14)

May those who fear You rejoice when they see me, for I have put my hope in Your Word. (Ps. 119:74) My soul faints with longing for Your salvation, but I have put my hope in Your Word. (Ps. 119:81)

You, Lord, delight in those who fear You, who put their hope in Your unfailing love. (Ps. 147:11)

> *And as we mature, we begin to realize that the Spirit of Christ is actually within us. The cross emerges off the printed page, it stands upright before us, confronting us with our own Gethsemanes, our own Golgothas—but also our own resurrections through which we ascend spiritually into the true Presence of the Lord.*
>
> Francis Frangipane, Holiness, Truth and
> the Presence of God

Lord, according to Your Word, hope deferred makes the heart sick, but a longing fulfilled is a tree of life. (Prov. 13:12) Lord, You are keenly aware of any hopes that have been deferred in my life. Help me to put my hopes in You for You will fulfill my longings.

Wonderful Savior, You tell me that there is surely a future hope for me, and my hope will not be cut off. (Prov. 23:18)

When I hope in You, Lord, I will renew my strength. I will soar on wings like eagles; I will run and not grow weary, I will walk and not be faint. (Isa. 40:31)

Lord, help me hear this word as one from You to me: "So there is hope for your future," declares the Lord. (Jer. 29:17)

Lord God, Your glorious Word exhorts me to return to my fortress, O prisoners of hope; even now You announce that You will restore twice as much to me. (Zech. 9:12) O, Lord, I am not a prisoner of darkness! I am a prisoner of hope!

Lord, You are the God of hope. Fill me with all joy and peace as I trust in You, so that I may overflow with hope by the power of the Holy Spirit. (Rom. 15:13)

You, O God, have delivered me from such a deadly peril, and You will deliver me still. On You I have set my hope that You will continue to deliver me. (2 Cor. 1:10)

I pray also that the eyes of my heart may be enlightened in order that I may know the hope to which You have called me, the riches of Your glorious inheritance in the saints, and Your incomparably great power for us who believe. (Eph. 1:18–19)

Lord God, cause my work to be produced by faith, my labor prompted by love, and my endurance inspired by hope in my Lord Jesus Christ. (1 Thess. 1:3)

Lord Jesus Christ, may You and God my Father, who loves me and by His grace gave me eternal encouragement and good hope, encourage my heart and strengthen me in every good deed and word. (2 Thess. 2:16–17)

Help me, Lord, to hold unswervingly to the hope I profess, for You who promised are faithful. (Heb. 10:23)

O God, turn to me and be gracious to me, for I am lonely and afflicted. The troubles of my heart have multiplied; free me from my anguish. Look upon my affliction and my distress and take away all my sins. (Ps. 25:16–18)

I believed; therefore I said, "I am greatly afflicted." (Ps. 116:10) Lord, help me to believe You enough to admit when I am greatly afflicted. You want me to pour out my heart to You because You are my Refuge! (Ps. 62:8)

Shout for joy, O heavens; rejoice, O earth; burst into song, O mountains! For the Lord comforts His people and will have compassion on His afflicted ones. (Isa. 49:13)

O God, I will be glad and rejoice in Your love, for You saw my affliction and knew the anguish of my soul. (Ps. 31:7)

If Your law had not been my delight, I would have perished in my affliction. (Ps. 119:92) Teach me Your Word during this season of my life like I have never known it before, and make this verse my testimony when I emerge from this place.

O God, speak to me so clearly through Your Word that I recognize Your voice. Help me to understand what You are making known to me, delighting me with Your Word so that I may celebrate with great joy! (Neh. 8:12)

> *I write this with all reverence: God Himself cannot deliver a person who is not in trouble. Therefore, it is to some advantage to be in distress, because God can then deliver you. Even Jesus Christ, the Healer of me, cannot heal a person who is not sick. Therefore, sickness is not an adversity for us, but rather an advantageous opportunity for Christ to heal us. The point is, my reader, your adversity may prove your advantage by offering occasion for the display of divine grace.*
>
> *Charles Spurgeon,* Spurgeon on Prayer and
> Spiritual Warfare

O God, You have made known to me the path of life; You will fill me with joy in Your presence, with eternal pleasures at Your right hand. (Ps. 16:11)

Your precepts, O Lord, are right, giving joy to the heart. Your commands are radiant, giving light to my eyes. (Ps. 19:8)

Surely, Lord, You have granted me eternal blessings and made me glad with the joy of Your presence. (Ps. 21:6)

You, God, turned my wailing into dancing; You removed my sackcloth and clothed me with joy that my heart may sing to You and not be silent. O Lord my God, I will give You thanks forever. (Ps. 30:11–12)

O *God,* let me hear joy and gladness; let the bones You have crushed rejoice. . . . Restore to me the joy of Your salvation and grant me a willing spirit, to sustain me. (Ps. 51:8, 12)

O *God,* those living far away fear Your wonders; where morning dawns and evening fades You call forth songs of joy. . . . The meadows are covered with flocks and the valleys are mantled with grain; Help me to shout for joy and sing. (Ps. 65:8, 13) You care for me far more than the land You enrich abundantly. Flood my dry soul with the streams of God and fill me with joy. (Ps. 65:9)

> *Whatever happened, happened. We can't remake our pasts.* But with God we can handle the past. *With God, whatever has happened in the past need not destroy us. Of course we'll face and many times reap the consequences of the past. But for the child of God there is hope. God is God, the God of all hope. No matter what has happened in our backgrounds, with God there is grace, peace, and hope if we'll run to Him and bring every past disappointment captive to faith in His Word.*
>
> Kay Arthur, As Silver Refined

Blessed, merciful God, Your Word promises that those who sow in tears will reap with songs of joy. If I go out weeping, carrying seed to sow, I will return with songs of joy, carrying sheaves with me. (Ps. 126:5–6) Help me to see that the promise is not made to those who simply have tears but to those who are willing to sow seed in the midst of their tears. Your Word tells us in Luke 8:11 that the seed is the Word. If I'm willing to keep believing and sowing Your Word, even when I am desperately hurting, You will bring me forth from this difficult season with songs of joy.

Lord, because of Your faithfulness, with joy I will draw water from the wells of salvation. (Isa. 12:3)

I will find joy in You, my Lord. You will cause me to ride on the heights of the land and to feast on the inheritance You have given my spiritual forefathers. The mouth of the Lord has spoken. (Isa. 58:14)

Now is my time of grief, but I will see You again and I will rejoice, and no one will take away my joy. In that day I will no longer ask You anything. . . . I can ask and I will receive, and my joy will be complete. (John 16:22–24)

Lord Jesus, You want me to have the full measure of Your joy within me. (John 17:13)

God of hope, please fill me with all joy and peace as I trust in You, so that I may overflow with hope by the power of the Holy Spirit. (Rom. 15:13)

Father, I want You to be able to have great confidence in me and take pride in me. In all my troubles, let my joy know no bounds. (2 Cor. 7:4)

The fruit of Your Spirit, Lord, is love, joy, peace, patience, kindness, goodness, faithfulness, gentleness, and self-control. (Gal. 5:22)

Lord, many have run this difficult race faithfully. I want to be among them. Therefore, since I am surrounded by such a great cloud of witnesses, help me throw off everything that hinders and the sin that so easily entangles, and help me run with perseverance the race marked out for me. Help me fix my eyes on You, Jesus, the author and perfecter of my faith, who for the joy set before You endured the cross, scorning its shame, and sat down at the right hand of the throne of God. (Heb. 12:1–2)

As a bridegroom rejoices over his bride, so will You, my God, rejoice over me. (Isa. 62:5)

I have gained access by faith into this grace in which I now stand, and I rejoice in the hope of the glory of God. (Rom. 5:2)

My soul glorifies the Lord and my spirit rejoices in God my Savior, for You have been mindful of the humble state of Your servant. (Luke 1:46–48)

Your anger, merciful Lord, lasts only a moment, but Your favor lasts a lifetime; weeping may remain for a night, but rejoicing comes in the morning. (Ps. 30:5)

You bring out Your people with rejoicing, Your chosen ones with shouts of joy; . . . We fall heir to what others have toiled for! (Ps. 105:43–44)

You have written me a new command; its truth to be seen in You and me, because the darkness is passing and the true light is already shining. (1 John 2:8)

O God, I know how the psalmist felt when he said, "My life is consumed by anguish. . ." (Ps. 31:10) You are the God who restored his life from such anguish. You will not withhold Your love from me.

I often feel very grateful to God that I have undergone fearful depression. I know the borders of despair and the horrible brink of that gulf of darkness into which my feet have almost gone. But hundreds of times I have been able to give a helpful grip to brethren and sisters who have come into that same condition, which grip I could never have given if I had not known their despondency. So I believe that the darkest and most dreadful experience of a child of God will help him to be a fisher of men if he will but follow Christ.

Charles Spurgeon, 2200 Quotations from the Writings of Charles H. Spurgeon

---

OTHER SCRIPTURES YOU CAN PRAY

Joshua 1:9
Philippians 1:6
Psalm 79:8
Psalm 141:8
Psalm 118:18
Mark 1:35
Job 29:3
Psalm 107:12–14
Psalm 139:11–12
1 Corinthians 4:5
Ephesians 5:8
Colossians 1:13
Psalm 13:3

Psalm 27:1
Psalm 76:4
Psalm 118:27
Isaiah 2:5
Matthew 5:14
Psalm 62:5
Ecclesiastes 9:4
Romans 8:24–25
1 Thessalonians 4:13
Psalm 30:10
Psalm 45:7, 15
Romans 14:17

PRAYING GOD'S WORD

PERSONALIZING YOUR PRAYERS

Chapter 13

OVERCOMING SEXUAL STRONGHOLDS

Satan has done a masterful job of shaming those who are caught in sexual strongholds into a continuous cycle of defeat. He seduces, then he shames, keeping his eye steadfastly on the goal of scandal. Let's reiterate that Satan cannot take our salvation from us, so he does everything he can to steal, kill, and destroy our character, testimony, and effectiveness. Defeated Christians work far more effectively in Satan's scheme to undermine the church than successful non-Christians ever will!

None of us will question that he is having a field day in our present generation in the area of sexual strongholds. Satan's attacks on sexuality have become so outright and blatant that we're becoming frighteningly desensitized and are unknowingly readjusting the plumb line to a state of relativity. In other words, instead of measuring our lives against the goal of Christlikeness, we are beginning to subconsciously measure our lives against the world's depravity. We can point to any amount of trash heaps around us and say, "I'll never be as bad as that." A Christian teenager might reason, "At least I sleep only with my boyfriend. Anyway, we're going to get married one day." A Christian spouse might justify his or her lusts with words like, "I may not get to order the dish, but there's no harm in checking out the menu." The virus of relativity is especially contagious in the media industry. We're tempted to choose one compromising movie over another because it's not nearly as bad as the other. We are wise to become very alert to the venomous snakebite of relativism. Satan is increasing the dosage of sexually immoral provocation with such consistency that we don't realize how much poison we're swallowing.

First of all, let's be sure to state that sexual intimacy is an absolute gift of God given to a husband and wife for their mutual joy and satisfaction. Most of us realize that sex itself is not the problem. It's what we're doing with it beyond its stated purpose that becomes the problem. Incalculable numbers of believers suffer from sexual strongholds. Even believers who really want to live victoriously often find themselves in what Neil Anderson, author of *The Bondage Breaker*, calls "the trap of sin-confess, sin-confess."[1] Many singles who fall back and forth into sexual sin are extremely remorseful about their actions and suffer terrible guilt, but they can't seem to avoid falling back into the trap.

We'd be extremely naïve to think that sexual immorality is limited to the defeated single. Not only are extramarital affairs rampant, but couples who are physically monogamous may be far from emotionally and mentally monogamous. Christ blew the door off marriage as an assumed impenetrable fortress against sexual immorality with Matthew 5:27: "You have heard that it was said, 'Do not commit adultery.' But I tell you that anyone who looks at a woman lustfully has already committed adultery with her in his heart." Alarming numbers of believing couples have unhealthy marriages because sexual perversion and pornography entered the home under the guise of "spicing things up." *God* can spice things up. And His choice of spice brings edification, healing, and the kind of romance that lasts. When a marriage is wholeheartedly surrendered to Jesus Christ's authority by both a husband and a wife, sooner or later, that marriage is going to spice up! If you think God is stuffy, you might want to take another look at the Song of Songs!

Most of us will agree that Satan's present employment of blatant sexual tactics is unparalleled in human history. Pockets of it existed to a stunning degree in ages past, but Satan has never had the kind of universal audience he has presently. I'm not sure he has ever before scored the points in favor of sexual strongholds that Internet access has accomplished for him. Prior to the Internet, society's access to pornography was a far more public affair. In other words, partakers had to have nerve enough to walk into an establishment and make a purchase. No longer. We can now sit in our Beaver Cleaver homes with our white picket fences and open the attic door of pornography through the Internet. It's now a private affair. The rate of Christians being snared daily is staggering. Satan gets his pawns trapped in secret shame, living miserable lives of deception. Please read this carefully: *we are being sexually assaulted by the devil*. The church must start mentioning the unmentionable and biblically address issues that are attacking our generation. God's Word applies to the strongholds of promiscuity, perversity, and pornography just as it does to any other. God is not shocked. He has the remedy. He is awaiting our humble, earnest cry for help.

What's this stuff all about, anyway? Why do sexual strongholds seem to be some of Satan's specialties? As I traveled and heard story after story of sexual strongholds in believers' lives, I began to ask God to give me some insight. No doubt far more answers exist than these, but I'd like to share a few things He's showing me:

- *Satan is trying to distort what God ordained a marriage to be.* According to Ephesians 5:22–32, God instituted marriage between one man and one woman to be the closest earthly representation of a much greater reality: Christ and the Church. We established earlier in this book that Satan's primary problem is that he is driven by a manic jealousy of Jesus Christ. He is seeking relentlessly to undermine and counterfeit the relationship that God ordained for the purpose of revealing a "type" of Christ and His Bride.

- *Satan desires to undermine the sanctifying work of Christ.* He knows that all believers have been "set apart" from the unclean to the clean, and from the unholy to the holy. He also knows that when believers act like the sanctified people they are, God is released to do powerful wonders among them. (Josh. 3:5) No purity—no power. Purity—boundless power. Satan is a fool, but he's no dummy.

- *Satan knows the overwhelming effects of sexual sin.* We must resist "ranking" sin since every sin causes us to miss the mark and require grace. All sin is equal in the sense of eternal ramifications, but not all sin is equal in its earthly ramifications. Satan knows that sexual sin is unique in its attack and impact on the body of the individual believer. First Corinthians 6:18–19 says, "Flee from sexual immorality. All other sins a

231

man commits are outside his body, but he who sins sexually sins against his own body. Do you not know that your body is a temple of the Holy Spirit, who is in you, whom you have received from God? You are not your own; you were bought at a price. Therefore honor God with your body." Since the Spirit of Christ now dwells in the temple of believers' bodies, getting a Christian engaged in sexual sin is the closest Satan can come to personally assaulting Christ. That ought to make us mad enough to be determined to live victoriously. Sins against the body also have a way of sticking to us and making us feel like we *are* that sin rather than the fact that we've *committed* that sin.

- *Sexual engagement forms a soul tie that was meant for marriage alone.* First Corinthians 6:13–16 says, "The body is not meant for sexual immorality, but for the Lord, and the Lord for the body. By His power God raised the Lord from the dead, and he will raise us also. Do you not know that your bodies are members of Christ himself? Shall I then take the members of Christ and unite them with a prostitute? Never! Do you not know that he who unites himself with a prostitute is one with her in body? For it is said, 'The two will become one flesh.'" These Scriptures tell us that when we engage in any realm of sexual intimacy with someone besides our marriage partner, we are tying ourselves to them. The original Greek word for "unites" in this verse is *kollao* meaning "to glue together, to make cohere."[2] In other words, it can form a soul tie that is absolutely out of the will of God and must be renounced severely in order for such surrendered ground to be reclaimed. A soul tie to *anyone* besides our spouse is outside the will of God and becomes an open target for the continuing, destroying schemes of the devil.

So, is there any hope of earthly recovery, or are we doomed to be defeated by the excess baggage and emptiness that wrong relationships left behind? The believer in Christ *always* has hope, but God means for hope to become a vivid reality through complete restoration. We are called to some radical responses with guaranteed results: we must repent wholeheartedly, receive the Lord's loving discipline, and cooperate fully with His plan for recovery. The process can be hard, painful, and somewhat lengthy *because we have to allow God to remove all the broken remnants of the ties to the ungodly relationship and fill in the holes with His loving Spirit until we are smooth and whole.* No matter how hard, the resulting freedom will be worth it. Incidentally, someone who has had many sexual partners may be thinking, *I don't have soul ties to* any *of them. I don't give them a second thought.* Please understand that you may be in one of the most binding sexual strongholds of all because you have completely segregated your emotions and are not only abusing your own body but others' too. I speak the truth to you in love, not judgment. You are in a serious situation, and heavy-duty consequences are no doubt pending. Please seek God and ask Him to heal you and give you appropriate godly sorrow so that you can be free. You are being terribly but successfully deceived.

- Sexual sin is highly habitual and addictive, so it has the long-term effects Satan prefers. He is many things, but he's not very creative. He much prefers a long-lasting yoke to the flimsier brand. Satan uses the same thing over and over as long as he's getting results. If you believe you may be dealing with or risking sexual addiction, don't forget to also use the Scripture-prayers on overcoming addiction (chap. 7).

- *One reason Satan has turned up the heat so furiously in temptations toward sexual sin in our generation is because he sees the signs of the times, and he knows that the Bride of Christ is supposed to be making herself ready for the Marriage Supper of the Lamb.* In 2 Corinthians 11:2–3, the apostle Paul expressed the heart of God in his desire that the Church be presented to Christ as a "pure virgin to Him." He went on to say, "But I am afraid that just as Eve was deceived by the serpent's cunning, your minds may somehow be led astray from your sincere and pure devotion to Christ." What better way to get to people who are supposed to be presented as pure virgins to Christ? I have wonderful news for every person who says, "It's too late for me! I gave up my virginity years ago!" Only in Christ Jesus, our Merciful Redeemer and Blessed Hope, can we regain our vir-

ginity. No, not physically. But emotionally, mentally, and spiritually. We can also allow Him to set apart these bodies that He has chosen to be the temple of His Holy Spirit henceforth to be sanctified, clean vessels. Not only is this possible, *this is God's will!*

Before we proceed to our Scripture-prayers for overcoming sexual strongholds, we are wise to address another deadly sexual assault of the evil one in our society: *homosexuality.* I have wonderful news for anyone who has struggled with homosexual sin. God indeed can deliver you and anxiously awaits your full cooperation. Do not let Satan shame you into not seeking forgiveness, fullness, and complete restoration in Jesus Christ. I know complete transformation is possible not only because God's Word says so, but because I have witnessed it with my own eyes. I know *plenty* of believers who have been set free from homosexuality. If you have a sound, Spirit-filled, restoring church, you probably sit near someone who has been freed and yet you have no idea. Why? Because the subject is still so tragically taboo in our churches that they are afraid to give their testimony. I am convinced that God wants us to speak freedom from our pulpits to every kind of captive . . . not just the socially "acceptable" ones. Ironically, one reason some former captives return to their previous homosexual lifestyle is because they find more "community" among their fellow sinners than their fellow saints. Oh, how we need the heart of Christ as we minister in the Body of Christ! We must learn how to deal with the issue of homosexuality in our churches because God's Word clearly tells us it will only increase as the return of Christ draws nearer.

When asked for the signs of His coming, Christ compared both the society of Noah and the society of Lot (Luke 17:26, 28), pointing to the increase of heterosexual *and* homosexual sin. Noah's generation is described in Genesis 6:5: "The Lord saw how great man's wickedness on the earth had become and that every inclination of the thoughts of his heart was only evil all the time." The uprising of homosexual sin in particular becomes obvious in Genesis 18 and 19 in the city of Sodom where Lot and his family lived. It's no accident that God's Word compares the generation preceding Christ's return with those of Noah and Lot. The dramatic increase in every kind of sexual sin is one of the most obvious signs of our times.

Yes, freedom is possible for the person who will seek Christ with all his or her heart no matter how long the bondage of homosexuality has continued. You must, however, be ready for the fight of your life. A fight that will have a magnificent harvest . . . but a fight nonetheless. Experts in the area of "homosexuality and the Christian" agree virtually across the board that homosexuality is as powerful and binding a yoke as exists. I believe it is one of Satan's "pet" yokes. One of his favorites. It is the ultimate slam against the man-woman relationship that prefigures Christ and His Bride, the Church. I believe the assault of homosexuality specifically against the people of God is Satan's devious means of infiltrating the Church with perversity at the exact time when the Bride is supposed to be "making herself ready" for the Marriage Supper of the Lamb (Rev. 19). Please don't misunderstand me. One of God's priority purposes for the Church is for her to be a welcoming place of restoration and recovery for all who desire to be freed from the captivity of sin. Homophobia is the last thing I'm suggesting for the Church; however, our current unwillingness to admit the problem, embrace the repentant, and aid in biblical restoration—all symptomatic of homophobia—has left us more vulnerable to evil than helpful to the captive.

Homosexuality is one of Satan's primary agendas in our current society. He is selling it at every corner both blatantly and subtly. Deception is never more active in any yoke of bondage than this one. If deception is indeed the glue that holds every stronghold together, the glue of deception in homosexuality is more like concrete. Our society is falling for a huge lie. Contrary to current propaganda, the same-sex "monogamous" relationship is not "just like the opposite-sex relationship." Every person liberated from the homosexual lifestyle I've ever talked to or read about has described it as obsessive, controlling, and increasingly absorbing. In a way only understood in the unseen world, a satanically induced web is associated with this particular yoke. This webbing of victims is methodically woven through a full-scale attack on the mind and emotions, taking advantage of every loophole in the lives involved. As the enemy draws one person after another into the web, his victims replace sound reasoning with rationalizing, lifelong value systems with a big lie called "tolerance," and become "feelings"-driven rather than "truth"-driven. One woman who wanted to be free admitted, "I want to be out because I know it's sin. It's just that I've never had anyone love me like that before."

Please hear this with your whole heart: it isn't *love*. It may feel like love because it is an overwhelming takeover of the heart, but it's not love. Jeremiah 17:9 tells us that *the heart is deceitful above all things*. Nowhere is the heart infiltrated by more deception than in homosexuality. I've never known anyone to be finally freed from the web as long as he or she still characterized his or her former feelings as "genuine love"—*including the woman I mentioned a few sentences earlier*. A few months after she allowed God to reprogram her heart and mind with truth, she came back to me and rephrased her sentence: "I've never had anyone *control* me like that before." Homosexuality's genuine escapees rarely fail to describe the inexpressible relief from an overwhelming oppression. As God begins to instill genuine "heart" health, they are often stunned to realize just how unhealthy their emotions really were.

If you have been yoked by the powerful bondage of homosexuality, I want to thank you from the depths of my heart for having the courage to pick up this book and read this commentary. God loves you with all His heart. With His Son's life, He's already done everything necessary to set you free. Now He just wants you to let Him apply it to your life. He can transform the desires of your heart and the entire nature of your passions, but first you must let Him change your thinking. That's an important purpose in the Scripture-prayers that follow. Please don't limit yourself to these, however. A strong dose of truth is the prescription for strong doses of captivity. Please get into the in-depth study of God's Word and let Him deprogram your mind of all deception and reprogram your mind with truth. Then, your feelings will begin to be dramatically transformed. In the in-depth process, you will discover something far more priceless than even your deliverance. You will discover your Deliverer. Only He can set you free, but in the process, you will build a relationship with Jesus Christ that will heal every heart disease and fill in every empty place that made your life an accident waiting to happen.

One of the Christian counselors I respect most in this world is a former captive webbed by Satan's lie of homosexuality. She offered me these words to share with anyone seeking to be free: "You cannot break out alone! Because you will only trade the unhealthy dependency for another kind if you don't walk through the healing process. Too often people will stop the outward manifestation of the root problem and believe they are free. But they are not free if they have not resolved the root issues. What they have done is controlled the outward manifestation while still being in bondage in their inner man. They continue to miss the true victory because they still believe the lies."

Ceasing outward behavior is a huge step in the right direction, but we can't stop there. Isaiah 1:16–17 says, "Stop doing wrong, learn to do right." In other words, God's Word tells us to follow up the cessation of sinful actions by learning how to live righteously. Our strongholds are certainly not limited to external behaviors; in fact, our unhealthy actions are simply more obvious indicators of an internal problem. Many men and women are engaged in binding, nonsexual affairs, whether with the opposite sex or the same sex. The cure takes place in the inmost places of the heart and mind. More than anything, the key to deliverance is not just being *delivered from* but being *delivered to*. The reason we keep going back to our old strongholds is that we have temporarily been delivered *from* the sin practice, but we did not follow through with deliverance straight *to* the healthy heart of God.

No matter what kind of sexual stronghold you seek to overcome, God's remedy is His truth. As you pray and claim these Scriptures through prayer, choose to believe God's truth even when you still feel the lie. Even state out loud when possible, "God, I know what Your Word says is true even though I still have feelings to the contrary. Your Word will remain the same, but my feelings will change. Help me to know that the first step is to believe with my mind and soon my heart will change too."

You can do it, believer, because God will do it through you if you'll let Him. Give Him *time* and *truth* and there's nothing He can't do. Reject Satan's lies that you can never be free. Don't you see? He is afraid of you! He is afraid of what you'll become and the power of your testimony if God sets you free. Go to whatever lengths God takes you. He's already provided the blood. Now you be willing to provide the sweat and tears. I promise you based on the authority of the Word of God that your liberation will be worth it.

The following Scripture-prayers specifically address sexual strongholds, but several other chapters in this book involve root issues that also strongly apply. Please consider incorporating some of the Scripture-prayers in "Overcoming Unbelief," "Overcoming Pride," "Overcoming Guilt," and "Overcoming the Enemy" as well. WARNING: The moment the enemy sees that you are becoming serious about being delivered from strongholds and being freed to pursue holiness, he will turn up the heat of temptation. Be alert and stand against him; however, if you happen to fall at times in your journey toward freedom, *do not quit.* Stand up, seek forgiveness, and get back on the freedom trail. Remember, God desires to completely renew our thinking and change our habits. It's a process that takes time. God is not expecting totally unblemished earthly perfection. His Son alone filled that requirement. He is looking for hearts in constant pursuit of Him and His righteousness. Long-term victory results from many short-term victories that finally collide, forming new habits.

Please understand that all of us are utterly powerless to overcome strongholds unless we've accepted Jesus Christ as our Lord and Savior. If you have never actually received Christ for yourself, I would be honored beyond measure to lead you through this simple transforming prayer:

Lord Jesus, I, _____ , have realized I am hopelessly enslaved to sin and that I am powerless to save myself. I acknowledge that You are the Son of God and You have already paid the debt for my sin. All I need to do is claim it personally. I realize now that You died for *me*. You bore every single one of my sins, past, present, and future, when You hung upon the cross. I accept the gift of grace offered to me through Your sacrificial death. I cannot be good enough to work my way into heaven and eternal life with You. You paved the way for me through Your perfect, sinless sacrifice, and I gladly accept Your gift. Come and dwell in me, Jesus, through Your Holy Spirit and set me free to live in Your resurrection life. Thank You, God, in advance that You will never leave me or forsake me.

Lord God, I do not understand what I do. For what I want to do I do not do, but what I hate I do. Sin is living in me. I know that nothing good lives in me, that is, in my sinful nature. For I have the desire to do what is good, but I cannot carry it out. For what I do is not the good I want to do; no, the evil I do not want to do—this I keep on doing. So I find this law at work: When I want to do good, evil is right there with me. (Rom. 7:15–21)

Lord God, in my inner being I delight in Your law; but I see another law at work in the members of my body, waging war against the law of my mind and making me a prisoner of the law of sin at work within my members. How wretched I am! Who will rescue me from this body of death? Thanks be to God—through Jesus Christ our Lord! (Rom. 7:22–25) Lord, You sent Your Son to rescue me from this body of death! Set me free to new life in You, Lord. I do not have to be a prisoner to sin. Please help me understand that the battle that rages over my body originates in my mind. Please help me to surrender my mind to You and to Your truth.

O Lord, You have searched me and You know me. You know when I sit and when I rise; You perceive my thoughts from afar. You discern my going out and my lying down; You are familiar with all my ways. (Ps. 139:1–3) Father, I thank You that while You love me completely, You know everything about me. Help me to be completely truthful with You. I don't need to hide anymore.

Lord God, if I claim to be without sin, I deceive myself and the truth is not in me. If I confess my sins, You are faithful and just and will forgive my sins and purify me from all unrighteousness. (1 John

1:9) Father, please help me to accept the fact that I have not out-sinned Your ability to forgive me! I am still forgivable as I come to You in sincere repentance.

You, God, created my inmost being; You knit me together in my mother's womb. I praise You because I am fearfully and wonderfully made; Your works are wonderful. I know that full well. (Ps. 139:13–14) Father, my body is not horrible. I have simply misused it. Please sanctify it and take it over completely.

Ah, Sovereign Lord, You have made the heavens and the earth by Your great power and outstretched arm. Nothing is too hard for You! (Jer. 32:17)

Lord, I acknowledge to You that I have been led astray. . . . The reason You, the Son of God, appeared was to destroy the devil's work. (1 John 3:7–8) Lord, I have been a willing party to the devil's work. Thank You that You appeared on this earth to die and be raised again to destroy his work. Please destroy the works he has accomplished in me and through me. Set me apart for Your work henceforth, O God.

Lord God, according to Your Word, no one who is born of God will continue to sin, because God's seed remains in him. (1 John 3:9) Please help me to understand and admit that I cannot simply go on and on indefinitely in my sin and claim to belong to You. O, God, if Your Spirit does not presently dwell in me and if I'm not saved from an eternal destiny in hell, please open my eyes and bring me to Your salvation!

This then is how I know that I belong to the truth, and how I set my heart at rest in Your presence whenever my heart condemns me. For You, God, are greater than my heart and You know everything. (1 John 3:19)

Lord God, I acknowledge to You that my body was not meant for sexual immorality, but for You, Lord. You, Lord, were meant to take authority over this body and bring it sanctification and meaning. I know that my body is a member of Christ, Himself. I shall not then take the members of Christ and unite them in an ungodly relationship. (1 Cor. 6:13–15)

In his excellent book, *The Bondage Breaker,* Neil Anderson stresses the importance of renouncing past sins and strongholds. He urges those who have struggled against sexual strongholds to earnestly pray the following:

Lord, I renounce all these uses of my body as an instrument of unrighteousness and by so doing ask You to break all bondages that Satan has brought into my life through that involvement. I confess my participation. I now present my body to You as a living sacrifice, holy and acceptable to You, and I reserve the sexual use of my body only for marriage. I renounce the lie of Satan that my body is not clean, that it is dirty or in any way unacceptable as a result of my past sexual experiences. Lord, I thank You that You have totally cleansed and forgiven me, that You love and accept me unconditionally. Therefore, I can accept myself. And I choose to do so, to accept myself and my body as cleansed. In Jesus' name. Amen.

I know, Lord, that my body is a temple of the Holy Spirit, who is in me, whom I have received from You. I am not my own; I was bought at a price. Therefore I desire to honor You, God, with my body. (1 Cor. 6:19–20)

Father, according to Your Word, a person can be handed over to Satan, so that the sinful nature may be destroyed and his or her spirit saved on the day of the Lord. (1 Cor. 5:5) O, God, please help me not to continue to resist repentance and be handed over to Satan for a season. Please help me to turn my life over to You now.

God, please don't give me over in the sinful desires of my heart to sexual impurity for the degrading of my body with someone else. I admit that I have exchanged the truth of You, God, for a lie. (Rom. 1:24–25)

Lord, if I remain stubborn and unrepentant in heart, Your Word says I am storing up wrath for myself for the day of Your wrath, when Your righteous judgment will be revealed. For those who are self-seeking and who reject the truth and follow evil, there will be wrath and anger. There will be trouble and distress for every human being who does evil . . . but glory, honor, and peace

for everyone who does good. (Rom. 2:5–10) Lord God, help me to see that the "good" You want me to do in response to my sin is to repent and receive Your help and turn my life entirely over to You. I do not have to settle for a life hopelessly entangled in sin. Set me free, Lord.

> *I'm continually amazed with my own failures. But the wonder of it all is that God keeps working on me and through me anyway. I'm convinced He's worked more through my failures than my successes. I'm so grateful the Bible is packed with failures who became champions of the faith: the Peters, the Davids, the Moseses, the John Marks, and the Jonahs. Their stories show me that God isn't looking at our achievements, but at us—and that even my failures can be used for His ultimate glory.*
>
> Tim Hansel, Holy Sweat

God, You demonstrated Your love for me in that while I was still a sinner, You died for me. (Rom. 5:8) Lord, help me to understand that You gave Your life to pay the debt for even the most heinous sins I could have committed. Your grace covers all sin if I will repent and receive.

Christ Jesus, I count myself dead to sin but alive to God in You. Therefore I will not let sin reign in my mortal body so that I obey its evil desires. I choose not to offer the parts of my body to sin, as instruments of wickedness, but rather I offer myself to God, as one who has been brought from death to life. I offer the parts of my body to You as instruments of righteousness. Sin shall not be my master, because I am not under the law but under grace. (Rom. 6:11–14)

Father God, when I've offered myself to sexual sin, I have offered myself as a slave to it. I am a slave to the one whom I obey whether I am a slave to sin, which leads to death, or to obedience, which leads to righteousness. (Rom. 6:16)

Thanks be to You, my God, that, though I used to be a slave to sin, I am wholeheartedly choosing to obey the form of teaching to which I was entrusted. I am being set free from sin and am becoming a slave to righteousness. (Rom. 6:17–18)

Lord, I willingly admit that I am weak in my natural self. I used to offer the parts of my body in slavery to impurity and to ever-increasing wickedness. I now offer them in slavery to righteousness leading to holiness. (Rom. 6:19)

> *Have enough faith, dear reader, to believe that you need mercy. Mercy is not for those who think they have merited it. Such people seek justice, not mercy. Only the guilty need and seek mercy. Believe that God delights in mercy, delights to give grace where it cannot be deserved, delights to forgive where there is no reason for forgiveness but His own goodness. Believe also that the Lord Jesus Christ is the incarnation of mercy. His very existence is mercy to you. His every word means mercy. His life, His death, His intercession in heaven, all mean mercy, mercy, mercy, nothing but mercy. . . . He is the Savior for you.*
>
> *Charles Spurgeon,* Spurgeon on Prayer and Spiritual Warfare

Lord, I admit that I reaped absolutely no benefit from the things I am now ashamed of. Those things result in death. But now that I have been set free, the benefit I am reaping leads to holiness and the result is eternal life. For the wages of sin is death, but the gift of God is eternal life in Christ Jesus my Lord. (Rom. 6:21–23)

Lord God, one of the most important principles I will ever learn about life in the Spirit versus life in the flesh is found in Romans 8:5. Those who live according to the sinful nature have their minds set on what that nature desires; but those who live in accordance with the Spirit have their minds set on what the Spirit desires. The mind of sinful man is death, but the mind controlled by the Spirit is life and peace. (Rom. 8:5–6) Lord, the key to the Spirit-led life is my mind-set. Teach me to feed the Spirit and starve the flesh.

Lord, as I approach You with repentance and the desire to live differently, who is he that condemns? You, Christ Jesus, who died—more than that, who was raised to life—are at the right hand of God and You are interceding for me! No, in all these things I will be more than a conqueror through You who loves me. (Rom. 8:33–34, 37)

Lord God, I know that the wicked will not inherit the kingdom of God. I choose to be deceived no longer: Neither the sexually immoral nor idolaters nor adulterers nor male prostitutes nor homosexual offenders nor thieves nor the greedy nor drunkards nor slanderers nor swindlers will inherit the kingdom of God. And I have been some of those things. But I have now been washed. I have been sanctified, I have been justified in the name of the Lord Jesus Christ and by the Spirit of my God. (1 Cor. 6:9–11)

Father God, Your Word says that I have been made holy through the sacrifice of the body of Jesus Christ. Being holy means that I have been set apart for sacred use rather than common use. I will be tempted at times to think like the unholy person I used to be. (Heb. 10:10) Keep me on track. Help me not to call anything impure that You have made clean. (Acts 10:15)

Lord God, when I was dead in my sins and in the uncircumcision of my sinful nature, You made me alive with Christ. You forgave me all my sins, having canceled the written code, with its regulations, that was against me and that stood opposed to me; You took it away, nailing it to Christ's cross. And having disarmed the powers and authorities, You made a public spectacle of them, triumphing over them by the cross. (Col. 2:13–15)

My merciful God, since I have been raised with Christ, set my heart on things above, where Christ is seated at the right hand of God. Help me set my mind on things above, not on earthly things. (Col. 3:1) Lord, please take my passions and redirect them first and foremost toward You. Be the chief focus of all my passions and create a new heart within me with healthy emotions.

Lord, I have come to understand that my heart is deceitful above all things. (Jer. 17:9) Please help me recognize ways my heart and my feelings are deceiving me.

Father God, help me, enable me, strengthen me to put to death whatever belongs to my earthly nature: sexual immorality, impurity, lust, evil desires and greed, which is idolatry. Because of these, Your wrath is coming. I used to walk in these ways, in the life I once lived. (Col. 3:5) Lord, help me to understand that "putting to death" means to cease empowering it or fueling it or doing things that arouse it to unholy life.

Father God, please help me not to shy away from praying about this extremely important problem. Your Word tells me to pray about everything! (Phil. 4:6) Help me to trust You and pour out my heart to You because You are my refuge. (Ps. 62:8) You will not shame me or turn Your back on me. You want to help me overcome every stronghold.

You wonder, "Am I doomed in my dilemma? I have left the door open for Satan, and he has taken advantage of my spiritual passivity. Can I get him out of the places he has wormed into?" The answer is a resounding yes! Jesus Christ is the Bondage Breaker. But in order to experience His freedom, we must find the doors we left open through which Satan gained engrace. We must say, "Lord, I confess that I am responsible for giving Satan a foothold in my life, and I renounce the involvement with him which has led to my bondage."

Neil Anderson, The Bondage Breaker

Thank You, God, for promising that no temptation has seized me except what is common to man. And You, God, are faithful; You will not let me be tempted beyond what I can bear. But when I am tempted You will also provide a way out so that I can stand up under it. (1 Cor. 10:13)

Lord, Your Word says how I can keep my way pure: by living according to Your Word. I will seek You with all my heart; help me not to stray from Your commands. Help me to hide Your Word in my heart that I might not sin against You. (Ps. 119:9–11)

Holy God, turn my eyes away from worthless things; preserve my life according to Your Word. Take away the disgrace I dread, for Your laws are good. (Ps. 119:37, 39)

Lord God, teach me knowledge and good judgment, for I believe in Your commands. Before I was afflicted I went astray, but now I obey Your Word. You are good, and what You do is good; teach me Your decrees. (Ps. 119:66–68)

Lord God, guard my course and protect my way as I pursue a righteous, victorious life in You. (Prov. 2:8)

Lord, help me not to despise Your discipline and not to resent Your rebuke, because You discipline those You love. (Prov. 3:11–12)

Lord God, Your Word says that You bless the home of the righteous but Your curse is on the house of the wicked. (Prov. 3:33) Lord, please help me cleanse my home of any kind of materials that support or fuel wickedness. Make this the kind of home You can fully bless.

Lord, You detest perversity, but You take the upright into Your confidence. (Prov. 3:32) Please make me a person You can take into Your confidence.

Lord God, help me to guard my heart above all else, for it is the wellspring of life. Help me to put away perversity from my mouth and keep corrupt talk far from my lips. (Prov. 4:23–24)

Lord, help me to keep my eyes looking straight ahead and fix my gaze directly before me. Make level paths for my feet and strengthen me to take only the ways that are firm. Help me not to swerve to the right or the left; keep my feet from evil. (Prov. 4:25–27)

According to Your Word, a man's ways are in full view of the Lord, and You examine all our paths. The evil deeds of a wicked man ensnare him; the cord of his sin holds him fast. He will die for a lack of discipline, led astray by his own great folly. (Prov. 5:21–23) Lord, self-discipline is a fruit of the Spirit. Please fill me with Your Spirit and empower me with a self-discipline only You can give. (Gal. 5:22–23)

God, please help me to love You with my whole heart, soul, mind, and strength, for this is Your priority for my life. (Mark 12:30) Help me also to love others so that I will not want to engage them in any kind of dishonoring activity. (Mark 12:31) Break my heart when I even think of doing what is dishonorable, Lord.

Lord Jesus, whatever is true, whatever is noble, whatever is right, whatever is pure, whatever is lovely, whatever is admirable—if anything is excellent or praiseworthy—help me to think about such things. (Phil. 4:8–9)

You, my God, made Christ who had no sin to be sin for me, so that in Him I might become the righteousness of God. (2 Cor. 5:21)

Lord, who can say, "I have kept my heart pure; I am clean and without sin"? (Prov. 20:9) Lord, I am powerless to possess a pure and clean heart on my own. Only You can do it for me. Create in me a pure heart, O God, and renew a steadfast spirit within me. . . . Restore to me the joy of Your salvation and grant me a willing spirit to sustain me. (Ps. 51:10, 12)

Lord God, You have promised me to one husband, Jesus Christ, and You want to present me as a pure virgin to Him. Please remake me into a pure virgin emotionally, mentally, and spiritually, and even set this body apart to be used as an instrument of righteousness from now on. Please help me not to be deceived by the serpent's cunning and

allow my mind to be led astray from my new commitment of sincere and pure devotion to Christ. (2 Cor. 11:2–3)

Lord God, since I have a great high priest who has gone through the heavens, Jesus Your Son, help me hold firmly to the faith I profess. For I do not have a high priest who is unable to sympathize with my weaknesses, but I have one who has been tempted in every way, just as I am, yet was without sin. Help me then to approach the throne of grace with confidence, so that I may receive mercy and find grace to help me in my time of need. (Heb. 4:14–16)

Father God, through constant use of the solid food of Your Word, help me to train myself to distinguish good from evil. (Heb. 5:14)

> *Why do I share my testimony? For several reasons. When God gave me the gift of life, I believe he coupled it with the desire to share my freedom with others. If I had known there was hope for those struggling with homosexuality, I would have sought it long before I did! I could never withhold salvation and hope from anyone, even though it means the regular sharing of my own deepest wounds and failures. Like Jesus, I was called to lay down my life and my reputation that others might see what redemption looks like.*
>
> *Dennis Jernigan,* This Is My Destiny

Lord of glory, You have a plan for me that no eye has seen, no ear has heard, and no mind has conceived. Your Spirit reveals this awesome plan to those who love You. (1 Cor. 2:9) I acknowledge that Satan's ploy is to keep me from fulfilling Your plan for my life. Please help me to resist him and overcome his assaults on my life. I want to do Your will, O God.

Lord God, I don't want to remain a carnal Christian. I want to be a spiritual believer to whom You can speak and through whom

You can minister. Please activate the mind of Christ in me daily that I may live in victory. (1 Cor. 2:16; 3:1)

> *In the Kingdom, there are no great men of God, just humble men whom God has chosen to use greatly. How do we know when we are humble? When God speaks, we tremble. God is looking for a man who trembles at His Word. Such a man will find the Spirit of God resting upon him; he will become a dwelling place for the Almighty.*
>
> *Francis Frangipane,* Holiness, Truth and the Presence of God

Since I have a great priest over the house of God, help me to draw near to You, God, with a sincere heart in full assurance of faith, having my heart sprinkled to cleanse me from a guilty conscience and having my body washed with pure water. Help me to hold unswervingly to the hope I profess, for He who promises is faithful. (Heb. 10:21–23)

Lord, help me to rid myself of all malice and all deceit, hypocrisy, envy, and slander of every kind. Like a newborn baby, help me to crave pure spiritual milk, so that by it I may grow up in my salvation, now that I have tasted that the Lord is good. (1 Pet. 2:1–2)

I am one of Your chosen people, O God, part of a royal priesthood, a holy nation, a people belonging to God, that I may declare the praises of You who called me out of darkness into Your wonderful light. I have now received mercy. You urge me as a stranger in this world to abstain from sinful desires, which war against my soul. (1 Pet. 2:9–11)

Lord Jesus, You Yourself bore my sins in Your body on the tree, so that I might die to sins and live for righteousness; by Your wounds

I have been healed. For I was like a sheep going astray, but now I have returned to the Shepherd and Overseer of my soul. (1 Pet. 2:24–25)

Lord God, You grant Your incomparably great power to those of us who believe. This same power is the mighty strength You exerted when You raised Christ from the dead. (Eph. 1:20) If You can raise the dead, You have all the power I need to live victoriously over every stronghold!

Christ Jesus, I have been crucified with You, and I no longer live, but You live in me. The life I live in the body, I live by faith in You, the Son of God, who loved me and gave Yourself up for me. (Gal. 2:20)

Lord God, cause my heart, soul, and mind to be so overtaken by Your grace that I share the testimony of the sinful woman who anointed Your feet. You said of her, "I tell you, her many sins have been forgiven—for she loved much. But he who has been forgiven little loves little." (Luke 7:47) Lord Jesus, make our story a love story.

Other Scriptures You Can Pray

Romans 8:8
Revelation 21:3–4, 7–8
Ephesians 5:1–2
Psalm 119:41–42

Isaiah 52:11
Hebrews 7:25–26
2 Peter 3:11

PERSONALIZING YOUR PRAYERS

Chapter 14

OVERCOMING THE ENEMY

J ust in case anyone is still clinging to a few doubts, let me assure you, *the devil is real.* You may be tempted to respond, "Oh, I've always known that." Remember a concept you and I learned in the chapter on "Overcoming Unbelief"? We live our lives not simply according to what we *know,* but what we really *believe.* Genuine belief is life-altering conviction. How we walk with our feet of clay on the hot pavement of life evidences what we truly believe. Like many of you, I was not adequately prepared for the warfare that lay ahead of me in my Christian life even though I had been raised in church. I'm not blaming anyone, but since I represent a serious casualty, I am compelled to tell everyone I know so that someone else might learn in the classroom what I unfortunately learned on a field trip.

Up to my twenties and early thirties, I really didn't give the doctrines concerning warfare and the devil much thought. Oh, I *knew* the basics to some extent. But I'm not sure I really *believed.* In retrospect, I find my ignorance rather ironic because he certainly had tallied numerous victories in my life by then. He is undoubtedly the author of all crimes against children, and he sought me out shamelessly from the time I was a small child. I simply did not realize my enemy was *him.*

My awakening came in my early thirties right after I wrote my first Bible study. At that time I had no idea I would ever write another one and certainly had not the least thought that anything would ever be published. I simply wrote the study for a wonderful group of women I was teaching at the time. I describe part of this time of my life in the chapter entitled "Overcoming Depression" because Satan surrounded me with such darkness *immediately* following the conclusion of that study. Writing the Tabernacle series was my first intensive season with God in our own version of the Holy of Holies, and I literally went skydiving when it was over. I do not want to take up time or space being redundant, so if you are interested in some of the background of the experience I'm about to share with you, please glance back at the chapter on "Overcoming Depression."

Satan wasted absolutely no time getting to me after the completion of my first intensely intimate season with God. The Lord withheld him from me while I was in deep study, but the lion was indeed crouching at my door the moment I came out. The Word clearly tells us that war is raging in the heavenlies over our lives (Eph. 6), and often we don't realize the contest that may be waging over us at any given time.

I am utterly convinced in retrospect that I, like every other servant of God, became of special interest to the devil the moment I surrendered to ministry as a college student. Although I did my best to serve God through serving my church, I was very little threat to the devil because I did not know the truth. In my late twenties, I realized how absolutely illiterate I was in the Word of God, and I surrendered sacrificially to my first Bible doctrine class. Instead of being bored stiff like this sanguine girl expected, my entire soul sprang to life. I began a love affair with Jesus Christ through His Word that has done nothing but spread like a wildfire in my soul since.

At that time I believe I went from being of "interest" to Satan to being a "concern" to Satan. That's when the turn came. I taught a lecture-style class every Thursday at a church in Houston. The ladies came to me and said, "We love coming to this class, and we really want to stay here, but we want homework like some of the other Bible classes are doing." The tears sting in my eyes as I think back on their approach because I now know they were totally influenced by the living God who loved me and gave His Son for me. I laughed and told them I couldn't possibly write homework. I didn't know how. They assured me God would teach me. The tears run down my cheeks as I say to the glory of God: *teach me He did*. In lots of hard ways. In lots of delightful ways. But all of them life-changing ways.

When I wrote the first series, my life transformed dramatically. The enemy watched a forest fire of unquenchable passion ignite my heart for God, and suddenly I went from being an "interest" and a "concern" to being a "threat." At that point, I, like hosts of others who are serious about God, went into the crosshairs of the devil's weapon. You see, we don't become a major threat until we begin to walk relentlessly in truth. Remember, the sword of the Spirit is what Satan wants to avoid at all costs. Satan is a methodical schemer, so while I spent time with God in our Holy of Holies, he went to work on a plan. Satan had a trump card. He knew that I had secrets buried deep within me that I knew nothing about in the conscious realm. He also knew, based upon my past—and my past *record*—that my heart was still deeply wounded and handicapped. I thought I had gotten my act together. I had lived successfully for years . . . but not victoriously. Oh, how wise we are to understand the mammoth difference. *Successfully* can describe how we handle relatively manageable challenges that the unbeliever could manage just as well. We are simply spared any overwhelming challenges for a while. *Victoriously* describes how we live as overcomers in the midst of Goliath opposition.

Please understand, I had no idea what bondage remained in my heart. I have often said that I did not know I was bound until God began to set me free. However, Satan certainly knew. I am utterly convinced that Satan asked to sift me like wheat, just as he has many other servants of God, and that God gave him permission because He knew that what Satan meant for evil, He, my God, would use for good. Satan orchestrated a string of events that still make me shiver. I'll share with you just a few: I finished the first Bible study on a Thursday morning. I felt an immediate and very foreign darkness descend on me like a cloak. I could not begin to comprehend what I was feeling. A lostness of sorts. A horrible feeling of fear as I faced life outside that "Holy of Holies."

The very next day, I had an appointment to meet with a woman from out of town who was also in ministry and had a background of childhood abuse. I believe with all my heart the Holy Spirit warned that I was ill-equipped to counsel this precious woman, but out of respect to the person who asked me to do him the favor, I foolishly agreed. While she was describing the graphic details of her abuse, I began to break out into a drenching sweat and ceased hearing anything she was saying. Somehow her descriptions triggered an excruciating string of memories of my own as if someone had thrown in a videotape recording every horrid detail of my childhood.

Good things also happened in my childhood, but I assure you they weren't recorded on the "tape." As soon as I could excuse myself, I made my way to the car. I was so physically ill, I had to rest my head on the steering wheel until the terrible wave of nausea and trembling subsided enough to drive. My mind was spinning. This was only the beginning.

Satan proceeded with a well-executed web of schemes to destroy me. Even today when I look back and calculate his methodical, perfectly timed assaults, I shudder all over. The intense onslaught of the enemy lasted for months. I suffered terrible nightmares, choking attacks, fear, confusion, unparalleled feelings of powerlessness, and life-despairing defeat. Satan attacked me from every side and continually caught me off guard. He confronted me in unexpected places where he knew I had no experience. As one wave of attack followed another, I feared I would lose all soundness of mind. For a while, if I hadn't loved my family so much, I would have been tempted to give up.

The master deceiver not only capitalized on things in my background that were true; he also interjected distortions and lies. Although the furious part of the battle only raged for a little less than a year, I was not able to sort out the lies from the truth and the distortions from accuracy for several years. God allowed the enemy a certain season of time in which to sift me like wheat . . . and for a little while, Satan held a victory celebration at my expense. I wish so much that I could say I fought him successfully from the beginning, but I did not. He came frightfully close to accomplishing his goal. In the end, Satan did not win. I am, however, not without scars. God uses them to remind me where I've been and where I never want to return.

I am anticipating a reaction I immediately want to address and redirect. I shared the previous testimony not to focus on the resur-

facing of childhood memories of abuse. I shared it so you will see how Satan can get a foothold in areas left untreated by the healing Word of God. I am not a counselor for victims of childhood abuse. Thankfully, God has raised up many trained counselors today, and they are the ones you are wise to contact if you are presently struggling with something similar. Ask your pastor to recommend someone to you if you need extra help. I certainly did. But I want to warn you that in some counseling of child-abuse victims, Satan is having a field day with the whole concept of "memory retrieval." It has almost become faddish. Please be advised that the devil can suggest virtually anything. *Just because we suddenly get a certain picture in our heads does not mean we've experienced it personally.* Please be aware of this rule of thumb: when memory retrieval is authentic, it comes like a missing puzzle piece in the midst of other pieces already out on the table. In other words, I had virtually all of the symptoms of a person who had been the victim of childhood abuse. I was a very tearful, paranoid child much of the time. I went through a period of time in which I pulled my hair out by the handfuls. My adolescent years were wrought with poor decisions in which I felt powerless and out of control. I was deeply unhappy and felt an overwhelming sense of shame that I couldn't even understand. The list could go on and on. You see, by the time the last puzzle pieces fell on the table, *they fit.* Beware of pieces that don't fit the rest of the picture!

You might also be interested to know that I was a successful, popular, well-dressed, well-groomed student working very hard to appear together. I believe that Satan saw a young woman in her early thirties whose heart was a shattered piece of glass still holding itself together. It just needed a good nudge to come crashing to the floor. He broke me, all right. But God brought biblical brokenness from those shattered pieces and humility from my humiliation. God lovingly came to me in my heap of despair and disaster and seemed to kiss the elbows and knees I had scraped in the fall. He said to my heart what I'll try to put into words: "My child, if you're really going to do this thing, you're going to have to give Me unhindered access to your entire heart, mind, soul, and body. Wholeness will come when you've given yourself to Me *wholly* and let Me fill every empty place in your life. Now you've learned what Satan can do. Are you ready to learn how to stand and fight?"

That was my crash course in warfare. I hope so much that you might be able to learn from my experience rather than one of your own. Satan is in a huff because he was hoping I'd be too embarrassed to share it. He was wrong. If my story could help you, it is worth whatever disparaging thoughts someone could think of me. You see, as much as I wish my testimony could be *defeat followed by salvation followed by consistent victory*, it is not. My testimony is *salvation, confusion, misery, defeat, success, more defeat, unmitigated failure, then victory*. . . . In essence, my testimony is that there is life after failure. Abundant, effective, Spirit-filled life . . . for those who are willing to repent hard and work hard! I have a feeling somebody needed to hear that. Yes, God can still use us, but we must fall on our faces in desperation, taking full responsibility for our own sin but no one else's, receive His loving discipline, and walk radically in the truth of God's Word. Without exception, every one of the overcomers I know personally who have come back to their feet after terrible defeat have lived in victory only through a radical walk with Jesus Christ in truth. For folks like me, there's not a lot of gray. I learned the hard way what can happen when you wander too close to a hole. You can fall in.

I'm presently living in victory over the many strongholds Satan had raised in my life. I have been for a matter of years; however, it's up to no one else but me now what my testimony will be. God has graciously allowed me a number of do-overs: hard tests I passed the second time around. I have no doubt more tests will come, but how I pray to pass them! How I pray that though I will undoubtedly stumble, I will not fall. If we're not careful, we can respond to a season of heated warfare with legalism and religious bondage. Beware of trading one area of bondage for another! A genuine walk in truth is a walk of glorious liberty!

Yes, I have surrendered my life to a very radical walk with God, but I'm not miserable, nor do I fight the feeling that "this is what I get for being defeated by the devil." I have come to a place where most often I delight to do God's will, and I see His precepts for me as green lights for victory, peace, joy, fullness, and passion. I was forced to make some radical decisions, but I wouldn't trade the relationship with Jesus Christ I discovered in my desperation for all the spotless track records in the world.

Let me be clear: I never want to go back to that kind of defeat, and I live in alertness daily. The pain was tremendous, and the cost was enormous! However, God used my defeat to bring me to a place of ministry and authenticity I would never have known. I nearly quit ministry over it, which I realize in retrospect was Satan's plan. I am very aware that a few legalistic folks who have rarely done anything wrong would have helped me quit had they known the details of my story . . . but what a shame that would have been. It was not until I was broken that God was released to create in me a new healthy heart and teach me the humility and compassion of a true servant. I have a long way to go, but I have put the devil on alert: he may make my life very difficult but he cannot make me quit. For I, like you, am one of God's dear children, and I have overcome the spirits of darkness because the One who is in me is greater than the one who is in the world (1 John 4:4).

What is my revenge after all the devil has done to me? To let God make me twice the foe of hell I would ever have been otherwise. What is my joy? Walking in truth, so aware of where I have been that I cleave to Christ Jesus like a sash around His priestly robe. My prayer in sharing this testimony is that . . .

- You may be warned that Satan can and will attack God-seeking believers, especially if they appear to pose a threat.
- You may be better equipped to handle your "sifting season" than I was.
- You may find hope if you, too, have been terribly defeated in the past.
- You will never put me on a pedestal because I am "weak in my natural self" just as you are (Rom. 6:19).
- You will walk radically, joyfully, and abundantly in the truth of God's Word.
- You will become a powerful foe of hell.

Tragically, Satan has successfully duped the vast majority of our churches into imbalance regarding all things concerning or threatening him. Our human natures are drawn like magnets to polar points, and we unfortunately apply our fleshly extremes to our pulpits. We tend to give the devil either far too much credit or not nearly enough. I cannot say this strongly enough: it is imperative in the days in which we've been assigned to occupy this earth that believers walk in truth and soundness of doctrine. Just as Christ warned in Matthew 24, we are living in days characterized by a rampant increase of deception and wickedness. Satan knows the biblical signs of Christ's imminent return far better than we do, and he is furious because he knows his time is short (Rev. 12:12). Therefore, he has moved into comparative nuclear arms in his war against us while we're still using popguns in our war against him. I am no expert on biblical warfare, but God has purposely chosen to burden my heart with the unnecessary defeat of believers in Jesus Christ and made me an ambassador of the message of victory. A war of unprecedented proportions is waging against the Church and the people of God. We must put on our armor, learn how to use our weapons, and fight with the confidence of those who know they are destined to win.

In addition to learning how to use the sword of the Spirit effectively, the time has come for us to pray fervently for great spiritual discernment to keep our feet balanced on the battlefield. The Word of God commands us not to be ignorant of Satan's devices, but we are also strongly warned to keep our focus on Jesus Christ. The Word of God poses a plumb line for how much attention we might give to concepts *concerning* or *applying* to Satan and victory over our enemies. The concept arises as early as Genesis 3; then we are warned in Genesis 4:7 that "sin is crouching at your door; it desires to have you, but you must master it." The Book of Exodus offers volumes of applications to those who are captive in their own Egypts, desperate for deliverance. Deuteronomy and Numbers also address the extreme importance of obedience to the Word of God if we intend to live in victory while surrounded by enemies. The Book of Joshua is perhaps unparalleled in its Old Testament applications to the New Testament believer who seeks to live as "more than a conqueror." The Book of Judges has plenty to say about the undeniable link between sin and defeat.

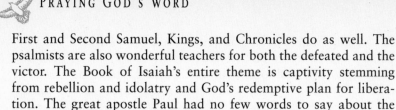

First and Second Samuel, Kings, and Chronicles do as well. The psalmists are also wonderful teachers for both the defeated and the victor. The Book of Isaiah's entire theme is captivity stemming from rebellion and idolatry and God's redemptive plan for liberation. The great apostle Paul had no few words to say about the tragedy of defeat and the call to consistent victory in his New Testament epistles. Peter's epistles also come from somewhat a resident expert since he had been personally "sifted like wheat" by the master of deception himself. The Bible, of course, concludes with the Magna Carta of war, judgment, and eternal victory in the amazing Book of Revelation.

As you can see, much of the Word applies specifically to the battles we face. However, the Bible consists of sixty-six books, most of which I have not named above. My point? The Bible has *much* to say about fighting the good fight of faith and becoming well-trained soldiers . . . but it also has far *more* to say about the pure pursuit of God, His righteousness, and His plan for us. I believe a wise conclusion to draw from the emphases in the Word of God is: give *much* time and thought to becoming well-equipped victors in the battle that rages, but give *more* time to the pursuit of the heart of God and all things concerning Him. Much about warfare. *More about God Himself.*

The following Scripture-prayers are for times when you are certain or suspicious that Satan is trying to defeat you. Believer, victory is your inherited right. Claim it.

O God, how I thank You for seeing my misery and hearing my cries because of Satan, the slave driver. You are concerned about my suffering. Come down to rescue me, O Lord, and bring me to the place of Your promise. (Exod. 3:7–8)

Lord God, You are the Great I AM. (Exod. 3:14) This is Your name *forever!* (Exod. 3:15) My enemy cannot begin to stand against You.

I will sing to You, Lord, for You are highly exalted. The horse and its rider You have hurled into the sea! You, Lord, are my strength and my song; You have become my salvation. You are my God and I will praise You. You, Lord, are a warrior! The Lord is Your name! (Exod. 15:1–3)

Your right hand, O Lord, is majestic in power. Your right hand, O Lord, shatters the enemy. In the greatness of Your majesty, You will throw down those who oppose You. You will unleash Your burning anger; it will consume them like stubble. (Exod. 15:6–7)

Lord God, the enemy boasted, "I will pursue, I will overtake them. I will divide the spoils; I will gorge myself on them. I will draw my sword and my hand will destroy them." But You can blow with Your breath and cause the sea to cover my enemy! You can cause my enemy to sink like lead in the mighty waters! (Exod. 15:9–10) Lord, Your power has not diminished since the days when You revealed Your power and glory as You fought for Israel. I am Your child too. Fight for me, God! Overpower the one who seeks to overpower me!

Who among the gods is like You, O Lord? Who is like You— majestic in holiness, awesome in glory, working wonders? Stretch out Your right hand and deal with my enemy, O God! (Exod. 15:11–12)

> *To topple the "stronghold of our experiences" we must "let God be found true, though every man be found a liar" (Rom. 3:4, NASB). The only One who has a right to shape our lives is Jesus Christ. We must determine to allow nothing and no one to shape us, not even our personal experiences, unless they are consistent with the promises of God. In truth, who is ruling our lives, God or our experiences?*
>
> Francis Frangipane, The Three Battlefields

Father God, I thank You that those who belong to You were meant to be the head, not the tail! If I am obedient to You, the Lord my God, and do not turn aside from Your ways, You will

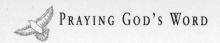

not allow the enemy to keep me at the bottom. (Deut. 28: 13–14)

There is no one like You, the God of Jeshurun, who rides on the heavens to help me and on the clouds in Your majesty! You, the eternal God, are my refuge, and underneath me are Your everlasting arms. You will drive out my enemy before me, saying, "Destroy him!" (Deut. 33:26–27)

Who is like Your children, O God, a people saved by the Lord? You are my shield and helper and my glorious sword. Cause my enemy to cower, Lord! Trample down his high places. (Deut. 33:29)

Lord God, when Your children, the Israelites, were defeated in a battle, You revealed to them that they were hanging on to something that did not belong to them. You said, "You cannot stand against your enemies until you remove it." (Josh. 7:13) Father God, I earnestly ask You to reveal anything in my life that could be hindering victory, then give me the courage to release it to You.

> *Satan dines on what we withhold from God.*
>
> *Francis Frangipane,* The Three Battlefields

Keep me safe, O God, for in You I take refuge. I say to You, Lord, "You are my Lord; apart from you I have no good thing." (Ps. 16:1–2)

Lord, my God, show the wonder of Your great love, You who save by Your right hand those who take refuge in You from their foes. Keep me as the apple of Your eye; hide me in the shadow of Your wings from the wicked who assail me. (Ps. 17:7–9)

Lord God, I feel like the enemy has tracked me down. I feel as if he has tried to surround me, with eyes alert, to throw me to the ground. He is like a lion hungry for prey, like a great lion crouching in cover. Rise up, O Lord, and confront him. Bring him down! Rescue me from his wickedness! (Ps. 17:11–13)

I love You, O Lord, my strength! You are my Rock, my Fortress, and my Deliverer; You, my God, are my Rock, in whom I take refuge. You are my Shield and the horn of my salvation, my Stronghold! I call to You, O Lord, who is worthy of praise, and I am saved from my enemies! (Ps. 18:1–3)

Lord God, the cords of death have entangled me; the torrents of destruction are overwhelming me. The cords of the grave have coiled around me; the snares of death are confronting me. In my distress I am calling to You, Lord. I am crying to You, my God, for help. From Your temple hear my voice; let my cry come before You, into Your ears. (Ps. 18:4–6)

Lord God, look upon the enemy that oppresses me and let smoke rise from Your nostrils! Let consuming fire come from Your mouth. Part the heavens and come down! Mount the cherubim and fly! Soar on the wings of the wind! Shoot Your arrows and scatter my enemy. (Ps. 18:8–10, 14)

Leap up at the sound of this promise! Believe it. Let it go down into your souls. "The LORD *looseth the prisoners" (Ps. 146:7,* KJV*). He has come to loose you. I can see my Master arrayed in His silk garments. His countenance is as joyous as heaven, His face is as bright as a morning without clouds, and in His hand He holds a silver key. "Where are you going, my Master, with that silver key of Yours?" I ask. "I go," He says, "to open the door of the captive and to loosen everyone who is bound." Blessed Master, fulfill Your errand . . . !*

Charles Spurgeon, Spurgeon on Prayer and Spiritual Warfare

Reach down from on high, my God and my Redeemer, and take hold of me! Draw me out of deep waters. Rescue me from my powerful enemy, from my foes, who are too strong for me! My enemy has confronted me in the day of my disaster, but You, Lord, are my support! Bring me to a spacious place; rescue me because You delight in me! (Ps. 18:16–19)

You, O Lord, keep my lamp burning; my God, You turn my darkness into light. With Your help I can advance against a troop; with You, my God, I can scale a wall! (Ps. 18:28–29)

As for You, my God, Your way is perfect; Your Word is flawless. You are a shield for all who take refuge in You. (Ps. 18:30)

Who is my God, except for You, Lord? And who is my Rock except for my God? It is You, God, who arms me with strength and makes my way perfect. You make my feet like the feet of a deer; You enable me to stand on the heights. You train my hands for battle. (Ps. 18:31–34)

You give me Your shield of victory, and Your right hand sustains me; You stoop down to make me great. You broaden the path beneath me, so that my ankles do not turn. . . . Arm me with strength for the battle; make my adversary bow at my feet. Make my enemy turn back in flight. Thank You, God! One day You will utterly destroy my foe! (Ps. 18:35–36, 39–40)

The Lord lives! Praise be to my Rock! Exalted be God my Savior! You are the God who avenges me, who subdues and saves me from my enemy! Therefore, I will praise You among the nations, O Lord; I will sing praises to Your name. You give great victories, Lord God; You show Your unfailing kindness to Your anointed ones. (Ps. 18:46–50)

Lord God, I will shout for joy when You make me victorious, and I will lift up a banner in the name of my God! Please, Lord, grant these requests! (Ps. 20:5)

Some trust in chariots and some in horses, but I trust in the name of You, the Lord my God. My enemy will be brought to his knees and ultimately fall, but I will rise up and stand firm. (Ps. 20:7–8)

Father, I joyfully celebrate the fact that one day, at the time of Your appearing, You will make my enemy like a fiery furnace. In Your wrath You will swallow him up, and Your fire will consume him. (Ps. 21:9)

Though my enemy plots evil against me and devises wicked schemes, he will not succeed if I am walking with You, O God. You will make him turn his back when You aim at him with drawn bow. Be exalted, O Lord, in Your strength! I will sing and praise Your might! (Ps. 21:11–13)

I trust in You, Lord, so I'll let You rescue me. Teach me to delight in You and deliver me, O God. (Ps. 22:8)

> *When the Archenemy finds a weak place in the walls of our castles, he takes care where to plant his battering ram and begin his siege. You may conceal your infirmity, even from your dearest friend, but you will not conceal it from your worst Enemy. He has lynx eyes and detects in a moment the weak point in your armor. He goes about with a match, and though you may think you have covered all the gunpowder of your heart, he knows how to find a crack to put his match through. Much mischief will he do, unless eternal mercy prevents.*
>
> *Charles Spurgeon,* Spurgeon on Prayer and Spiritual Warfare

Do not be far from me, Lord, for trouble is near and there is no one to help. . . . I feel like roaring lions tearing their prey open, their mouths wide against me. (Ps. 22:11, 13)

To You, O Lord, I lift up my soul; in You I trust, O my God. Do not let me be put to shame, nor let my enemies triumph over me. (Ps. 25:1–2)

Guard my life and rescue me, O Lord. Let me not be put to shame, for I take refuge in You. May integrity and uprightness protect me, because my hope is in You. (Ps. 25:20–21)

You, the Lord, are my light and my salvation—whom shall I fear? You, the Lord, are the stronghold of my life—of whom shall I be afraid? When evil advances against me to devour my flesh, when my enemy and my foe attacks me, cause him to stumble and fall. Though an unseen army besiege me, cause my heart not to fear; though war break out against me, even then will I be confident. . . . Because . . . one thing I ask of the Lord, this is what I seek: that I may dwell in the house of the Lord all the days of my life, to gaze upon the beauty of the Lord and to seek You in Your temple. (Ps. 27:1–4)

Lord God, in the day of trouble, keep me safe in Your dwelling. Hide me in the shelter of Your tabernacle and set me high upon a rock. Cause my head to be exalted above the enemy surrounding me. Then remind me to offer You the sacrifice with shouts of joy, and help me to sing and make music to You, Lord! (Ps. 27:5–6)

Turn Your ear to me, O Lord. Come quickly to my rescue; be my rock of refuge, a strong fortress to save me. Since You are my rock and my fortress, for the sake of Your name lead and guide me. (Ps. 31:2–3)

Mighty God, free me from the trap that is set for me, for You are my refuge. . . . You have not handed me over to the enemy but have set my feet in a spacious place. (Ps. 31:4, 8)

I trust in You, O Lord; I say, "You are my God." My times are in Your hands; deliver me from my enemies and those who pursue me. Let Your face shine on Your servant; save me in Your unfailing love. Let me not be put to shame, O Lord, for I have cried out to you. (Ps. 31:14–17)

> Victory begins with the name of Jesus on our lips. It is consummated by the nature of Jesus in our hearts. *Most Christians only engage in spiritual warfare with the hope of either relieving present distresses or attaining a "normal existence." However, the purpose of all aspects of spirituality, warfare included, is to bring us into the image of Christ. Nothing, not worship nor warfare, neither love nor deliverance, is truly attainable if we miss the singular objective of our faith: Christlikeness.*
>
> Francis Frangipane, The Three Battlegrounds

Let everyone who is godly pray to You while You may be found; surely when the mighty waters rise, they will not reach me! You are my hiding place; You will protect me from trouble and surround me with songs of deliverance. (Ps. 32:6–7)

Contend, O Lord, with those who contend with me; fight against those who fight against me. Take up shield and buckler; arise and come to my aid. Brandish spear and javelin against those who pursue me; say to my soul, "I am your salvation." (Ps. 35:1–3)

My whole being will exclaim, "Who is like You, O LORD? You rescue the poor from those too strong for them, the poor and needy from those who rob them." (Ps. 35:10)

O Lord, You have seen this; be not silent. Do not be far from me, O Lord. Awake, and rise to my defense! Contend for me, my God and my Lord. Vindicate me in Your righteousness, O Lord my God; do not let them gloat over me. (Ps. 35:22–24)

Father God, according to Your Word, the wicked lie in wait for the righteous, seeking their very lives; but You will not leave them in their power or let them be condemned when brought to trial. (Ps. 37:32–33)

Lord God, You are my stronghold in time of trouble. Help me and deliver me; deliver me from the wicked and save me, because I take refuge in You. (Ps. 37:39–40)

Do not withhold Your mercy from me, O Lord; may Your love and Your truth always protect me. For troubles without number surround me; my sins have overtaken me, and I cannot see. They are more than the hairs of my head, and my heart fails within me. Be pleased, O Lord, to save me; O Lord, come quickly to help me. (Ps. 40:11–13)

Blessed is he who has regard for the weak; for You, Lord, deliver him in times of trouble. You, Lord, will protect Him and preserve His life; You will bless him in the land and not surrender him to the desire of his foes. (Ps. 41:1–2)

Gird Your sword upon Your side, O Mighty One; clothe Yourself with splendor and majesty. In Your majesty ride forth victoriously in behalf of truth, humility, and righteousness; let Your right hand display awesome deeds. (Ps. 45:3–4)

Lord of heaven and earth, help me to be still and know You are God; You will be exalted among the nations. You will be exalted in the earth. You, Lord Almighty, are with me; the God of Jacob is my fortress. (Ps. 46:10–11)

God, You have ascended amid shouts of joy, the Lord amid the sounding of trumpets. For You, God, are the King of all the earth; I will sing to You a psalm of praise. You reign over all, and You are seated on Your holy throne. (Ps. 47:5–8)

Listen to my prayer, O God, do not ignore my plea; hear me and answer me. My thoughts trouble me, and I am distraught at the voice of the enemy. (Ps. 55:1–3) I will cast my cares on You, Lord, and You will sustain me. (Ps. 55:22) As for me, I trust in You. (Ps. 55:23b)

From the ends of the earth I call to You, O Lord. I call as my heart grows faint; lead me to the rock that is higher than I. For You have been my refuge, a strong tower against the foe. (Ps. 61:2–3)

Praise You, my God! Let the sound of Your praise be heard; You have preserved my life and kept my feet from slipping. For You, O God, tested me; You refined me like silver. (Ps. 66:8–10)

May You arise, God, may Your enemies be scattered; may Your foes flee before You. I desire to sing to You, O God, and sing praises in Your name. I extol You who rides on the clouds—Your name is the Lord. I rejoice before You! (Ps. 68:1, 4)

O God, Your chariots are tens of thousands and thousands of thousands! The Lord has come into His sanctuary. Praise be to the Lord, to God my Savior, who daily bears my burdens. My God is a God who saves; from the Sovereign Lord comes escape from death. (Ps. 68:17, 19–20)

I pray to You, O Lord, in the time of Your favor; in Your great love, O God, answer me with Your sure salvation. Rescue me from the mire, do not let me sink; deliver me from those who hate me, from the deep waters. Do not let the floodwaters engulf me or the depths swallow me up or the pit close its mouth over me. Answer me, O Lord, out of the goodness of Your love; in Your great mercy turn to me. Do not hide Your face from Your servant; answer me quickly, for I am in trouble. (Ps. 69:13–17)

O Lord, be my rock of refuge, to which I can always go; give the command to save me, for You are my rock and my fortress. (Ps. 71:3)

I am always with You, O God. You hold me by my right hand. You guide me with Your counsel, and afterward You will take me into glory. Whom have I in heaven but You? And earth has nothing I desire besides You. My flesh and my heart may fail, but God is the strength of my heart and my portion forever. (Ps. 73:23–26)

Father God, You said of Your children long ago, "If my people would but listen to me, if Israel would follow my ways, how quickly would I subdue their enemies and turn my hand against their foes!" (Ps. 81:13–14) Lord God, please help me to listen carefully to You and follow Your ways so that I will not hinder my own victory through disobedience.

Help me to dwell in the shelter of You, the Most High, so that I may rest in Your shadow, Almighty One. Cover me with Your feathers, and help me to find refuge under Your wings. Let Your faithfulness be my shield and rampart. Help me not to fear the terror of night nor the arrow that flies by day. (Ps. 91:1, 4–5) Help me to make You, the Most High, my dwelling, and let no harm befall me nor disaster come near my tent. Thank You, Father, for commanding Your angels concerning me to guard me in all my ways. (Ps. 91:9–11)

Father, allow my eyes to see the defeat of my adversary. Let my ears hear the rout of my wicked foe. (Ps. 92:11) Cause me to still bear fruit in old age, . . . proclaiming, "The LORD is upright; he is my rock, and there is no wickedness in him." (Ps. 92:14–15)

> *We must realize that it is not Satan who defeats us; it is our openness to him. To perfectly subdue the devil we must walk in the "shelter of the Most High" (Ps. 91:1). Satan is tolerated for one purpose: the warfare between the devil and God's saints thrusts us into Christ-likeness, where the nature of Christ becomes our only place of rest and security. God allows warfare to facilitate His eternal plan, which is to make man in His image.*
>
> Francis Frangipane, The Three Battlegrounds

You, Lord, reign! You are robed in majesty and You are armed with strength! Your throne was established long ago: You are from all eternity. You are mightier than the thunder of the great waters, mightier than the breakers of the sea—the Lord on high is mighty! (Ps. 93:1–2, 4)

The Lord reigns; let the earth be glad; Let the distant shores rejoice. Fire goes before You, Lord, and consumes Your foes on every side. Your lightning lights up the world; the earth sees and trembles. The mountains melt like wax before You, Lord. The heavens proclaim Your righteousness and all the people see Your glory. (Ps. 97:1, 3–6)

In my anguish I cry to You, Lord. Answer me by setting me free! You, the Lord, are with me; I will not be afraid. The Lord is with me; He is my helper. I will look in triumph on my enemy. (Ps. 118:5–7)

O Lord, my God, though I walk in the midst of trouble, You preserve my life; You stretch out Your hand against the anger of my foes, with Your right hand You save me. You, Lord, will fulfill Your purpose for me; Your love, O Lord, endures forever—You will not abandon the works of Your hands. (Ps. 138:7–8)

Let the morning bring me word of Your unfailing love, for I have put my trust in You. Show me the way I should go, for to You I lift up my soul. Rescue me from my enemies, O Lord, for I hide myself in You. Teach me to do Your will, for You are my God; may Your good Spirit lead me on level ground. For Your name's sake, O Lord, preserve my life; in Your righteousness, bring me out of trouble. In Your unfailing love, silence my enemies; destroy all my foes, for I am Your servant. (Ps. 143:8–12)

Praise be to You, the Lord my Rock, who trains my hands for war, my fingers for battle. You are my loving God and my fortress, my stronghold and my deliverer, my shield, in whom I take refuge. Part Your heavens, O Lord, and come down; touch the mountains, so that they smoke. Send forth lightning and scatter the enemy; shoot Your arrows and rout them. Reach down Your hand from on high; deliver me and rescue me! (Ps. 144:1–2, 5–7)

Father, I pray that You will cause no weapon forged against me to prevail. Enable me to refute the tongue of my accuser. Thank You for giving this as a heritage to Your servants, O Lord. (Isa. 54:17)

Lord, I have heard of Your fame; I stand in awe of Your deeds, O Lord. Renew them in our day, in our time make them known. (Hab. 3:2)

Father God, help me to remember how Your Son responded when repeatedly tempted by the devil when He was in the wilderness. He responded to Him with Your Word! (Matt. 4:1–11) Help me to hide Your Word in my heart (Ps. 119:11), so that I am ready to resist when the enemy taunts me with temptation.

> *In the battles of life, your peace is actually a weapon. Indeed, your confidence declares that you are not falling for the lies of the devil. You see, the first step toward having spiritual authority over the adversary is having peace in spite of our circumstances. When Jesus confronted the devil, He did not confront Satan with His emotions or in fear. Knowing that the devil was a liar, He simply refused to be influenced by any other voice than God's. His peace overwhelmed Satan, His authority then shattered the lie, which sent demons fleeing.*
>
> Francis Frangipane, The Three Battlegrounds

Dear Lord, please lead me not into temptation but deliver me from the evil one. (Matt. 6:13)

Father God, according to Your Word, wickedness will increase as the time of Your return draws nearer. (Matt. 24:12) Prepare me through prayer and Your Word to stand firm when I am under the attack of the evil one.

Lord God, if You ever give Satan permission to sift me as wheat, I earnestly pray to be faithful to You and to emerge from the difficult season with a fresh ability to strengthen my brothers and sisters in Christ. (Luke 22:31)

Father, help me to understand that Satan, the ultimate thief, comes only to steal and kill and destroy; You came so I could have life and have it more abundantly. (John 10:10)

Thank You, God, that You know Your sheep. You give us eternal life and we shall never perish. No one can snatch me out of Your hand. (John 10:27–29)

Father God, I thank You that because I am in Christ, Satan, the prince of this world, has no hold on me. (John 14:30)

Father, according to Your Word, in this world I will have trouble, but I am to take heart! You have overcome the world! (John 16:33)

Father God, protect me by the power of Your name. (John 17:11) Your Son's prayer for me is not that You presently take me out of the world but that You protect me from the evil one. (John 17:15)

Father God, according to Your Word, the devil is an enemy of everything that is right, full of all kinds of deceit and trickery, perverting the right ways of the Lord. (Acts 13:10) Please help me not to be influenced by him in any way.

Victorious God, I celebrate the fact that You, the God of peace, will soon crush Satan under Your feet, and until then the grace of our Lord Jesus Christ is with us. (Rom. 16:20)

Lord, Your Word is clear that there is no harmony between You and the devil. (2 Cor. 6:15) Make me aware of any possible ways I am unknowingly in harmony with any of his works.

Father God, as a spouse, please make me aware of the enemy's schemes against marriage. Help my spouse and me not to deprive one another of physical intimacy except by mutual consent and for a time, so that we may devote ourselves to prayer. Even then we must come together again so that Satan will not tempt us because of our lack of self-control. (1 Cor. 7:5)

My Father, please help me to be on my guard; stand firm in the faith; be a person of courage; be strong; and to do everything in love. (1 Cor. 16:13)

Lord God, according to Your Word, the god of this age has blinded the minds of unbelievers, so that they cannot see the light of

the gospel of the glory of Christ, who is the image of God. (2 Cor. 4:4) Your Word also says that only in Christ is the veil removed. (2 Cor. 3:14) O, Father, please cause my lost loved ones to turn to You so that the veil will be taken away. (2 Cor. 3:16)

Mighty God, Your Word clearly states that Satan himself masquerades as an angel of light. Help me to be very discerning because his servants also masquerade as servants of righteousness. (2 Cor. 11:14)

Almighty God, help me to be strong in You and in Your mighty power. Help me to put on the full armor of You, God, that I can take my stand against the devil's schemes. For my struggle is not against flesh and blood, but against the rulers, against the authorities, against the powers of this dark world, and against the spiritual forces of evil in the heavenly realms. I must, therefore, put on the full armor of God, so that when the day of evil comes, I may be able to stand my ground, and after I have done everything, to stand. (Eph. 6:10–13)

Help me, God, to stand firm with the belt of truth buckled around my waist, with the breastplate of righteousness in place, and with my feet fitted with the readiness that comes from the gospel of peace. In addition to all this, help me to take up the shield of faith, with which I can extinguish all the flaming arrows of the evil one. Help me to take the helmet of salvation and the sword of the Spirit, which is the Word of God. Help me to pray in the Spirit on all occasions with all kinds of prayers and requests. With this in mind, help me to be alert and always keep on praying for all the saints. (Eph. 6:14–18)

My Father, please help me always to know You are near and not to be anxious about anything, but in everything, by prayer and petition, with thanksgiving, present my requests to You. If I do, Your peace, which transcends all understanding, will guard my heart and mind in Christ Jesus. (Phil. 4:5–7)

Glorious God, I thank You for qualifying me to share in the inheritance of the saints in the kingdom of light. For You have rescued me from the dominion of darkness and brought me into the kingdom of the Son You love, in whom I have redemption, the forgiveness of sins. (Col. 1:12–14)

Father God, thank You for making me alive with Christ when I was dead in my sins and in the uncircumcision of my sinful nature. You forgave me all my sins, having canceled the written code, with its regulations, that was against me and that stood opposed to me. Christ took it away, nailing it to His cross. And having disarmed the powers and authorities, Christ Jesus made a public spectacle of them, triumphing over them by the cross. (Col. 2:13–15)

> *Let us recall that the Lord delivered the ancient Hebrews out of Egypt so He could bring them into the Promised Land. Likewise, we are delivered out of sin, not that we might live for ourselves, but that we might come into Christlikeness. Our goals must align with God's, for if our nature does not change, we will invariably find ourselves entangled in the same problems that caused our difficulties in the first place.*
>
> Francis Frangipane, The Three Battlegrounds

Lord, the Spirit clearly says that in later times some will abandon the faith and follow deceiving spirits and things taught by demons. (1 Tim. 4:1) Please, heavenly Father, help me to stand firm in the faith and not be deceived in a time of growing deception.

Lord God, Your Word tells me that I must be self-controlled and alert. My enemy the devil prowls around like a roaring lion looking for someone to devour. Please empower me to resist him, standing firm in the faith, because I can know my brothers and sisters throughout the world are undergoing the same kind of sufferings. (1 Pet. 5:8–9)

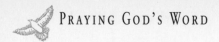

Father God, deliver me from the lion's mouth just like You did the apostle Paul. Rescue me from every evil attack and bring me safely to Your heavenly kingdom. To You be glory for ever and ever. Amen. (2 Tim. 4:17–18)

Father God, how I praise You that the reason the Son of God appeared was to destroy the devil's work. No one who is born of God will continue to sin, because God's seed remains in him; he cannot go on sinning, because he has been born of God. (1 John 3:8–9)

Lord, Your Word tells me not to believe every spirit, but to test the spirits to see whether they are from God, because many false prophets have gone out into the world. (1 John 4:1) Father, please teach me how to follow this command accurately and effectively. Thank You for assuring me that because I am Your dear child, I have overcome all spirits not of God because the One who is in me is greater than the one who is in the world. (1 John 4:4)

My faithful Father, help me to have absolute assurance that I am a child of God because the whole world system is presently under the control of the evil one. (1 John 5:19)

Father God, help me to recognize and understand how Satan's role as accuser of believers affects me. Your Word says he accuses Christians day and night. (Rev. 12:10) Please help me to discern the difference between true conviction of sin from the Holy Spirit and wrongful accusation from the kingdom of darkness.

Father, Your Word tells me that the accuser of believers is overcome by the blood of the Lamb and by the word of our testimony. (Rev. 12:11) Please help me to use the power You have given me to overcome the enemy when he wars against me.

Lord God, according to Your Word much woe has come to the earth and the sea because the devil has come down to us. He is filled with fury because he knows his time is short. (Rev. 12:12) I rejoice, Father, that the enemy's time is short. Please give me wisdom and power to respond effectively when I am subjected to his wicked fury.

Spiritual authority is not a tug-of-war on a horizontal plane; it is a vertical chain of command. Jesus Christ has all authority in heaven and on earth (Matt. 28:18); He's at the top. He has given His authority and power to His servants to be exercised in His name (Luke 10:17); we're underneath Him. And Satan and his demons? They're at the bottom, subject to the authority Christ has invested in us. They have no more right to rule your life than a buck private has to order a general to clean the latrine. Why, then, does the kingdom of darkness exert such negative influence in the world and in the lives of Christians? In a word, the lie. Satan is not an equal power with God; he is a vanquished foe. But if he can deceive you into believing that he has more power and authority than you do, you will live as if he does!

Neil Anderson, The Bondage Breaker

Christ Jesus, I acknowledge that You are the ultimate mighty warrior. There is none like You! No power equals Your power! You are transcendent over all! When I feel overwhelmed with evil all around me, help me rejoice in the vision of the apostle John, who saw heaven standing open and there before him was a white horse, whose rider is called Faithful and True. With justice You will judge and make war. Your eyes will be like blazing fire, and on Your head will be many crowns. You have a name written on You that no one knows but You Yourself. You will be dressed in a robe dipped in blood, and Your name is the Word of God. The armies of heaven will follow you, riding on white horses and dressed in fine linen, white and clean. Out of Your mouth will come a sharp sword with which to strike down the nations. You will rule them with an iron scepter. You will tread the winepress of the fury of the wrath of God Almighty. On Your robe and on Your thigh You have this name written: King of kings and Lord of lords. (Rev. 19:11–16)

Lord God, I thank You for the assurance that my enemy and accuser is a defeated foe. He will be judged for all his deception, wickedness, perversion, and lust to see people lost and tormented. The devil, who has deceived so many, will be thrown into the lake of burning sulfur where he will be tormented day and night forever and ever. (Rev. 20:10)

Father God, how I look forward to an eternity void of the kingdom of darkness. No longer will there be any curse. The throne of God and of the Lamb will be in the city, and Your servants will serve You. We will see Your face, and Your name will be on our foreheads. There will be no more night. We will not need the light of a lamp or the light of the sun, for You, the Lord God, will give us light. And we will enjoy Your reign forever and ever. (Rev. 22:3–5)

> *Oh, Archfiend, how you are taken in your own net! You threw a stone that fell on your own head. You made a pit for Job, but fell into it yourself. You are taken in your own craftiness. . . . Beloved, let us commit ourselves in faith to the care and keeping of God. Come poverty, come sickness, come death, we will in all things through Jesus Christ's blood be conquerors. By the power of His Spirit, we will overcome at the last. . . . And God will have all the praise in us all, forevermore. Amen.*
>
> *Charles Spurgeon,* Spurgeon on Prayer and Warfare

OTHER SCRIPTURES YOU CAN PRAY

Exodus 3:9–10
Exodus 15:13, 16, 18
Joshua 1:8
Joshua 1:9
Psalm 16:7–8
Psalm 21:1
Psalm 21:7
Psalm 33:20–21
Psalm 34:22
Psalm 40:1–3
Psalm 62:5–8
Psalm 69:33

Psalm 80:3
Psalm 86:1–2
Psalm 102:17, 19–20
Isaiah 64:4
Matthew 22:37–39
John 17:17
1 Corinthians 15:24–25
Philippians 1:27–28
2 Thessalonians 3:3
2 Timothy 2:9

PERSONALIZING YOUR PRAYERS

Chapter 15

NOW, IT'S YOUR TURN!

Perhaps you've looked in vain to find your most overwhelming personal obstacle addressed in this book. One vital goal I have for this resource is that you would be able to follow the approach on your own. Using a Bible concordance or a topical Bible resource, search for Scriptures pertaining to any issue that is preoccupying you and robbing you of abundant life. You may not find a detailed description of your stronghold in Scripture, but you will most definitely be able to find verses that apply. First of all, ask God to guide you (Ps. 25:4–5) and to open Your eyes to His Word (Ps. 119:18). Second, if you're not sure how to use Bible resources like a concordance, ask your pastor or a Christian friend or Bible teacher to help you. Once you've found a list of pertinent Scriptures, simply rewrite them into prayer and start using them! You will be immensely blessed by searching for various topics in Scripture and in the process, you'll discover treasures you didn't even know to hunt!

The following section is provided to give you a head start in practicing your own Scripture-prayers. Two common strongholds many people struggle to overcome are fear and anger. In this final chapter, I have supplied several Scripture references that pertain to each stronghold. Whether either of these issues is a stronghold for you or you simply want the practice, read the references then rewrite the Scriptures into prayers in the space provided. I've also provided space for you to continue on with the Scriptures you find on your own. At the conclusion of the book, you will find lined pages so that you can fill them in with your own subjects and Scripture-prayers.

Beloved, you will never waste time in God's Word.
Your Bible is filled with indescribable treasures! Enjoy the dig!

OVERCOMING FEAR

Psalm 27:1 _____

_____

_____

Psalm 46:1–2 _____

_____

_____

Psalm 56:3–4 _____

_____

_____

Romans 8:15 _____

_____

_____

Psalm 34:4 _____

_____

_____

Isaiah 41:10 _____

_____

_____

Isaiah 41:13–14 _____

_____

_____

Isaiah 43:1–3 _____

_____

_____

Hebrews 13:5–6 _____

_____

_____

Proverbs 14:26_____

_____

_____

Isaiah 35:3–4 _____

_____

_____

Hebrews 2:14–15 _____

_____

_____

PRAYING GOD'S WORD

OVERCOMING ANGER AND BITTERNESS

Ephesians 4:30–31 _____

_____

_____

James 1:19–21 _____

_____

_____

Colossians 3:15–16_____

_____

_____

Psalm 71:20 _____

_____

_____

Hebrews 12:15 _____

_____

_____

James 3:14 _____

_____

_____

Ephesians 4:26 _____

_____

_____

Proverbs 29:8 _____

_____

_____

Proverbs 29:11 _____

_____

_____

Jonah 4:2 _____

_____

_____

Romans 12:17–21 _____

_____

_____

PRAYING GOD'S WORD

PERSONALIZING YOUR PRAYERS

_____
_____
_____
_____
_____
_____
_____
_____
_____
_____
_____
_____
_____
_____
_____
_____
_____
_____
_____
_____
_____
_____
_____
_____
_____
_____

PERSONALIZING YOUR PRAYERS

PERSONALIZING YOUR PRAYERS

PERSONALIZING YOUR PRAYERS

_____

_____

_____

_____

_____

_____

_____

_____

_____

_____

_____

_____

_____

_____

_____

_____

_____

_____

_____

_____

_____

_____

_____

NOTES

INTRODUCTION

1. Spiros Zodhiates, ed., *The Complete Word Study Dictionary: New Testament* (Iowa Falls, Iowa: World Bible Publishers, Inc., 1992), #1411, 485.
2. Louie Giglio, from a sermon at First Baptist Church, Houston, Tex., 8 August, 1999.

CHAPTER 4

1. Zodhiates, *Word Study Dictionary,* #3900, 1113.
2. Ibid., #266, 130.

CHAPTER 5

1. Oswald Chambers, *He Shall Glorify Me* (Ft. Washington, Penn.: Christian Literature Crusade, 1965), 134.

CHAPTER 8

1. Zodhiates, *Word Study Dictionary,* #37, 69.

CHAPTER 11

1. Zodhiates, *Word Study Dictionary,* #863, 299.

CHAPTER 13

1. Neil T. Anderson, *The Bondage Breaker* (Eugene, Ore.: Harvest House Publishers, 1990), 201.
2. Zodhiates, *Word Study Dictionary,* #2853, 875.